W9-AXI-716

America's Ancient Civilizations

Other books by A. Hyatt Verrill

ALONG NEW ENGLAND'S SHORES

THE SHELL COLLECTOR'S HANDBOOK

America's Ancient Civilizations

by A. HYATT VERRILL
and RUTH VERRILL

G. P. Putnam's Sons
New York

Contents

Destruction by earthquakes and a volcanic eruption. Dr.
Lothrop's excavations. The question of antiquity. Evidences
of extreme age. Decomposition of rock. Depth of soil and
strata. Who were the Coclés?

A most romantic search. The Gilded Man and the Golden
City. New lands discovered and explored. The truth about
El Dorado. The sacred lake. The Chibchas and others.
Strange cultures of Colombia. The Canarias and their neigh-
bors. Stone seats of Manabi. Microscopic gold beads. The
question of lenses. Missing links.

The great city of Chan Chan. Destructive rains. The ruins
of today. Capital of the Grand Chimu. Chimus and Moujiks. Remarkable pottery. Moulds. Records in pottery. Portrait jars. Surgery of the ancient Chimus. Trepanning and
amputations. Artificial limbs. Dentistry. Masters of all trades.
Wood carving, feather work, weaving, metallurgy. Gold
plating. Origin of the Chimus. Conquest by the Incans.

Area of the city. Outlying suburbs. Canals and docks.
Streets. Public baths. Reservoirs. Houses and palaces. Temples. Water supply. Sanitary measures. Vast irrigation
system. Gigantic burial mounds. Treasures in the ancient
graves. Some facts and figures.

The ancient city of Cajamarca. A Chavin city. Unique form
of architecture. Ground plan of the city. A city and a fortress. The great plaza. Reservoirs and running water. Dual
deities. The cemetery of Amencay. Stone coffins. Sculptured
figures. Destruction and vandalism. Ruins of old Cajamarca.
The mysteries of Chavin. Thishti—Keeper of the Cats.
The Owl and the Pussy-cat.

Pachacamak, the sacred city of the ancient Peruvians. Dual
temples. A vast necropolis. Tens of thousands of graves.
Priceless relics. Excavations and vandalism. Wanton destruc-

tion. Extreme antiquity. Puzzles and problems. What the
Spaniards found. Looting of the temples. Hidden treasures
of Lurin.

equalled. Plants that were developed. Stock raising. Llamas, alpacas, ducks, dogs, Guinea pigs. Human burden bearers. Arts and industries. The world's most expert weavers. Finest known textiles hand woven. Lifelike pottery. Metallurgy. The "lost" art of laquer work on wood. Implements and weapons. Spoons and forks. Pins. Knives. Bows and arrows. Battle axes. Maces. Shields. Spears. Throwing sticks. The Atlatl. Slings. A regular army. Uniforms and training. An Incan West Point. Sham battles. Professional schools. Theology.

*Three sections of plates may be found
following pages 110, 142 and 238.*

Introduction

In the twenty-three years that have passed since I wrote *Old Civilizations of the New World* much additional material has been obtained, many new discoveries made, many theories and conclusions have been cast aside and many others that were ridiculed in 1929 have been accepted. It would seem at first thought that considering the fact that archaeologists and anthropologists have been studying the remains of the ancient Americans, excavating in the ruined cities, disinterring the dead, puzzling their brains over inscriptions, for several centuries, that there would be little or nothing new to learn or discover. But the surface scarcely has been scratched as yet. Even ruins and burial places that have been known for hundreds of years are only partially excavated and there are hundreds—probably thousands—in the vast Andean regions of South America or hidden in the dense jungles and mighty forests of Central America and Mexico, that have never been located.

Dr. Rubin de la Borbolla of the Museo Nacional in Mexico City told me that in the State of Chiapas alone over two hundred sites had been located but never yet investigated, and even in the vicinity of great cities in Peru there are countless burial mounds never yet excavated, many pyramids and numerous ruined cities that never have been studied.

Among the Andes, in remote defiles and valleys far from the beaten track there are ruins of great cities that, in their heyday, must have been inhabited by tens of thousands of persons, yet these never have even been visited by scientists. So vast are the remains of Peru's ancient civilization alone that as one eminent archaeologist expressed it, "It would take a thousand men a thousand years to even partially study and excavate all of the Incan and pre-Incan remains in Peru."

It is true that we have acquired a very great knowledge of many of America's ancient civilizations, but for every fact that has been firmly established there are a dozen puzzles still unsolved. Progress, however, is constantly being made. The antiquity of remains, which was a short time ago largely a matter of guess work, can now be fairly accurately determined by means of the radioactive-carbon test.

Theories of the origins of the ancient Americans and their amazing cultures and attainments that, a few years ago, would have met with ridicule and been deemed preposterous by the old school of archaeologists are now accepted as factual by many of the leading authorities on the subject. Yet even on many basic matters scientists do not agree.

Their estimates of the age of many of the remains varies from several centuries before the Christian era to several centuries A.D. Neither do they agree as to which of the ancient civilizations is the oldest, whether they are related or connected, whether or not one was influenced by another, the identities of the deities of the ancient Americans and many other important matters.

In writing this book I have been guided mainly by my own first hand studies and observations over more than an average lifetime, and by my familiarity with the living Indians of Mexico, Central and South America, and my understanding of their psychology, mental reactions, superstitions and craftsmanship. I have been guided by common sense, logical conclusions, and obvious facts rather than by the assumptions and theories of others. If my conclusions are sometimes at variance with those of some archaeologists, the question of who is right is up to the reader to decide.

In setting forth my theory of the Old World origins of the ancient American civilizations I have confined myself to established facts and recorded historical evidence. In this connection I have drawn freely upon the results of Mrs. Verrill's intensive studies of the ancient Asiatic civilizations and dynasties, a work to which she has devoted fifteen years and more of research during which she has learned to decipher the archaic Sumerian Linear Script used on the inscribed tablets and monuments of the Sumerians. Her monumental work, *Gods Who Were Men,* still in manuscript form, has been commended and accepted by many eminent archaeologists, among them Dr. Junius Bird, Dr. Gordon Ekholm, Dr. Rubin de la Borbolla, Dr. Antonio Costello Branca, Dr. Charles F. Elvers, and others.

No doubt I will be criticised for using the terms "King," "Emperor," "Kingdom," and "Empire," when referring to the greatest of the ancient civilizations of America and their rulers. I am quite aware that, strictly speaking, there were no kings, princes, queens or princesses among the majority of American Indian tribes, and that, in most cases, the rulers or chieftains were chosen because of their bravery and prowess in battle, their fame as "medicine men," their wisdom and oratorical ability or some other outstanding characteristics. But even so it is splitting hairs to maintain that these tribal or confederation rulers were not kings, for the dictionaries define KING as: "A male ruler or sovereign," and KINGDOM as: "A territory ruled by a king or queen. Any sphere of influence;" and EMPEROR as "The sovereign or supreme ruler of an empire:" the term EMPIRE being defined as "Supreme power or dominion, the region ruled by an emperor or sovereign."

Therefore, any chief or "Great Lord" who ruled a tribe or a nation, was technically and properly a "king" unless we restrict the terms "king" and "emperor" to men of royal blood. In that case the rulers of both the Aztecs and Incans—as well as those of the Mayas, the Zapotecs, and others, were literally Kings or Emperors, for the rulers of the ancient Mexicans and Peruvians were both of royal families. In fact the members of the Panaka family, who were the Incas of Peru, always married their sisters in order to preserve the purity of royal blood (a custom that was also followed by the Pharaohs of Egypt). I feel justified therefore in referring to the Incas as emperors and to the Aztec rulers as kings. Moreover, the Mexican archaeologists refer to the Aztecs as the *Imperio Mexicano* or Mexican Empire.

Much as we do know of America's ancient civilizations, much as we have learned, vast as is the material on which scientists do agree, there is far more to be learned, for much of the history of the ancient Americans is as great a mystery as ever, which makes it such a fascinatingly interesting subject.

A. HYATT VERRILL

July, 1952

CHAPTER 1

Analysis of Ancient Civilizations

At the time when Columbus reached America the entire continent, including the West Indies, was inhabited by thousands of tribes and races of aborigines whom Columbus called "Indians" under the mistaken idea that he had reached India. Although the geographical error was soon discovered, yet for some inexplicable reason the misnomer remained, and despite countless attempts to change it and adopt some distinctive name for the native American, they are still referred to as "Indians," although the British call them Red Indians to distinguish them from the inhabitants of India, while we refer to the latter as East Indians.

At the time of the arrival of the Spaniards many of the Indians were primitive savages, others had developed various degrees of culture and some had reached amazing heights of civilization. I have often been asked, "What is the difference between a culture and a civilization?"

Cultures are stepping stones from primitive savagery to the civilized state. In its broadest sense a culture begins when a primitive race takes to making and using weapons, builds homes or shelters and cooks food. But in its more common and restricted sense a culture implies a knowledge of certain crafts and arts, such as weaving, pottery making, or carving. With the establishment of permanent villages, the cultivation of the soil, a more or less organized government, codes of laws or regulations, the development of a numerical system, a concrete religion and definite deities, and a high proficiency in many arts, the culture begins to approach a civilization. But there is still a gap to be crossed. The Pueblo people of our Southwest attained a very high cultural state but could not have been included among the civilized races. Neither could the Iriquois or "Six Nations" Confederation despite their advanced form of government, their huge, well built houses, their established villages or towns, their skill in many arts and crafts, their numerical and calendrical systems, their pictorial ideographic writing, their religion and deities, their agricultural attainments and other matters. But when a highly cultured race reaches the point where it establishes true cities, constructs massive buildings of stone or other permanent materials, builds roads and bridges, erects carved monuments and inscribed stelae, possesses a knowledge of mathematics, astronomy and other sciences, irrigates the arid soil to render it productive, develops accurate calendrical and numerical systems, possesses a written, inscribed or otherwise recordable language, has an organized systematic government, maintains a well-drilled, well-equipped army, attains the highest proficiency in all the more important arts and crafts, produces metallurgists of the highest skill, then a true civilization is attained.

Just why some tribes or races advanced so much further than others living under similar conditions and environment, is a puzzle. The first steps toward culture were of course due to necessity. To protect himself man had to have weapons, to keep himself warm he had to have some sort of covering for his body, and although a cave served very well for a shelter, caverns were not always available, so artificial shelters were devised. Each upward step along the cultural highway led to another and with the improvement in weapons, with better homes and better garments, man's lot steadily improved until he was able to devote some of his attention to the making of basketry, pottery and weaving.

We must also remember that men of all races and all ages have been blessed or cursed with ambition, with an overwhelming desire to improve conditions, to better themselves and their fellows; and the more they succeeded in this the greater their ambition to accomplish more and greater things. It is very largely this urge that has lifted our own civilization to its present height. All great inventions and discoveries, all improvements in living, economic and other conditions, have been the direct results of this basic ambition. Of course there always are a certain number who are entirely lacking in any desire to improve themselves or their conditions. They are perfectly content to vegetate, to continue leading a humdrum, uneventful life, to eschew all modern improvements and inventions. We have excellent examples of this among the "Hillbillys" and isolated mountain people of our own country and to a lesser extent among the "Crackers" of our southern states. Although they are included in our civilization yet in reality they are merely in a cultural state, and a rather low state of culture at that.

Similar conditions undoubtedly obtained among the various tribes and races. Some were ambitious and constantly sought improvement while some were content to remain as they were, with the result that whereas some of the ancient Americans attained civilizations that equaled and in many ways excelled those of the Old World, others who were their neighbors possessed only cultures.

Apparently neither geographical, climatic nor meterological conditions had any great bearing upon the development of the ancient civilizations of America. In the bleak and barren heights of the Andes, miles above the level of the sea, on the desert coastal strip of Peru, in the hot tropical jungles of equatorial America, on the plains of the Mexican highlands, and in the humid tropical valleys near the coasts, the great civilizations flourished equally well and reached equally astounding heights. Neither were these ancient civilizations developed by any one type of aborigine. There were desert tribes, forest tribes, lowland and highland tribes, races accustomed to hot arid districts, tribes inured through the ages to steaming, rain-drenched humid forest areas; people whose ancestors always had dwelt by the sea and others whose homes were amid snow-capped peaks.

Among the makers of America's ancient civilizations were warlike and peaceful races. Some were born conquerors who organized wars on their neighbors and subjugated them as ruthlessly and as successfully as Caesar. Others, whose civilizations had reached equal heights gave battle only in defense of their homes. Some were cruel, bloodthirsty, and gloried in human sacrifices, suffering and even cannibalism, while others, fully if not more advanced, were gentle and kindly, passionately fond of music and amused themselves with innocent games, sports, contests, and dancing.

But in one respect all were similar. All possessed a highly developed esthetic and artistic taste, a remarkable genius for organization, a superior mentality, great creative ability, an extreme sense of idealism, and indomitable will power. Perhaps these more than any other factors were what led certain races to attainments so far surpassing all other ancient Americans that it seems scarcely possible that they were of the same ancestral race.

Another remarkable feature of the ancient American civilizations is that while they were so similar in a great many ways they differed so greatly in others. All constructed enormous massive buildings, imposing temples, magnificent palaces and huge populous cities, but in the details these were not at all alike. No other American race, nor Old World race for that matter, ever equaled the Mayas when it came to the construction of decorative, ornate buildings. On the other hand the buildings of the Aztecs were plain by comparison, but they were so beautifully proportioned, so thoroughly artistic in their severe type of decoration that in some respects they were more attractive than those of the Mayas. Moreover, they were placed on the summits of titanic pyramidal mounds which rendered them all the more impressive and imposing.

In the high civilization of the pre-Incans and Incans, that in many respects was the most advanced of the three major civilizations of ancient America, ornate decorative architecture held no place. Their buildings, enormous, impressive and magnificent, were constructed of huge stone blocks of many forms and angles all so carefully cut and fitted that even with no cement or other binder they remain today as solid and indestructible as when first erected thousands of years ago.

Although the Mayas, the Aztecs and the Peruvians all had excellent numerical systems and accurate calendrical systems, and all possessed a deep knowledge of mathematics and astronomy, each was distinctive. The Aztecs used a decimal numerical system, the Mayas' numerical system was vigesimal and that of the Incans was based on the primitive digital five or bi-decimal count. All three calendrical systems were based on the lunar year of three hundred and sixty days, and in order to make this coincide with the solar year, five nameless days were added, with an additional day every four years as in our leap years. But among the Aztecs and Mayas the five extra days were regarded as unlucky and were feared, whereas among the Peruvians they were days for rejoicing, when no work was done and the people spent the time in merrymaking, dancing and celebrating until the period ended with the Rebirth of the Sun ceremonies and the lighting of the New Fires.

It is quite possible, in fact probable, that all three of these major American civilizations were offshoots, or I might say the developments, of a single advanced culture, or that one had been strongly influenced by another. In fact there are many evidences to prove that the Central American and Mexican civilizations had their beginnings on the coastal area of South America where, according to the most recent carbon tests, there are the most ancient known remains of an advanced culture in America.

During the past few years archaeologists, for some unknown and inexplicable reason, have constantly been reducing the estimated ages of ancient American remains, but now that the carbon test has been discovered they no longer can guess and juggle dates to suit themselves.

Also, for some equally incomprehensible reason, certain archaeologists belittle the ancient American civilizations. They have stated that Montezuma's so-called palace was merely an adobe house like those used by the Mexican Indians of today and that the Incans were ignorant, untutored semi-savages. How any sane and intelligent person can believe such tommy-rot is inconceivable, for there is abundant evidence, both documentary and in the form of remains, to prove the utter falseness of such statements.

Despite the stupendous amount of study, investigation, exploration and excavatory work that has been carried on by archaeologists for several centuries, the fact remains that what we actually know of the ancient civilizations of America is far less than what we do not know.

But each year, each month, new facts are being learned, new links in the chain discovered. All we can do is to watch and wait with open minds, casting aside matters that are proved untenable and treasuring those that are proven facts. And we must learn not to consider anything impossible.

In the past many a matter regarded as an impossibility has been proven a fact. At any time, somewhere, some exploration or excavation may reveal a revolutionary and epochal discovery, something utterly undreamed of, some remains that will prove the master key to the unsolved puzzle of America's ancient civilizations.

CHAPTER 2

The Mystery of the Indian

The builders of America's ancient civilizations are always referred to as Indians, but if they were Indians, how did it happen that of all the thousands of tribes of Indians in North, South, and Central America only a few tribes in South and Central America and Mexico ever developed a high state of civilization, originated and perfected remarkable and accurate numerical and calendrical systems, erected magnificent buildings, reached unparalleled skill in many arts and crafts, performed engineering feats that put those of the Old World to shame, evolved extremely complex religions with a multiplicity of deities, worked out most efficient yet unique forms of government, developed agriculture to the highest degree, possessed a deep knowledge of astronomy and the higher mathematics, instituted the greatest irrigation systems that ever had existed, were expert metallurgists and gem cutters, and had well-drilled, well-equipped armies and efficient officers?

But if these builders of America's ancient civilizations were *not* Indians, as we know them, who were they? For that matter who *are* the Indians?

Many theories have been advanced to explain the presence of the so-called Indians in America. Some have claimed that they migrated to America from the Old World in prehistoric times when the continents were connected by land bridges or when the open water areas were far smaller than today. Some have maintained that these first human beings to reach America came over via northern Europe and Greenland; others with equally plausible arguments have expressed the opinion that they crossed from one continent to the other not far from the equator and perhaps by the

way of Atlantis. A few have believed that the Indians were truly
indigenous, that their ancestors were evolved or created in America,
and have defied anyone to prove that like conditions and like environment could not have produced human beings in one part of
the world as well as in another and that even if ape-like fossil men
never have been found in America, as in Asia and Africa, it did not
prove that they did not exist and that sooner or later, they might
be discovered. But the theory that has had the most adherents was
that our Indians were *all* descendants of Asiatics who crossed over
by way of the Behring Straits and the Aleutian Islands.

All of these various theories had their strong as well as their weak
points. There was also the question of the age of man in America,
the approximate time of his appearance on the scene. For a long
time it was thought that he arrived in the New World comparatively recently, only a few thousand years ago—but gradually, as
more extensive and more systematic archaeological work was carried
on, man's age in America was steadily pushed back. Remains of his
handiwork; stone weapons, camp sites and fire sites, kitchen middens and once-inhabited caves, potsherds and even human bones,
proved that man had lived in America for an almost inconceivable
length of time. Then came the Folsom Man, so-called because
proofs of his presence were first found near Folsom, New Mexico.
These consisted of an entirely unique form of stone arrow and
spear heads. Long, slender, rounded rather than flat, they were beautifully made and proved that Folsom Man had advanced far along
the road toward culture. The depth at which the artifacts were
found and the stratification of the soil proved their great antiquity.
Then an even greater discovery was made. Associated with the Folsom weapons were the bones of long extinct animals; mammoths,
primitive elephants, giant bison, camels, three-toed horses, giant
ground sloths and others, all fossil creatures of the remote Pleistocene Period. And as stone arrow and spear heads were *beneath* the
bones it proved the presence of man in North America for ten thousand years or more.

Had there been but one such find the great age of the relics
might have been questioned but as time went by more and more of
the Folsom points were found in association with the remains of
Pleistocene animals in more than fifty localities. Then, near Colo-

rado, Texas, the typical stone weapons were found embedded in the bones of animals, proving that they had been hunted and killed by men in the almost inconceivably distant past when the great glacial cap covered much of North America and strange beasts of gigantic size roamed over what is now the United States.

Moreover, the easily recognizable Folsom points were turning up in countless localities far from their original source, until they had been obtained from all but one or two of the states in the Union. But still more was yet to come. In strata far beneath the remains of Folsom Man, anthropologists found the remains of an even older race whom they called Sandia Man and who, unless all accepted evidences and data are worthless, inhabited North America in pre-glacial days—perhaps over fifty thousand years ago.

The adherents of the comparatively recent immigration of man theory could not stand for this, but as they could not alter the evidence they re-dated the time of the last glacial era and brought it down to about ten thousand years ago, a time that did not greatly conflict with their own ideas on the subject. Then, in Mexico, archaeologists discovered skeletons of men beneath very ancient lava flows, and others under strata, that proved them to be even more ancient than Folsom Man. The skulls of these extremely ancient Mexicans were in such good condition that the heads and faces could be reconstructed. When this had been done it was found that these extremely ancient people of Mexico differed not at all from the present day Indians, proving that even in the incalculably ancient period in which they lived the so-called Indians were highly developed intelligent human beings far superior to their fellows of the Old World of the same era and far more advanced in their culture.

Perhaps even more ancient than any of the human remains and weapons so far discovered in America are the drawings on the walls of various caves in Hava Supai Canyon, Arizona. These clearly show men attacking and killing the long-extinct North American ibex, the woolly rhinoceros, primitive imperial elephants and even one creature that looks suspiciously like a dinosaur. Possibly the well-executed drawings, done by scraping away a layer of one color of sandstone to expose another, a crude form of cameo, may have been the work of some Folsom Man artist or perhaps even a Sandia

Man. No one can say for no human bones or weapons have been found in the caves.*

These discoveries seemed to bolster up the theory of the Indians having originated in America, but the opponents of this theory came back with the question: If so why had no one discovered remains of anthropoid apes in America and no trace of primitive ape-like men?

That such evolutionary fossils had not been discovered was merely negative evidence, and for all anyone could say, they might exist somewhere. As if just to prove this the case, fossil remains of lemur-like animals *were* discovered in fossil beds in our western states.

Meanwhile the adherents of the trans-Atlantic immigration theory piled up evidence in support of their contentions. They pointed out that a great many, in fact the majority, of Indian tribes of eastern America had traditions of their ancestors having come from the east or "Sunrise."

Moreover, there was abundant evidence, in the form of ancient Phoenician records of various sorts, to prove that thousands of years before the Christian era these famed voyagers had large ocean-going well-rigged ships and made regular trips between the Mediterranean and England, around Africa to India and across the China Sea, and therefore might easily have crossed the Atlantic (Fig. 1).

Throughout all of this controversy the adherents of the Behring Sea immigration stuck to their guns. Although they admitted that if the Asiatics did cross over to Alaska they were fairly well-advanced in culture and that they were comparatively few in numbers, yet they did not or could not explain why the Asiatics had not brought food-plants, or domestic animals with them. And although they claimed that *all* the Indians of the three Americas had descended from these few wanderers who crossed to America by the way of Behring Sea they did not take into consideration the

* This would not indicate that those who made the carvings actually knew living dinosaurs. They may have found the fossil skeletons and reconstructed them. It has been stated that the footprints of three-toed dinosaurs together with those of ancient pachyderms, have been found in the rock in the canyon. I doubt if the footprints of three-toed dinosaurs can always be distinguished from those of some of the fossil three-toed giant birds that may well have been contemporaneous with the Imperial elephants, woolly rhinoceros and pleistocene man.

enormous length of time it would have required for them to have increased and multiplied and found their way across the continent to the Atlantic coast and as far southward as Tierra del Fuego, a length of time that was greater than they were willing to admit human beings had exised in the New World.

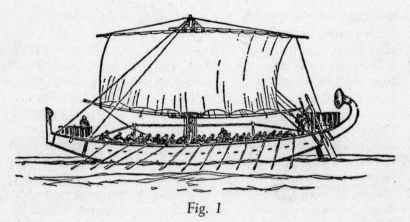

Fig. 1

The chief propagandist of this theory was Dr. Aleš Hrdlička who in order to explain the presence of Indians using the Athabascan language in our far Northwest, claimed that some of his Behring Sea immigrants had crossed the continent, remained in the east until they evolved and developed an entirely new language and culture, and then had trekked back to Alaska! But he could not find a way to explain how it happened that if his theoretical Asiatic migrants arrived in a fairly advanced cultural state, their descendants wandered southward for tens of thousands of miles to southern Chile and Patagonia and there left remains of a most primitive character; the crudest of crude stone implements, skulls of human beings who were of a very primitive type and descendants such as the Onas and Alakaleuts who are probably the lowest, most primitive Indians in all America.

In addition to his pet Behring Sea theory, Dr. Hrdlička divided all Indians into two types—the "long-headed" and "round-headed" races, and he and his followers maintained that the relationship and status of any tribes or individuals could be determined by the type of craniums they possessed.

It would have been just as reasonable to have attempted to separate and classify the races or tribes by the colors of their skins or hair, for among members of any race or tribe, or even in the same family, there often are some round-headed and some long-headed individuals not to mention those whose skulls are intermediate in form. In fact I have a photograph of three brothers belonging to the Kuna tribe of Panama, one of whom is of the extreme long-headed type, another equally typically round-headed while the third has a head that cannot be classified as either long or round.

Unquestionably the real truth is that man came to America from the Old World via all of these various routes. Some came from Europe by the way of Greenland, others across the Atlantic to South America, some via the Behring Straits, and others across the Pacific; the intermingling of all of these widely diverse peoples—and for all we know some truly indigenous races—resulted in the American Indians that inhabited the New World before the Vikings reached America.

Even those who have steadfastly held to the Behring Straits theory are beginning to have their doubts. In a paper published in the *Museum Journal* of the University of Pennsylvania from a lecture delivered by Dr. J. Alden Mason he states that there was nothing to indicate Old World influences on the ancient American civilizations, that *all* were "wholly, distinctively of pure blooded American Indian origin."

When I asked Dr. Mason just what he meant by a "pure blooded Indian" if, as he had contended, *all* our Indians were descendants of Mongols who had reached America via the Behring Straits, he was somewhat at a loss but stated that the paper was written twenty-five years ago and that opinions had changed since then!

Even the most skeptical cannot ignore or cast aside scientifically established facts and when the new carbon radioactive method of determining the antiquity of remains came into use it was found that a number of cultural sites throughout North, Central, and South America far antedated those of the oldest known human remains in Alaska. Charcoal from a pre-Aleut village site on Unimak Island was found to date from 1067 B.C. or some three to eight thousand years after North America was quite thickly populated by a large number of distinct tribes, each with its own culture and its own language.

Until quite recently the ages of the various extremely ancient Americans were largely a matter of guesswork but, with the recently discovered carbon radioactive method, dates with a margin of some five hundred years are obtainable, provided there is available carbon in the remains.*

In the case of the Folsom Man, charcoal and partly burned bones that have been tested give the following results:

Folsom site near Lubbock, Texas: Burned bones of extinct bison, 9900 B.C.

Nevada gypsum cave: Dung of ground sloth associated with presence of man, 8404 B.C.

But perhaps the most surprising and significant fact brought to light was the extreme antiquity of the tribal cultures of a number of our living North American Indians.

In Arizona charcoal of the Cochise (Apache) culture was dated as 4982 B.C. Burned bones from the Sage Creek, Wyoming, Yuma Indian culture were definitely dated as 4925 B.C. Deer antlers from Indian Knoll, Kentucky, were dated as 3352 B.C. Charcoal from the Lamoka III site in New York State dated back to 4332 B.C. Wood found among human remains in Bat Cave, New Mexico, was dated as over 1000 B.C. and even at that time the people were agriculturists and cultivated maize, for cobs of corn were found associated with the human remains. Finally, rope sandals taken from beneath lava in Fort Rock Cave, Oregon, were found to date from 7002 B.C.**

---

* This process is based on the radioactive deterioration of carbon. It is a highly technical and involved, but very certain, process; but unfortunately only comparatively few of the most ancient evidences of man's presence include carbon on which to make the test. Stone weapons and implements, pottery, uncharred bones, etc., afford no opportunity to make the test. Thus in the case of the mysterious Coclé culture in Panama, although there were thousands of stone monuments, tens of thousands of pieces of pottery, many bones and other remains, not a single trace of charcoal or carbon was found. Moreover, it is often very difficult to be certain that charcoal in association with other remains is of the same age. Remains of fires, charred bones, etc., cast aside as refuse might be much more recent than the oldest human remains at or near the same site, although they certainly could not be older. Despite its shortcomings the method is scientifically accurate as far as it goes and is perhaps the most important and far reaching advance in archaeological research.

** Recent tests by this method have given the following dates: Bark and charcoal from the Hopewell, Ohio, mound, 748 B.C.; Atlatls from a Nevada rock

Recent discoveries of exceedingly ancient artifacts in Ontario, Canada, would seem to prove that men fairly well advanced in culture inhabited North America some 17,000 years ago. According to Dr. Emerson Greeman of the Museum of Anthropology of the University of Michigan, stone artifacts found on an ancient beach about 225 feet above Lake Huron at Killarney, Ontario, date back to about 15,000 B.C. More recently a new site with great numbers of artifacts has been found at Sheguiandah Bay, Ontario. According to Mr. Thomas E. Lee, who discovered the site and is leader of the expedition carrying on the work, these stone artifacts are more recent than those found at Killarney and date back to 5000 to 7000 years ago. Mainly these very ancient Ontario stone implements are of quartzite and consist of scrapers, pounders and knives, often of very large size, some being as much as ten inches in length and weighing up to two pounds. However, until some material such as charcoal or burned bone is found the remains cannot be accurately dated by the radioactive carbon method.

With this steadily increasing antiquity of the ancient Americans it seems more and more probable that we have placed the cart before the horse as it were. That instead of the ancient American civilizations having been influenced if not established by immigrants from the Old World they had their beginnings in America, were carried to the Old World by the so-called Indians and, thousands of years later, were brought back to America by the Sumerians and others in their fully developed state. A theory made more plausible by the fact that the most ancient known culture of Mesopotamia has been definitely dated as 4756 B.C. or over 4000 years after the earlier American cultures.

---

shelter, 5086 B.C.; El Arbocillo, Mexico, early Zacatenacan, 1600 B.C.; Cerro Sechin, Peru, Chavin culture, 400-500 B.C.

CHAPTER 3

Opinions That Have Changed

Until quite recently, even to suggest that there was any connection between the civilizations of the Old World and those of America was rank heresy in the eyes of most archaeologists. Those of the old school were especially antagonistic to any such theory and maintained that there was nothing to indicate, much less prove, any contacts, declaring that ancient American art, pottery, sculptures, textiles, buildings, and everything else pertaining to so-called American Indian cultures were typically, unmistakably, American. There were no cultivated plants, no domesticated animals known to both continents prior to the coming of the Spaniards, they claimed, nothing to indicate racial or linguistic affinities, and, most important of all, the wheel was absolutely unknown to the pre-Columbian American races.

In all of these contentions they were wrong and—wonder of wonders—they are now beginning to admit it.

The pre-Columbian Americans *did* know the wheel and the archaeologists were well aware of the fact, yet when I reported the discovery of huge stone wheels at Tiahuanaco and pointed out that they were buried under huge slabs of stone from fallen buildings and could not have been of European workmanship as the savants claimed, I was ridiculed. In a preliminary report on his excavations at Tiahuanaco, Wendell Bennett stated that among other things he found a "stone wheel or grindstone." Later however, when his report was published, all reference to the wheel was omitted.

The archaeologists of Mexico had long known that the ancient Mexicans knew and used the wheel and there were numerous specimens of wheeled toys, etc., in the Museo Nacional, but for some unknown and mysterious reason, perhaps merely to sustain their denial of any Old World contacts, no North American scientist would publicly and openly admit the existence of the wheel in pre-Columbian times. However, in certain scientific papers never seen or read by the layman, there were, from time to time, brief references to wheels having been known to the early Americans, not only in pre-Columbian days but in the earlier days of the so-called Toltec-Aztec culture, and in Vol. XI, No. 4 (April 1946) of *American Antiquity*, Dr. Gordon F. Ekholm had an article, "Wheeled Toys in Mexico." Once the truth had been revealed it was useless to continue to maintain that wheels were unknown in ancient America and in *Natural History* (October 1950), the official organ of the American Museum of Natural History, there was an article in which it was admitted that the wheel *was* known to the pre-Columbian races, with illustrations of a wheeled toy found in Mexico and another wheeled toy from the Old World. The specimen from Mexico is of pottery while the specimen from the Old World, used for comparison, is of bronze. The comparison, however, would have been much more to the point if a pottery wheeled toy from the Old World had been shown, for a number of these, strikingly like those from Mexico, have been discovered in ancient remains in northern India and Iraq.

Having finally openly admitted that the ancient Americans did know the wheel, the consciences of the "die hards" were salved by stating that even if the early Americans did know the wheel, they made no practical use of it; which was all guesswork, for if the Mexicans or others *did* use wooden vehicles with wooden wheels the chances are that no traces of them would remain. After all, why should these ancient people have used wheels or wheeled vehicles for practical purposes? They had no draught animals and, lacking these, rollers and stone balls served every purpose and were far easier to provide than wheels.

Once these anti-Old-World-contacts archaeologists had been forced to admit the presence of the wheel in ancient America they began to see the light and to change their opinions in many ways. Sylvanus Morley states in his *The Ancient Maya* that these people were probably a mixture of aborigines and Asiatics and pointed out that the Mayan infants are born with the "Mongolian spot,"

which "as its name implies, is an almost universal physical characteristic of the Mongoloid peoples of eastern Asia. It is an irregular-
shaped spot located at the base of the spine, varying in size from a
dime to a dinner plate, more often nearer the former than the latter, bluish to purple in color, but fading to a slaty shade as it gradually disappears. It is present at birth in both sexes but disappears
in most cases before the tenth year is reached. It is found throughout eastern Asia, and is very common among Maya babies of
northern Yucatán today, as presumably it also was in ancient times."

Dr. Morley also points out that: "The patterns of certain lines
in the palms of the hands of both modern Maya and Chinese so
closely resemble each other as to indicate a remarkable degree of
racial similarity between the two peoples," and he also mentions
the occasional oblique eyes and epicanthic fold of the eye lids of
the Mayas of northern Yucatán.

Then came the epical voyage of Thor Heyerdahl from Peru
to Raroia Reef in Polynesian waters in 101 days, landing August
7, 1947. Making the voyage on the rudely built balsa raft Kon-
Tiki, proved beyond contention that migrants from South America
could have populated the Pacific Islands or vice-versa and that the
Maori tradition of the kumara (Peruvian name of the sweet potato) having come from South America with their ancestors was
plausible.

There was also the fascinating book by the Chinese Buddhist
priest, who in the fifth century A.D. visited the Americas and accurately describes many Central and South American cultural features ages before the coming of Columbus. The priest was known
as Hoei-shin (schin or shen) and his original document was entitled *Fusang* and entered in the *Year Books* or *Annals* of the
Chinese Empire for 499 A.D.

Little by little undeniable evidences of very ancient contacts
between the continents have been accumulated. Unmistakable
carvings and sculptures of elephants have been found and under
conditions which precluded all chances of their having been brought
over after the arrival of the Spaniards. Ancient inscriptions in
archaic Sumerian Linear Script, that could not have been faked,
have been found and even deciphered. In the Old World there
were records of voyages to the "Land Beyond the Sunset" and "The
Western Sunset Land" and in the time of Sargon of Agade, his son

King Menes and grand-son Narām-sin or Narmer, there were "Sumerian" (First dynasty Egyptian) inscriptions telling of colonies established in the Sunset Land and of "a holding" being built at the Lake of the Peak in "Urani Land." Also papyri tell of the "Red Beings" met when voyaging up a Great River. Such evidences could not lightly be cast aside. Moreover, I have a list of several hundred words, many almost exactly the same and having the same meanings in the ancient Peruvian and "Sumerian" dialects.

But the most noteworthy changes of opinions on the part of the anti-Old-World-contacts archaeologists came when Mrs. Verrill completed her monumental work—*Gods Who Were Men*, and presented copies to various museums and universities. Dr. Junius Bird of the American Museum of Natural History, in New York City, wrote: "Both Gordon Ekholm and I have read your book with considerable interest and appreciation of the time and effort you have put into it. Frankly, neither of us is qualified to evaluate much of your comparative material for it falls outside our experience and is from fields in which we have no training. . . . Many of your comparisons are significant. . . . Is it your intention that we should keep the volume on file here? If so, it will be available to anyone you may send in to see it."

She had been warned that her work and conclusions would be completely discredited by the Mexican archaeologists but when she talked with Dr. Rubin de la Borbolla she was amazed when he stated that the Mexican scientists had been convinced of the Old World influence for a number of years and that they not only agreed with her but asked her to continue her studies and researches along the lines being followed. But he was immensely surprised when he learned of Dr. Bird's change of heart, and read his letter. "This is wonderful!" said Dr. Rubin.

Years of patient research went into *Gods Who Were Men*. The entire lineage of the main-line ancient Sumerian-Aryan kings and Biblical characters were studied and relationships worked out, innumerable inscriptions were deciphered and translated and every available source of reliable information was meticulously studied. No one could question or deny facts and hence no one could any longer bring up any sustainable arguments in rebuttal of the evidences of Old World influences.

Moreover, with new evidences of Old World contacts with ancient America constantly cropping up, more and more of the archaeologists are abandoning their former attitude and are—in most cases rather reluctantly—admitting that there were numerous contacts between the Old World and the New World in the dim and distant past, ages before the arrival of the Spaniards.

One of the most ardent of these converts is Dr. Gordon F. Ekholm, Associate Curator of Archaeology, American Museum of Natural History. When Mrs. Verrill called his attention to the similarity between a stone image fourteen feet in height from Cyprus and supposed to represent Hercules, and a small pottery figure from the Rio Balsas area in Mexico, the two heads being identical in many details even to the beards combed and curled in the same manner, the same facial expressions and both with moustaches trimmed in an identical style, Dr. Ekholm wrote to her as follows: ". . . your letter with the photographs of the famous Bearded Mystery and your curiously similar example from the island of Cyprus . . . interests me very much for I have had in mind an attempt to try to solve the curious mystery of the figurine supposedly from Guerrero, Mexico. The Cyprus piece is indeed very similar, especially in that the curls of the beard are laid down in horizontal lines. . . . I am really very much interested in this problem—and would like very much to keep your photographs to add to a file on this particular subject which I have been keeping."

And in a paper presented at the meeting of the International Congress of Americanists in September, 1949, he says among other things: "The close relationship between the *patoli* game of Mexico and the *pachisi* game of India . . . has called attention to the similarity between the Mexican *volador* ritual and the Indian rite of hook swinging. . . . No less striking is the use of the parasol as a sign of royalty and rank among the Maya and in Asia. To this may be added the use of the throne, the litter and fans mounted standard-like on long poles as insignia of rank and royalty, all of them closely resembling similar paraphernalia of rank and royalty in southern and eastern Asia." (The same insignia were used by the Incans in Peru and were often depicted on carvings, frescoes and on pottery.)

Dr. Ekholm states further: "In reading descriptions of the palace and court of the Aztec emperor anyone familiar with Southeast

Asia cannot fail to be reminded of the courts of Burma, Siam and Cambodia, not only in a general way but even in minor details. The same applies to the form of government. Thus the four chief officials in Mexico corresponded to the four ministers of state and governors of the four quarters of the kingdom in the Hindu-Buddhist empires of Southeast Asia. . . . In general, the great stress laid on the four quarters of the world and the colors attributed to them, in both Asia and Mexico, seems particularly significant since it indicates a similar conception of the world."

In Peru the Incas' name for their Empire was the Empire of Tiahuantisuyo or "The Four Corners of the Earth."

Dr. Ekholm continues: "The large number of highly specific correspondences in so many fields precludes any possibility of mere accidental coincidence. Nor would it help us to take refuge in any kind of explanation based on some psychological laws. There is no psychological law which could have caused the people on both sides of the Pacific to stylize the lotus plant in the same manner and to make it surge from the mouth of a jawless demon's head, to invent the parasol and use it as a sign of rank and to invent the same complicated game. There is no other explanation than the assumption of cultural relationship. We must bow to the evidences of facts, even though this may mean a completely new start in our appraisal of the origin and development of the American Indian higher civilization. . . . The character of the correspondence which we have indicated precludes the possibility of attributing Hindu-Buddhist influence in Mexico and among the Maya to mere accidental contacts, such as might have resulted from ships driven on the coasts of America by storms and ocean currents. . . . This indicates the existence of some kind of two-way traffic between Southeast Asia and America in ancient times." Referring to the matter of ocean-going ships in ancient times, Dr. Ekholm says: "When the Chinese Buddhist scholar, Fa-hien, returned from India around A.D. 400 he embarked on a ship which carried more than two hundred sailors and merchants and which therefore must have been larger than the ships of Columbus and other Spanish explorers. This ship sailed directly across the ocean from Ceylon to Java. At Java Fa-hien embarked in another merchant ship which carried more than two hundred persons. This ship sailed right across the China Sea to northern China."

Speaking of resemblances between the architecture of Asia and ancient America, Dr. Ekholm says: "The similarities between the buildings of the Puuc [an epithet at one time applied to the Phoenicians] style and the Cambodian temples, particularly those of Isvarapura, indicate connections around the tenth century A.D.."

In his paper Dr. Ekholm confines himself to evidences of trans-Pacific contacts between the Hindu-Buddhists and the Mexicans and Mayas, but there are even more numerous and more convincing evidences of trans-Atlantic contacts between the Sumerians (Phoenicians) and the pre-Incans in far earlier times. Moreover, these contacts are recorded in Sumerian Linear Script in Mesopotamia and elsewhere. And we must not overlook the fact that the Gangetic culture of India, (the Hindu-Buddhist) was introduced to that country by the "Sumerians" several centuries before Christ, for the traditional founder of Buddhism was a former Brahman of high caste and the Brahman caste was a branch of the early Aryan race according to some authorities.

Among the ancient Sumerian records, a number tell of voyages to the Sunset Land and the establishment of colonies there and the conquests of the people by the Sumerian warrior kings, Sargon of Agade, King Menes, Narām-sin and others. There have been numerous finds in America that appear to verify these ancient records, the most important of them being the sculptured stone and pottery images, and statues, carvings, and paintings, of rulers and deities. Moreover, these are not restricted to South and Middle America but are also found here and there over a considerable portion of North America, especially in the vast areas drained by the Colorado River and its tributaries. Throughout this area there are pictographs and glyphs cut and painted on cliffs and in caves that certainly are not the accepted North American type. There are also objects unlike anything else found in America and there are carved stone heads and amulets unquestionably of Old World origin. Finally there are the Santa Rita frescoes in British Honduras, all of which will be fully described and discussed in Chapter 8, "The Plumed Serpent."

One of the most important alterations in the opinions of the many archaeologists who were strongly opposed to any suggestion of Old World influence or pre-Columbian contacts with America is that the most eminent authorities in their field now doubt the American origin of maize.

The long-sustained theory that maize was developed from the wild teosinte plant of the Central American highlands has been rejected by a number of scientists, among them Dr. Edgar Anderson of the Missouri Botanical Garden in St. Louis, who wrote me: "Teosinte is not the ancestor of maize but is a weed resulting probably from a mixture of maize with some wild grass or grasses."

CHAPTER 4

The Mayas*

Of all the ancient civilizations of America that of the Mayas in Yucatán, Guatemala, and Honduras has received the most attention, the most study and, in some ways, the most publicity. Yet despite the fact that for two centuries or more the most learned, experienced and famous archaeologists have devoted years of study to Mayan remains, have cleared hundreds of acres of forest and jungle to reveal forgotten ruins of temples, palaces and cities; have cleaned and examined thousands of stelae and have excavated millions of tons of earth and rubble and have almost completely restored such imposing structures as the temples of the Warriors, Temple of the Serpents, the Ball Court at Chichen Itzá, and other edifices; although countless papers, monographs, reports, and voluminous works on the Mayas have been published, the fact remains that we really know very little about them or their civilization.

No one has ever discovered a means of deciphering the thousands upon thousands of inscriptions in sculptured stone. The only glyphs that scientists have learned to interpret are the calendrical and numerical symbols, and they do not agree in regard to these. No two

---

* In pronouncing Mayan and Mexican names all vowels have the broad Spanish sound. H is silent as in Spanish. X when following E, I, or O, has the sound of Sh; for example: Holbox is pronounced Allbosh; Ixtepec is pronounced Ishtepeck. X when following A has the sound of H as in Oaxaca, pronounced Oahaka. As a rule, however, J has been substituted for X in such names and it is now Oajaca. Z has the sound of our S and the two letters are interchangeable as in Serape or Zerape. Ll is as in Spanish Lya. The terminal Tl is pronounced very much like Te-le with the final E almost silent. C usually has the hard sound of K except before I when it may have the sound of our S as in Usamacinta.

archaeologists are even in accord as to the ages of the inscriptions or the exact dates recorded by them. Some insist that the stelae bear dates corresponding to centuries before the Christian era while others claim, with apparently equally learned arguments, that no Mayan date is older than a century or two A.D. Moreover, they are not even consistent in their opinions, for at least one famed archaeologist has placed Mayan dates as several centuries B.C. and later on, has declared them to be a few centuries A.D. One Mayan authority, the late Sylvanus Morley, when referring to a pottery plaque with date glyphs, stated that it could not possibly be so old and that the artizan must have made a mistake! He thereupon worked out a date according to his own ideas and found—to his apparent amazement—that his date was still too early! The great trouble is that while simple date and numerical glyphs are quite easy to decipher there are a great many that have curlicues and "trimmings." These may all have their purpose and a very small variation or addition to a glyph may completely alter its meaning, although archaeologists consider all such as purely decorative.

No authority is positive as to all of the identities of the Mayan deities, their statues or attributes or whether they were borrowed from the Aztecs and Toltecs or whether these people borrowed their deities from the Mayas. Unfortunately there are no complete codices or records of the Mayas. All they could lay their hands on were destroyed by the fanatical Spanish priests, and the few fragments that escaped, such as the *Dresden Codex,* cannot be deciphered without a key or "Rosetta stone" which so far is non-existent.

According to tradition a complete history of the Mayas was recorded in the *Golden Book of the Mayas* which, if it actually existed, as it probably did, was so carefully hidden to prevent it from falling into the hands of the Spaniards that it never has been found. The most complete account of these ancient people is the *Popol Vuh* written by a Christianized Maya with the approval of an unusually broad-minded and intelligent priest. But even the *Popol Vuh* is somewhat sketchy and as it was done entirely from memory, and was censored by the Church, its actual scientific value is somewhat in doubt.

It must be admitted, however, that we have accumulated a vast amount of well established facts in regard to the cultural remains

Fig. 2. Maya full figure glyphs

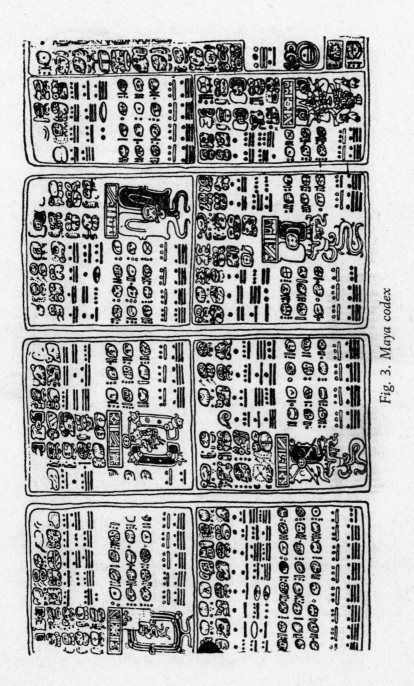

Fig. 3. Maya codex

of the Mayan civilization. We know that there were two distinct
stages or eras known as the Old Empire and the New Empire and
we know much in respect to the migrations of the people, their
religion, customs, costumes, wars, and games.

Although we ordinarily speak of the people of the Mayan Empire as Mayas, yet they belonged to numerous races or tribes. The
most important of these were the Quiché Maya, the Lacandons and
the Xius (pronounced She-use). All three of these races still dwell
in Yucatán, southern Mexico and Guatemala.

In their physical characteristics, their dialects and their life and
customs they are very distinct. The Lacandons, who are brown-
skinned and rather tall for Indians of the tropics, live in scattered
villages in the forest-clad mountains of Chiapas and northern
Yucatán. They are shy, suspicious of strangers and rarely visit the
larger towns. They depend mainly upon agriculture and hunting
but formerly, when chicle gum commanded a high price, they carried on a large trade with the Mexicans and today they do consid-
able lumbering.

The Quichés are scattered over most of Yucatán, southern Mexico, and Guatemala, where there are many tribes and sub-tribes.
Among them are the true Quichés, the Kakchiquels, Zutugils,
Pipils, and Coxohcholes, all speaking dialects of the Maya language
and having similar arts, customs, and industries, but they are easily
distinguishable by their costumes and by the designs of their beautifully hand-woven textiles. In color they vary from pale ocherous
to light brown and many of them, especially those in Mexico, have
the high sloping forehead, the receding chin and the large beak-
like nose so typical of the figures in ancient Mayan sculptures.

In Guatemala they practically control the smaller industries.
The markets, produce, pottery and wooden ware, baskets and fur-
niture, textiles and poultry, and many another business and trade
are in the hands of the Indians. In fact Guatemala is basically and
economically Maya Indian and it is largely the Indians in their
colorful, picturesque garments that attract the tourists, for without
them as drawing cards the tourist trade of Guatemala would be of
little importance.

In Yucatán the Xius are most numerous; they are laborers,
kitchen gardeners, lumbermen, and the keepers of small shops and
eating places. They are the artizans and mechanics, the taxi drivers

and the street car conductors. In fact they are everywhere and while many are of mixed blood there are thousands who are pure Indian. Although the women adhere to their native dress, which varies in pattern and ornamentation with the tribe and locality, these are not as striking or colorful as those of the Guatemalan Mayas but consist of a long cotton skirt and loose sleeveless blouse more or less covered with beautiful embroidery in floral designs.

In color the Xius vary from olive to very light yellowish-brown. Their features are regular, the girls and women are often truly beautiful and the Hebraic noses of the Quiché are lacking. Of course there has been a great deal of mixture of the Quiché, the Xius, and the Lacandons, as well as with other non-Mayan Indians, but the facial characteristics of each of the Maya races are so marked that a person familiar with them can tell at a glance whether an Indian is a Quiché, a Lacandon or a Xiu. Undoubtedly a cross section of the population of an ancient Mayan city would be almost identical with a similar cross section of the native Indian population of Mérida, Campeche or Progreso today.

Thanks to the accurate and painstaking restoration of Chichen Itzá and other ancient Mayan sites, one can revisualize the past to some extent and to make it more realistic the government stages elaborate spectacles in which the present day Mayas, attired in accurate replicas of the ancient Mayan costumes, enact scenes from the past of their ancestors. Probably no race anywhere ever evolved such amazing, colorful, complex and, it would appear, awkward and cumbersome dress and decorations as were those worn by the Mayan priests, officials and warriors. Most conspicuous were the enormous headdresses of metal, wood, cloth, and feathers which are so clearly and accurately preserved on frescoes, sculptures, and carvings.

The Mayan architecture is perhaps the most striking feature of their civilization and is so distinctive that it is recognizable anywhere. For some reason—perhaps to render the structures more impressive or perhaps to protect them from inundations—the temples and palaces were built upon the summits of artificial hills or mounds of stone and rubble known as *kus* which were usually higher than the building itself. The Mayan buildings were constructed by a stepping-in method and were therefore rarely over one story in height, but this shortcoming was often overcome by erecting a building in the usual way and then adding to the height of the mound in its rear until it reached the roof level of the first structure. Then a second building was constructed on this so the effect was of a two story edifice.

By again adding to the height of the mound and building another structure the appearance of three or four story buildings was obtained. In nearly every case the roof of the building was topped by a high and often ornate roof-comb of stone work, wood, or stucco, often as high or higher than the building itself, so that the actual edifice, although low and squat, had the appearance of being high and imposing.

Another typical feature of Mayan architecture is the stucco work, often made in molds like our modern concrete, and usually modeled in striking and elaborate designs of human figures, geometrical designs, scrolls and various animals' heads. So hard and enduring was this stucco that it is almost indistinguishable from stone and often has been mistaken for stone sculptures.

Regardless of whether actual stone or stucco were used, the elaborate sculptures and carvings of the buildings are their most striking features. Everything from the largest blocks of stone to the smallest was sculptured, carved or covered with glyphs. The style and type, however, varied greatly according to the locality. In the more northerly areas bas-reliefs were the favorites. In Honduras human figures and caryatides predominated. At Copán, once the metropolis of the Mayas, there are such deeply undercut bas-reliefs that they appear like sculptures in the round about to be cut from the rock. And there are buildings with depictions that are a combination or mixture of all.

Probably the finest of all known Mayan buildings if not the finest example of prehistoric architecture in the world, is the great temple of the Foliated Cross, at Palenque in Chiapas, Mexico. With its numerous great rooms, with their stepped-in arched ceilings and the double-sloped roof surmounted by an enormous roof-comb of carved stonework, the temple is a most striking and imposing structure, but its most unusual features are the subterranean hallways and apartments with their stone altars.

Like Pachacamak in Peru (See Chapter 16), Palenque, discovered by Calderon in 1774, was a sacred or holy city and contains eighteen magnificent temples in addition to twenty other large buildings. Being a sacred or holy city the sculptures and decorations on the buildings are all of a religious character and there are no carvings or paintings depicting warriors, battles, kings or similar subjects.

Chichen Itzá—now so familiar to thousands of tourists—was also a holy city and was dedicated to Kukulcan or the Plumed Serpent god identical with Quetzalcoatl of the Aztecs. Here the Temple of the Jaguars is perhaps the most outstanding example of Mayan architecture and surpasses all other known prehistoric American buildings in the beauty of its design, its elaborate frescoes and carvings, and its coloring.

CYCLE (BAKTUN)   TUN

KATUN   UINAL

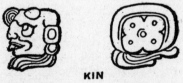

KIN

Fig. 4. Maya time symbols

As is the case with the other temple of the city, the main entrance is flanked by enormous carved snake-gods with the bodies and heads of the rattlesnake. Originally (and in restoration) these and the entire front of the building and the high roof-comb of open stonework, were painted in red, green, and white, the sacred colors of the Plumed Serpent. Leading up to the temple is a magnificent stone stairway flanked by jaguar heads.

In addition to this imposing structure there are the Hall of the Warriors, the Iglesia or Church, the Red House, and the Ball Court wherein the ancient Mayas played a game very similar to our modern basketball but far more difficult, for instead of striving to toss the ball into a basket the Mayas' ball had to be thrown through a stone ring.

To attempt to describe or even mention the innumerable Mayan buildings that are scattered from Chiapas, Mexico, to Copán in Honduras, would require a volume. However, there is such a striking similarity between them that this is not essential. Far more important are the Mayas' numerical and calendrical systems. I doubt if any people who ever lived had such a mania for dating everything as did the Mayas. There is scarcely a building, a monument, an idol or any other object in the entire Mayan area that is not covered with numerical and calendrical glyphs, and, in addition, there are countless stone columns or stelae with date glyphs that were carved and erected at regular intervals—stone calendars as it were. It is mainly from these that archaeologists have derived what knowledge we have of Mayan history, but as I have already mentioned, the glyphs that recorded other matters—wars, organization, the rulers, history, life and all matters of human interest remain undeciphered and undecipherable.

The Mayas numerical system was vigesimal instead of decimal as is ours. That is, they counted by units of twenty instead of ten. And instead of arbitrary figures to record numbers they used dots and horizontal bars. Each dot was a unit and each bar denoted five. The highest number recorded by this method was nineteen, indicated by three bars and four dots. It might seem as if it would be almost impossible to make a mistake in deciphering such a simple system of numbers but in a great many cases where there are only one or two dots above the bars the vacant space is filled in with crescents, crosses, squares, etc., while the bars may be plain or ornamental (Fig. 5). It has been assumed that these have no meanings but merely served as decorations to fill up empty areas which the Mayas considered inartistic. But who knows? It is quite possible that every one of these decorations added to the plain everyday date glyphs had a meaning which might completely alter the date itself. And the fact that no two authorities can agree as to the dates or ages of Mayan remains would rather indicate that such is the case. The same holds true of the calendrical glyphs.

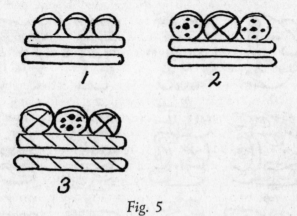

Fig. 5

In addition to the dot and bar numerals the Mayas used head symbols denoting numbers (Fig. 6), but just as the dots and bars were embellished with additional figures the face numbers may be plain and easily deciphered or they may have curlicues and otheɩ decorations added, while elaborate full figure glyphs in which the numerical face signs appear are common. No one knows with certainty whether or not such additions to the date figures or the use of full figures instead of heads convey a meaning and hence no one can with absolute certainty fix a Mayan date.

The Mayas calendrical system was perhaps their greatest and most remarkable attainment for it was the most accurate of all calendrical systems until the Gregorian calendar was devised.* Originally it was based upon the lunar year and started with an arbitrary count of 260 days but later it was modified to coincide with the solar year. The result was a series of 360 day periods and to correct this five "unlucky" days were added.

* In addition to their other attainments the Mayas had a very deep and accurate knowledge of astronomy. They possessed complete data on the eclipses of the moon, fully as accurate as any we have at the present time, and were thus able to foretell an eclipse long before it occurred. We have no real knowledge of their astronomical devices other than their tower observatories such as the *Caracol* at Chichen Itzá which has been carefully restored.

Fig. 6. *Maya numerals and symbols*

The original basic year of 260 days was still retained, however. This was divided into periods of thirteen weeks of twenty days each. In other words it was similar to our series of seven day weeks and just as each day of our week has a name, so the twenty days of the Mayan week had their names. These were:

1 Imix	6 Cimi	11 Chuen	16 Cib
2 Ik	7 Manik	12 Eb	17 Caban
3 Akbal	8 Lamat	13 Ben	18 Enzab
4 Kan	9 Muluc	14 Ix	19 Cauac
5 Chicchan	10 Oc	15 Men	20 Ahau

and were represented by symbols (Fig. 7).

Any single day indicated by its sign or symbol fixed its position in the twenty day period in exactly the same way as we fix the name of any day in our week count. With these day names the Mayas combined numerals from one to thirteen. As twenty and thirteen have no common factor higher than one, twenty times thirteen or two hundred and sixty days elapsed before any certain day, such for example as *1 Imix*, reappeared in a time count.

This period known as a "round" is most important as it was used as a sacred or ritual calendar by the priests and ran in a constantly recurrent cycle through the entire Mayan date system. The Mayan secular year consisted of eighteen periods or "months" of twenty days with the addition of five "unlucky days" and were known as:

1 Pop	7 Yaxkin	13 Mac
2 Uo	8 Mol	14 Kankin
3 Zip	9 Chen	15 Muan
4 Zotz	10 Yax	16 Pax
5 Tzec	11 Zac	17 Kayab
6 Xul	12 Ceh	18 Cumhu

Five unlucky days of Uayeb

These were indicated by symbols or signs as shown on Fig. 8. The names or signs together with numerals in addition to the day name and its number were used to definitely fix a day's position in the year. Thus a date such as *Ahau 4, Cumhu 8* would in a way correspond to our Friday, January 10th, the name Friday establishing the sixth day in our seven day week, just as the Mayan *Ahau 4* fixed the position of the day in their two hundred and sixty-

Fig. 7. *Maya day signs*

POP UO ZIP

ZOTZ TZEC XUL

YAXKIN MOL CHEN

YAX ZAC CEH

MAC KANKIN MUAN

PAX KAYAB CUMHU UAYEB

Fig. 8. Maya month signs

day period, and just as our 10th of January establishes that day's position in our year, so the Mayas' *Cumhu* 8 fixed the position of the day in the Mayas' year.

The Mayan system, however, was very different from ours when it came to numbering the month days. In our system the days run from one to thirty or thirty-one, whereas the Mayan month of twenty days had its days numbered from one to nineteen, for the Mayas measured only elapsed or past time.

For example, the date *Cumhu* 0 would record that the month of *Kayab* had ended but the first day of *Cumhu* had not been passed. In a way it was very similar to reckoning time by a clock and saying "four-thirty," thus indicating the last hour and the minutes of the next hour; or speaking of a person being in his twenty-second year when he has passed his twenty-first birthday.

As the Mayan day signs ran in a continual circle of twenty, and as there were twenty days in the Mayan month, it followed that every month began with the identical day sign and each day always occupied the same place in every month. Had there not been the five *Uayeb* or unlucky days at the end of every year, the positions of the day signs would have remained the same always, but the additional *Uayeb* days resulted in each day sign shifting five places back every new year. As a result, every year, as well as every month in a year, commenced with a day sign that was five days later than in the preceding year. As twenty is divisible by five four times, it follows that only four day signs could possibly become initial days in the Mayan year, and that each day sign could only hold four positions in any one month. The various positions of these are shown more clearly in the following table:

Positions 0.5.10.15	Positions 2.7.12.17	Positions 1.6.11.16
Ik	Kan	Akbal
Manik	Muluc	Lamat
Eb	Ix	Ben
Caban	Cauac	Enzab

Positions 3.8.13.18	Positions 4.9.14.19
Chicchan	Cimi
Oc	Chuen
Men	Cib
Ahau	Imix

Therefore in inscriptions where a date is questionable the choice of the day is limited to four. If a day sign in such an inscription is followed by a month date with a number that seems impossible it is often assumed that a mistake was made by the sculptor. But if, as I believe, any curlicues, or other additions to the numeral, signified a different number this assumption may be wrong.

Although every fourth year the day signs held their same relative positions, their accompanying numerals did not. Thirteen divides three hundred and sixty-five twenty-eight times with a remainder of one, hence each new year began with a day sign one more than the preceding year. For example the New Year's Days would be *1 Ik, 2 Manik, 4 Caban* and so on.

The highest common factor of both four and thirteen is one, so four times thirteen or fifty-two years had to pass before the same day and number combination would reappear in the same position in any one month. This fifty-two year period of 18,980 days is known to us as the "Calendar Round." Where a day and month date are shown together as *4 Ahau, 8 Cumhu* for example, the exact position of the day may be determined within the fifty-two year period. In addition to this fifty-two day Calendar Round there was the so-called "Long Count" which was a combination of the Mayas' numerical and calendrical systems.

Their numerical system was, if anything, more remarkable than their calendrical system and never has been excelled even by Europeans. Unlike our numerical system which is decimal, that of the Mayas was vigesimal. That is, while we count by tens the Mayas counted by twenties.

When we see or write down such a number as 152 we know that the five has ten times the value of the two and that the one has ten times the value of the five. In the Mayan system, however, the figure five would have twenty times the value of the two and the figure one would have twenty times the value of the five so that the number 152 by the Mayan system would indicate two plus five times twenty plus one times twenty times twenty or, expressed in numerals, 552. However, when numerals were employed for reckoning time the one would have but eighteen times the value of the five owing to the fact that a figure in the position of the five would indicate five periods of 365 days or twenty times eighteen and hence was equal to the number of days in eighteen months omitting the unlucky days.

Thus when used for computing time the Mayan figure would be 488 instead of 552. In the calendrical count the unit was a day with an involved numerical indicating the total sum of the days grouped in periods corresponding to the numerical system.

To the Mayas a day was known as a *kin* or sun and was indicated by a number corresponding to the position of our units. Twenty of these *kins* equalled a *uinal* or month that was represented by a numeral in the position of our tens. Eighteen *uinals* made a year or *tun* of three hundred sixty days with its numeral in the place of our hundreds. Twenty *tuns* made a *katun* with its numeral in the position of our thousands and twenty *katun* made a *baktun* or cycle indicated by a numerical in the position of our ten thousands. This will perhaps be more plainly shown by the following:

Indicated by our position of

1 kin . . . . 1 day . . . . units
20 kins . . . 1 uinal or month . . . . . . tens
18 uinals . . 1 tun (360 days) . . . . . . hundreds
20 tuns . . . 1 katun (7200 days) . . . . . thousands
20 katuns . . 1 baktun (144,000 days) . . tens of thousands

This may all seem very complex and puzzling but to archaeologists who have made a study of Mayan remains it is very simple and readily understood. For example, an archaeologist examining Stela A at Copán in Honduras might jot down: 9.14.19.8.0. To him this would mean that the inscription read: 9 baktun, 14 katun, 19 tun, 8 uinal, 0 kin, which would read as follows:

days

0 kin . . . . (1x0)   0
8 uinal . . . (8x20)   160
19 tun . . . . (19x360)   6,840
14 katun . . . (14x7200) . . .   100,800
9 baktuns . . (9x144000) . . . 1,296,000
                                 _____
                                 1,403,800 days

—a trifle less than 3,846 of our years. The inscription I have explained above is a very good example of a Mayan "Long Count" inscription. These are invariably followed by a month and a day

sign, together with their respective numbers. In the case of the inscription on the Copán monument the Long Count is followed by
the date 12 *Ahau, 18 Cumhu* of the Calendar Round.

These are most important when deciphering an inscription, for
if the 1,403,800 days of the Long Count are reckoned in reverse
from the date 12 *Ahau, 18 Cumhu,* we obtain the Calendar Round
date of 4 *Ahau, 8 Cumhu.*

Every known Initial Series date, followed by a Calendar Round
date, results by means of this series in the mysterious 4 *Ahau, 8
Cumhu.* In other words the Mayan calendrical system was calculated from a certain day (4 *Ahau, 8 Cumhu*) far back in the dim
and distant past. It was, in fact, similar to our system of beginning
our calendrical dates with the birth of Christ or A.D. 1. On a stela
at Quiriguá, Guatemala, there is an inscription dating the erection
of the monument as:

9 baktuns or cycles . . .	1,296,000 days	
17 katuns	122,400	
5 tuns	1,800	
	1,420,200	

after the 5 *Ahau, 8 Cumhu* starting point. If, as archaeologists
estimate, this monument was erected about 750 A.D., the starting
point of the Mayan calendrical system must have been 1,420,200
days earlier or approximately 3135 B.C. In this connection it is of
interest to note that according to their traditions the Mayas were
descendants of the four "Becabs" who came over seas to escape
the flood, and that Biblical students estimate that the Flood described in the Bible was about 3000 B.C.

Up to the present time no one has discovered any Mayan inscriptions that are dated earlier than the second half of the ninth cycle
so that to correlate accurately our years with Mayan dates is largely
a matter of guesswork and individual opinion and, as a result, the
ages of Mayan remains as estimated by various archaeologists vary
greatly. Some maintain that no Mayan remains date back beyond
500 A.D. while others, equally fitted to judge, declare that the
Mayas' civilization dates back to many centuries B.C. This may,
perhaps, be due to a misinterpretation of some of the glyphs. It
has been assumed that the so-called variations and decorations of
Mayan numerals and signs have no significance, but who can be

certain that such a glyph as No. 1, Fig. 5, which expresses thirteen may not have a totally different meaning if inscribed as in Nos. 2 and 3? If this is the case it would upset all or nearly all interpretations and completely alter the age of Mayan remains.

There is also the possibility of the inscriptions being in a code, while finally, as the explanatory or descriptive portions of the inscriptions cannot be interpreted, it is impossible to state with certainty that the dates are those on which the monuments were erected and did not refer to some event that took place in the past.

If we should find a book printed in some language which we could not read but in which the dates were in the same numerals as in English, could we assume that they referred to the events described on the pages where they appeared?

If we could not read the text how could we be sure they did not refer to some event mentioned on other pages? There is still another quite reasonable explanation of the apparently incongruous dates on certain Mayan inscriptions. If, as many archaeologists believe, the earliest records were on wood or other perishable substances, it may be that some of them were copied in stone and hence the dates on the later monuments would appear to be far too old. Not until the entire inscriptions can be interpreted can anyone be absolutely sure of the significance of the calendrical symbols.

We must also remember that there were two "Periods" of the Mayan civilization as the OLD EMPIRE, divided into three stages, and the NEW EMPIRE. Roughly these are dated as follows:

OLD EMPIRE

    Archaic . . .   Earliest known remains up to A.D. 104
    Middle . . .   Remains from A.D. 104 until A.D. 200
    Great . . . .   Remains from A.D. 200 until A.D. 350

NEW EMPIRE

    . . . .   Remains from A.D. 350 until the Conquest.

Up to the present time *all* known inscriptions that have been deciphered are of a calendrical character and of the "Hieratic" type or that used by the priests, rulers and wise men.

Nowhere, among all of the known decipherable glyphs, are there any of the "Demotic" type that relate anything regarding the lives of the Mayas, the names of their rulers, their habits or their history. All that we know of such matters has been learned from carvings, sculptures and effigies showing the people, the priests and the kings engaged in various activities and ceremonies. From these, which are very accurate and lifelike, we know how the Mayas dressed, how they worshiped and many other details of their lives and customs. Also, we must not forget that remnants of the Mayan civilization were still in existence at the time of the arrival of the Spaniards whose priests recorded quite a lot about the Mayas, although mainly interested in destroying the civilization, the religion, and the records of the subjugated people.

Unquestionably the Mayan written or sculptured language was their greatest achievement. In fact, in the opinions of many, it was the greatest achievement of any race either ancient or modern. It must have been developed at a very ancient date and appears to have sprung into use fully perfected for there are no known truly archaic or evolutionary forms of the inscriptions.

Those of the OLD EMPIRE are all of the same type throughout that period, but those of the NEW EMPIRE appear very different, although they are merely more complicated, involved and elaborated. That such a written language could have been invented in its perfected form is of course inconceivable and the only explanation appears to be that either the earliest or evolutionary forms were made on wood or some other perishable substance that has vanished, or that the amazing pictorial writing was brought fully developed from some other locality or culture of which we have no knowledge.

But until someone, somewhere, discovers a key to the Mayan picture writing the bulk of countless carvings and sculptures of the Mayas will remain a sealed book wholly undecipherable.

The first real progress in deciphering any of the Mayan inscriptions was made by Diego de Landa, the second Bishop of Yucatán, in 1524 to 1579, who wrote a history of the Mayas and explained their calendrical and numerical systems and the date symbols. In addition to this there were the *Books of Chilam Balam* compiled by Yucatán Indians of Mayan blood and written during the first century after the Spanish Conquest. These "Books" are chronicles and bits of history of the Mayas and throw a great deal of light upon the meanings of glyphs relating to the Mayan calendar.

Finally, there is the *Popol Vuh* (pronounced Popol-ou) or Book of the People.

This is the Sacred Book of the Quiché Maya, and is analogous to our Bible. No one knows who wrote or compiled this most interesting and illuminating work, aside from the fact that it was first written in the Quiché Maya language with Latin letters about the middle of the sixteenth century. The original was lost, but fortunately it had been copied about the end of the seventeenth century by Fray Francisco Ximenez, at that time the parish priest of Santo Tomas, Chichicastenango, in Guatemala. It is a most complete and fascinating book to anyone interested in the Mayas for it contains the traditions, mythology, history and genealogy of the Quiché Mayas and the chronology of their kings down to A.D. 1550. It has been translated into several languages including Spanish and English and in the latter form is published by the University of Oklahoma Press.

Finally, there were the *Golden Books of the Mayas* which tradition states were fifty-two golden plates threaded on gold bars and engraved with characters relating the entire history of the Mayan people. Whether or not such records ever existed, whether they were found and melted down to bullion by the Spaniards or whether, as tradition declares, they were hidden by the Mayan priests and never have been found, no one really knows.

In addition to their written language inscribed on stelae, monuments and elsewhere, the Mayas had codices. Only a few of these are preserved as far as known. The most important and perfect being the *Codex Peresianus* in Paris, the *Dresden Codex,* and the *Troano Codex* in Madrid.

Unlike the Aztec codices that were largely pictorial and are quite easily deciphered, those of the Mayas had few pictures and were covered with much the same type of characters as are inscribed on stone monuments. All are thought to deal mainly with the Mayan mythology but no one has yet been able to fully decipher them, although portions of some have been interpreted.

The mythology of the Mayas was very complicated and involved and there is a great deal of confusion as to the actual identity of some of their deities as several were known by more than one name while their attributes were not infrequently duplicated. Regardless of such details the Mayas were thoroughly priest-ridden and must have lived in constant fear of offending some of their innumerable mythological deities. Prominent among these, if not the most important of all, was the Plumed Serpent known to the Mayas as KUKULCAN (Kukul—the Quetzal and Kan—serpent) and also called GUCUMATZ in Guatemala. To the Mayas, Kukulcan was fully as important a deity or hero-god as he was to the Aztecs to whom he was known as QUETZALCOATL. (See Chapter 8.) Then there was the Mayan sun-god or KINICH AHAU (literally, Face of the Sun), who was analogous to INTI of the Incans and was also known as KINICH KAKMO (Fire Bird) and was identified with red macaw or *Arara* (Fire Bird). Primarily the Mayas were sun worshipers and in nearly all of their myths the origin of the race was solar. As the sun rises in the east, the Mayas' gods, who were credited with having introduced their civilization and culture, were believed to have come from the east. Even more important than their sun-god in many ways, and in fact the greatest of all Mayan deities, was the invisible and supreme god known as HUNAB-KU. He was worshiped by all the Mayan tribes and was regarded as the unity of all gods and in a way held the same position in the Mayan religion as our God Almighty holds in the Christian and Jewish religions.

There was also the Moon god named ITZAMA, "The Father of Gods and Men," a name derived from his legendary words: *"Itz-en-caan; itz-en-muyal"* or "I am the dew of Heaven. I am the dew of the clouds." This epithet appears to establish a connection between Itzama, Tlaloc, and the deity Chac as the god of rain. Undoubtedly these seemingly various deities are but one and the same god under different names. Itzama was also credited with having introduced cacao, the culture and use of rubber, and other produce. If he was the original Kukulcan, as Dr. Spence formerly of the British Museum believes, then Itzama was the Creator god who, according to tradition, introduced maize and its culture, as well as other vegetables.

Itzama was the personification of the east, the rising sun, and associated with esoteric ideas of light, life and knowledge. Tradition gives him the credit of having invented writing, and introducing books. He was regarded as a great healer and as the first priest of the Mayan religion.

XAMAN-EK was regarded as "the Guide of Merchants," and is associated with picture writing and symbols of peace and plenty. He was also referred to as the "North Star god" and in connection with this fact it is of interest to note that the North Star was for a considerable length of time known to Old World sailors and merchant mariners as the "Phoenician," due to its value in navigation by the stars.

ZOTZILHA CHIMALMAN, known as the "Bat god" was the Mayas' god of night and darkness and was believed to dwell in a cave. Throughout the mythology and religion of the Mayas, as well as in their legends, there is always conflict between darkness and light, with Kinich Ahau the Sun god battling with Zotzilaha-Chimalman. In fact it is quite possible that the whole Mayan religion was built around the never-ending conflict between life and death or day and night.

Then there was IXCHEL, goddess of childbirth, the moon, the rainbow, medicine and weaving, who also personified water as a destroying agent. She was believed to be the sister-wife of the Creator-god Itzama.

The rain-god known as CHAC-MOOL was undoubtedly identical with Tlaloc of the Toltecs and archaeologists have never been able to decide whether the Mayas borrowed Chac-Mool from the Aztecs or inherited this deity from their Toltec background. Although usually represented as a man resting on his back with flexed knees and with his hands clasping a bowl held on his stomach, he is often depicted, both in frescoes and in sculptures, as having a long nose or rather a snout like that of the tapir, which is thought to be symbolic of a spout for pouring water.

The termination of each religious or priest year of the Mayas was marked by a feast day and ceremonies of great importance. This was known as the *Tzolkin* (Aztec: *Tonalamatl*) which came at the time of the spring florescence beginning at sundown but with the actual feast and ceremonies commencing at dawn the next day.

One of the few occasions when the Mayas made human sacrifices took place at this time when young and carefully selected beautiful virgins were sacrificed to Kinich Ahau by being cast into the sacred well at Chichen Itzá. We need not, however, feel either horror or sympathy for the victims, for they considered it a great honor to be the chosen ones and competition for becoming "brides" of their god was as keen as among young ladies of today in their rivalry for selection as the Queen of this, that or the other. Moreover, they implicitly believed that by their sacrifice they would be transported directly to the Mayan heaven and literally would become brides of the deity.

Besides their true gods or deities the Mayas' mythology contained four BACABS, who were known as KAN, MULUC, IX and CAUAC, considered semi-deities or genii, who were symbolical of the four cardinal points of the compass and were thought to support the four corners of the sky. Each had its own color by which it was identified, Kan being yellow; Muluc white; Ix black and Cauac red.

In addition to all these I have mentioned there were a number of unidentified strange gods or deities depicted on codices and at times in carvings and known to archaeologists by letters (Fig. 9).

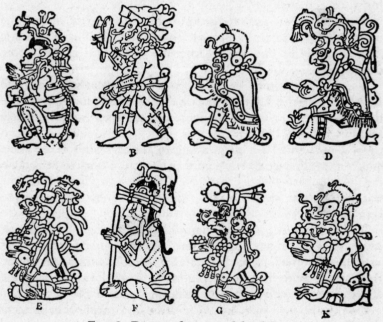

Fig. 9. Deities designated by letters

Whether these were merely elaborated representations of the well-known deities of the Mayas or whether they were distinct gods or perhaps "proxies" who took the places of the regular gods, no one knows. Although they have been identified as gods of certain matters by means of their characteristics, this is little more than guesswork and may be wrong. Thus *A* has been designated as the god of Death on account of his fleshless skull and skeleton body, while the glyph that accompanies him shows a death's head with closed eyes, a skull and a sacrificial knife.

As the figure *B* has a long snout-like nose he is thought to be the god of water or Chac-Mool. *C* is surrounded by the symbols of the planets and is supposed to be the god of the North Star. *D* represents an aged man with the symbol of night, and as his glyph is encircled by stars and has the numeral 20, the time of the moon's duration, the figure is regarded as the Moon god. *E* wears a headdress supposedly made of ears of maize and with a parrot over his forehead. He is considered the god of Harvests or the Corn god, but it takes a most vivid imagination to see anything in the least resembling ears of maize in the figure's headdress. *F* is supposed to be the god of sacrifice as there are "wound" marks on his face and body. He may be the same as XIPE the Flayed god of the Aztecs. *G* is considered the Sun god and has the glyph KIN. The figure *K* is mainly remarkable for its elaborate branched nose with which it appears to be eating fruit from a dish. It is considered the same deity as Chac-Mool but as the figure *B* is regarded as the Rain god, figure *K* is called the Thunder god.

As I have said, the identification of these figures is based on supposition and the chances are that every odd decoration and detail had its particular meaning and that these, if separated from the figure of the person, would, to one who knew the key, tell a complete story of the figure in its entity and its significance.

Moreover, it is not at all improbable that all of these figures are intended to represent the same personage or deity under his various manifestations or titles. Many, in fact most, of the Mayan deities held more than one niche in the Mayas' mythology. Thus Itzama was not only the Moon god but was also god of the East, god of Birth and Death, god of Nature and probably a Sun god under certain conditions. Even more varied in his attributes was Hunab-ku the traditional father of Itzama, who was the invisible unity of all the Mayan deities.

The uncertain lettered gods of the codices may well represent this supreme god in his various personalities. This theory is rendered the more logical owing to the fact that each of the figures has certain elements common to all. Finally they may have some calendrical significance, for many of the Mayan deities were more important from a symbolic than from a religious standpoint, and each of the Mayan weeks was believed to be under the auspices of a certain deity. All of which goes to show how very little we actually know of the Mayas. Even their traditions tell us little concerning who they were, or where they originated; in fact not much of anything is known concerning their early history.

Fig. 10. Portion of Maya Codex

The late Dr. Sylvanus Morley called attention to the fact that the majority of Mayan children had the "Asiatic blue spot" on the lower portion of the back as well as the epicanthic eye fold and other physical characteristics which are typical of certain races of northeastern Asia. He claimed that (as at that time was believed) they had migrated from Asia by the way of the Behring Sea. But he overlooked or ignored the fact that none of these natives of Asia have the huge convex nose, so typical of Mayan carvings, and still common among the present day Mayas, or the fact that neither the blue spot, the Asiatic type of eyes nor the other features occur among many tribes of North America.

Regardless of the origin of the so-called "Indians," it is now generally conceded that the Xiu Mayas were descended from, or were a branch of, the Toltecs who wandered over a large portion of Mexico and Yucatán before finally establishing themselves in the area about Chakanputun for more than two hundred years before they occupied Chichen Itzá and founded Mayapan and Uxmal. But there were also the Lacandons who were of Mexican ancestry and who established themselves in the vicinity of the Gulf of Carmen and along the Usumacinta River, but whose descendants at present are mainly in the State of Chiapas in Mexico. Finally there were the Zutuhils and the Quiché Maya who occupied Guatemala and parts of Honduras. According to their traditions and their *Popol Vuh,* they came from the east across the sea and documents of the Quiché and Cakchiquel, as well as those from Yucatán and Mexico, relate the same story of the origin of the inhabitants of the central Mexican plateau and the northern half of Central America. There is no real evidence that they were of Mexican origin but it is thought that they had a common origin or parent culture.

Recent discoveries and researches lead us to believe that their ancestors originally came from the area we know today as the Departments of Ancash and Junin, Peru. Many of the Ancash sculptures, carvings, and other remains are very similar to those of the Maya with symbolic and other details identical. Moreover, Ancash means blue, and many of the sculptures, etc., show the figure of a two-headed serpent (Plate 4). This two-headed serpent was a most important symbol of the Toltecs and the blue snake or Xiucoatl of the Mayas may have been employed as a totem for the Zutuhils who referred to themselves as the "People of the Blue Snake."

Regardless of whether the ancestors of the Mayas were of Toltec, Peruvian or Old World origin it must have required an incalculable length of time for the various races, each with its own dialect, to have invented and developed a common language, to have devised most amazing and accurate numerical and calendrical systems and a form of highly involved and decorative picture writing that has no counterpart in any other portion of the world.

Naturally, until a common language had been evolved and until the people had invented a method of recording events of their history, there was only tradition, and even the best and most reliable of traditions are often far from the truth and vary greatly. Apparently, however, the several tribes or clans were in an almost continual state of warfare. In the northern section of Yucatán the Tutul-Xius, clan of the cult of the Feathered Serpent (Kukulcan), together with the House of Cocom were constantly battling for supremacy with the priest clan of Ipa-Hanak who were of the cult of Kinich-Ahau or the Sun god. Moreover, the Quiché Mayas of the Guatemala highlands were at loggerheads with the Yucatán Mayas.

As I have already mentioned, the Mayan Empire of Xibalba or the Great Snake was a more or less loosely knit federation of many tribes, innumerable clans and cults. Each city or state had its own ruler or "king" yet all were somewhat under the domination of the Mayapan priests or priest-kings, who were of the Xiu clan and claimed direct descent from the original Kukulcan or Itzama who, it is now believed, were one and the same. Despite their civil wars the Mayas managed to reach great heights in architecture, in arts and in astronomy during their Old or First Empire, yet they attained even greater achievements during the New and Second Empire. It was at this time that Chichen Itzá and many of the famous and magnificent cities were built. The founders of Chichen Itzá, however, were not the priests but were of the warrior caste of the clan of Itzaes. But as is so often the case, with the development of art, religion, astronomy and other sciences, armies and warriors became of less and less importance until the Mayas were in no condition to resist an enemy who had hired Mexican mercenaries to bring about their destruction. In a comparatively short time they lost their grandeur, their Empire was disrupted and the lives, arts and customs of the people were greatly altered. Although the remnants took refuge in more remote city-states they never managed to form a third extended empire, and at the time of the Spanish conquest the Mayan civilization as an entity was at an end.

CHAPTER 5

Ancient Mexican Civilizations

When the Spaniards under Cortez arrived in what now is Mexico they found an amazing civilization with a king or ruler named Montezuma whose subjects were referred to as AZTECS. And when Prescott wrote his *History of the Conquest of Mexico*, he described and treated of the "Aztec Empire" with the result that the majority of persons, who are at all interested in the subject, have the erroneous idea that *all* the Mexican Indians were "Aztecs," that Montezuma ruled all of Mexico at the time of the conquest and that the magnificent buildings, the impressive monuments, the colossal pyramids and temples, the great cities, the religion and deities, the language and in fact everything that Cortez and his followers found in Mexico were Aztec. In fact most persons when speaking of any of the present-day Indians of Mexico refer to them as "Aztecs."

In reality the Aztecs were and are only a small percentage of all of the Indian tribes and races of Mexico, the term referring only to the Nahuas or the tribes who speak the Nahuatl language. Moreover, these people occupied only a comparatively small area of Mexico, mainly the high plateaus and valleys in the neighborhood of the City of Mexico which was the Aztec capital and was known to them as Tenochtitlán.

In addition to the Nahuas there were a number of other tribes who were under the Aztec rule, for the empire was a confederation of many tribes and cultures, but there were many others who never bowed to the Nahua yoke, who spoke languages very different from Nahuatl and who were constantly at war with the true Aztecs. To be sure there were a number of tribes living beyond the true boundaries of Montezuma's realm who, although not integral parts of his empire, paid annual tribute to him and thus saved themselves from extermination or slavery.

The most powerful of the tribes who were not under Aztec rule were the Tarascans whose capital was Tzintzuntzán near the shores of beautiful Lake Pázcuaro in the present State of Michoacán. Never conquered by the Aztecs and with a high culture and a civilization all their own, the Tarascans fell to the Spaniards. But they were of far firmer stuff than their Aztec enemies and even when put to the most fiendish tortures they never revealed the hiding place of the vast store of gold, silver, and precious stones they had accumulated, and the treasures still remain where the Tarascans concealed them centuries ago.

In the southern part of the country, on the Isthmus of Tehuantepec, there were the Zapotecs and the Tehuanas who had their own civilization that was far more ancient than that of the Aztecs and whose palaces, pyramids and other remains at Monte Albán and Mitla are perhaps the most wonderful as well as the most ancient of all in Mexico.

Others who were not of the Aztec race and had their own cultures were the Totonacs in the vicinity of the present State of Vera Cruz whose culture is now designated as the TAJIN. This culture has definite relationships with the Teotihuacán culture, the Otomis in the Guanajuato and Querétaro districts, the Pipils on the west coast of the country, the Mixtecs on the Gulf Coast and the Tlascalans who became allies of Cortez and without whose aid the invasion would have doubtless ended in the annihilation of the Spaniards. It is true that the superstitions of the people and the tradition of the prophecy foretelling the coming of the "Sons of Quetzalcoatl" (bearded white men from over the sea), led the Indians to believe that the Spaniards were deities and not ordinary human beings, and consequently immortal. But it did not take them long to discover that the Spaniards were far from being gods and that they were as mortal as anyone else when it came to a well-aimed arrow, a spear thrust or the blow of a jagged-edged Aztecan sword. Also, of course, the natives' fear of the Dons' horses and the terror inspired by their firearms played very important parts in the success of the conquest, but it was very largely the Spaniards' native allies and the influence of Malinche, the slave girl, that brought Montezuma and his empire to their tragic and dramatic ends.

In addition to the numerous tribes with their own cultures, their own rulers and their own cities, who were not integral parts of the Aztec Empire, there were numerous semi-savage, primitive tribes such as the Huicholes and Yaquis of northern Mexico and several jungle-dwelling tribes in the extreme south.

Just as so many persons are under the impression that the entire Indian population of Mexico are Aztecs and that, at the time of the conquest, Montezuma ruled them all, the majority of persons refer to all the ruins and remains of Mexico's ancient civilization as "Aztec." Actually many of the most remarkable, the most famous, the most impressive and the best preserved monuments, buildings, pyramids, carvings, metal work and other evidences of the advanced civilization of ancient Mexico were not the work of the Aztecs but others whose cultures far antedated that of the Nahuatl speaking Aztecs.

Just who the Aztecs were or whence they came has never been definitely established. That they were not indigenous to Mexico is proved by their codices or pictographic writings on paper, which record the history of the people. But most regrettably many of these are missing, having been destroyed, along with an incalculable lot of other material of inestimable archaeological value, by the fanatical Spanish priests.

The name Aztec means "People of the Cranes" and both their traditions and their codices agreed that their original home was at some unidentified locality known as Aztlan or "Place of the Reeds," which some archaeologists believe to have been California. The fact that the Aztecs established their capital on the marshy shores of a lake rather indicates that they did come from a marshy area where reeds abounded.

Other localities shown on the codices and mentioned in their traditions are the "Seven Caves" or Chicomoztoc, and the "Country of Bright Colors" or Tlapallan, which some authorities think refer to the Zion, Bryce or similar canyons and the Painted Deserts of our Southwest.

If, as many believe, the Aztec legends of the Toltecs are historically correct and the Aztecs were descendants of the Toltecs, then evidences of their presence are to be found as far north as northern

Utah where, near the Green River at Vernal, there are numerous pictographs, both painted and engraved upon the rocks, showing human figures some of which have been identified as representing Quetzalcoatl, of whom more later.

Whatever the truth may be in regard to the origin and migrations of the Aztecs and their history we know that they appeared in Central Mexico and founded their capital city of Tenochtitlán. However, there are several versions of the Aztecs' traditions regarding their migrations and their founding of the city and they are so interlarded with obvious myths and folklore that it is impossible to separate legend from history.

According to one of the traditions the Aztecs were led to the locality by a chief named Huitzilopochtli who, later on, became deified as the god of war. When the wanderers came to the spot indicated they saw an eagle with spread wings perched upon a cactus and grasping a serpent in its claws. Feeling that this was a good omen the Aztecs sank piles into the marshy ground and established their city.

Another version tells of the Aztecs seeking refuge on the western shores of the lake and there finding a sacrificial stone whereon, forty years earlier, a prisoner of war, the Prince Copal, had been put to death. A cactus plant had sprouted from the crevice in the stone and an eagle with a snake in its talons perched upon it. This the people decided was an omen and their high priest plunged into a small pond and there met Tlaloc, the god of waters, who granted permission to build the city. Very likely the site *was* selected because an eagle, or more likely a caracara hawk, was seen perched on a cactus and devouring a snake, for all Indians are forever looking for signs or omens and are greatly influenced by any event or occurrence that is in any respect out of the ordinary.

Moreover, all their legends relating to the founding of Tenochtitlán agree as to the eagle on the cactus so we may feel quite sure that the city that was destined to grow into the great, teeming, modern City of Mexico owed its existence to a snake-eating bird of prey perched on a cactus. It is, therefore, highly fitting that Mexico's national emblem is an eagle grasping a serpent while perched on a cactus.

Even if we cannot be quite certain as to how the Aztecs happened to establish Tenochtitlán on the Lake of Texcoco, we know that the "People of Anahuac" as they called themselves, were a rather small and alien tribe and it was truly remarkable that within a comparatively short time they had subjugated many other tribes and had formed an "empire" with a remarkable dynasty, a strange, cruel, and bloodthirsty religion; had developed innumerable arts and crafts; possessed accurate calendrical and numerical systems and had erected magnificent temples and titanic pyramidal mounds.

The fact that they *did* accomplish all this and more would appear to indicate that much of their culture was already developed prior to their founding of their capital and that they were the descendants or offshoots from some highly cultured race such as the Toltecs, who the Aztecs claimed were their ancestors, or that they had borrowed much of their culture from the others who had preceded them.

Fortunately the Aztec government was in full swing and at its peak when Cortez and his men arrived on the scene, and as a result we possess a wealth of definite knowledge of their civilization. But on the other hand, the Spaniards, and especially the priests, took little interest in matters ethnological and archaeological. They were seeking gold and other treasures and were obsessed with the purpose of salvaging the souls of the pagan Indians. As a result, everything that the priests could lay hands on, and that savored of paganism, was ruthlessly destroyed and everything of monetary value that Cortez and his soldiers found was broken up or cast into the melting pot. Only some of the stupendous pyramids and the most massive structures resisted the Dons' fanatical destructiveness.

However, one of the Spaniards, Bernal Díaz de Castillo, wrote a most voluminous and, as far as we know, a fairly accurate account of the campaign entitled *Historia Verdadera de la Conquista de Nueva España,* in which he gives quite a detailed description of the Aztecs' lives, customs, religion, gods, sacrifices, and other matters.

From these and other sources we know a great deal more about the Aztecs as they were at the time of the conquest than we know about the Mayas. On the other hand, we must not forget that a great deal of our supposed knowledge of these people is largely guesswork. Frequently contemporaneous writers disagreed and still more often they omitted all mention of important matters, which doubtless to them were uninteresting everyday affairs not worth recording. Also, even the most intelligent and highly educated of the

Spaniards were greatly at a disadvantage when it came to observing and describing matters that pertained to the Indians. And they were, of course, forced to rely for their information upon interpreters and hearsay until they had mastered the Nahuatl dialect with its strange guttural, clucking and throaty sounds so very different from the soft Castilian. Even their own spelling of Spanish names and words was often incorrect and when it came to Aztec names and words they found the letters of their Spanish alphabet wholly inadequate. All they could do was to spell the words phonetically and even this was often impossible as no letters existed to express the Aztec sounds. As a result, as well as because names of places, deities, and other things varied according to the locality and the tribal tongue of the area, a great deal of confusion occurred and today we cannot be sure of the names of deities, personages, tribes, and localities or whether or not the Indians' pronunciation of a name was at all the same as it would be according to the Spaniards.

However, we do know that the Aztec capital had developed into a large and very imposing city when the Spaniards arrived. According to the records of the invaders the city was then over twelve miles in circumference and contained more than fifty thousand houses with a teeming population of over a quarter million inhabitants or almost one-eighth the size of Mexico City today.

Moreover, on neighboring islands and on the shores of the lake, there were several towns almost as large as the capital itself so that even in those days the population of "Greater Tenochtitlán" must have totalled over a million—perhaps even more than Greater Mexico City of today.

According to the chroniclers, the city was admirably planned and laid out with broad avenues running from east to west and from north to south, thus dividing the city into equal-sized squares. There were also four main roads or highways crossing the lake on causeways or dykes while innumerable canals served as streets and lanes. There was even a public water supply consisting of an aqueduct with twin pipes of stone and cement that carried water from the hills to the center of the city where there were fountains and reservoirs. Smaller conduits piped water to the palaces and the more sumptuous residences. The homes of the upper classes were of stone, usually covered with stucco. Mainly they were one story in height with flat roofs on which were gorgeous flowers, for despite

their cruel religion and human sacrifices the people were passionately fond of flowers as are all Mexican Indians of today.

The written or inscribed language of the Aztecs was very different from that of the Mayas. Whereas the latter used symbols and
various characters in no way related to or suggestive of the subject
recorded, the Aztecs employed pictographs of the subject accompanied by numerical or other symbols. And whereas the Mayas
mainly employed glyphs cut in stone for recording events and their
codices were of secondary importance, the Aztecs used codices almost exclusively. A vast number of these are preserved and many
are readily interpreted. In addition, when recording calendrical matters they used various signs or symbols of the days, names of deities,
etc., and such records were often carved on stone. Although these
are far easier to decipher than are those of the Mayas yet there
are many matters on which archaeologists do not agree. We cannot state positively why various representations of some one deity
should be very different in details and we cannot be certain that
the correct meanings have been given many of the signs and
symbols.

Although, as I have said, the Aztecs used pictures to record
events and localities, these were often so highly conventionalized as
to be almost unrecognizable and, in addition, the Aztecs were de-
veloping a phonetic type of writing in which the phonetic value
of names or symbols were combined to form names of persons,
places and various objects of which the codex treated. Thus the
picture of a trap or *montli* followed by an eagle or *qhuauhtli* followed by a lancet, *zo* and finally a hand, *mail* might be used to
record the name *Monquauzoma* (or as we call it—"Montezuma")
by combining the first syllables of the objects thus: *Mon-quau-
zo-ma*.

The codices and other writings were not, however, intended to
be used by the public in general but were primarily official and
were mainly for use by the priests, the officials and what we might
call the educated classes. Also a great many were learned, just as
many historical events are learned by us, and were memorized and
handed down from generation to generation by word of mouth.

No one knows when the Aztecs first learned to make paper and
inscribe the codices which were written on long sheets of their
tough handmade paper which was then folded again and again to

form books. But the art must have been very ancient as some of the codices record events that took place long before the Aztecs reached Mexico. They were still made and used long after the Spanish conquest and even after the Indians had acquired a knowledge of Spanish, and numerous codices have explanatory supplementary Spanish words.

Although both the Aztecs and the Mayas possessed an amazing knowledge of mathematics and astronomy, yet they had progressed along separate lines and the results attained were very different.

Like the Mayas, the Aztecs' year was three hundred and sixty-five days but without the added day every fourth year. Because of this their calendar in time failed to correspond with the actual time and to correct and overcome this there was the "Binding of the Years" or *Nexiuhilpilitzli*. The years were divided into two cycles; one of fifty-two years of three hundred and sixty-five days, the other of seventy-three groups of two hundred and sixty days each. The first cycle of solar years consisted of eighteen periods of twenty months each, with the five *nemontemi* or unlucky days over. These were not included in the year but extended the yearly division of twenty months. The other cycle of the seventy-three groups of two hundred and sixty days each were split up into thirteen day divisions or "birth cycles."

The basis of reckoning time was the twenty day period or lunar month, each day of the period having its own name and symbol such as house, reed, wind, or serpent. Also, these lunar months were split up into four weeks of five days each and these were identified by the symbol or name of the third day in each week. The day names continued regardless of the length of the year which was known by the name of the middle day of the week on which it commenced. As there were only twenty day names there were four—the house (*calli*), the rabbit (*rochtli*), the reed (*acatl*), and the flint (*tecpatl*) that always appeared in the same order on account of the incidence of the solar year.

The "sun year" consisted of four common years and as the unlucky days did not count, the result was that the day names ran continuously year after year. However, the priests had their own religious calendar and always commenced this with the first calendrical date irrespective of the name it bore in the ordinary year.

There was also the "bundle" (*Xiumalpilli*) of thirteen years, four of which made up the fifty-two year period or "Binding of the Years." As a result of all this every year had a double aspect for each was a distinct period of time and each was also a part of the "sun year."

The five Unlucky Days were not only considered unlucky but were regarded with terror by the people who firmly believed that the world would come to an end at the close of one of these periods. As no one could foretell which cycle would bring this destruction the people always prepared for the worst. Then, when nothing happened and the Binding of the Years ceremonies were celebrated and all work stopped, sacrifices were made, the people grovelled before their god and at the dawning of the first day of the new (fifty-third) year all eyes were focused on the Pleiades, watching for the omen that meant a new lease of life or utter annihilation. Once the constellation had passed the zenith all knew that present danger was over and there was great rejoicing with innumerable human sacrifices while temple and hearth fires that had been extinguished were rekindled.

Originally the lunar cycle was the Birth Cycle of 260 days and was a portion of the civil calendar with its thirteen named "moons." Later it became a thing apart with nothing in common with the regular calendar and the "moon" names were given up, the days being known by numerals from one to thirteen. Oddly enough the number 13 occurs with suggestive frequency in the religious, calendrical and other important matters of the ancient American races. Practically all their prophecies were based on thirteen.

Quetzalcoatl, the Feathered Serpent god of the Aztecs, prophesied that in the thirteenth era white strangers would arrive from over seas and would overthrow the Aztec king and would enforce a new religion. The Maya priest, Chilam Balam, prophesied that at the close of the thirteenth age white men, "sons of Kukulcan," would arrive in Yucatán and in far-off Peru the Inca Huayna-Kapak prophesied on his death bed that during the reign of the thirteenth Inca white men would "come from the sun" and conquer and subjugate the Incans. And the most amazing part of it is that, in a way, all three of these prophecies were borne out. Cortez and his Spaniards reached Mexico in the thirteenth era; they conquered or rather overran the Mayas toward the close of the Mayan thirteenth age, and Pizarro and his followers reached Peru during the reign of Atahualpa, the thirteenth Inca.

Unlike us, these ancient American races all regarded thirteen as a propitious, in fact an almost sacred, number and all through their legends and folk lore it appears over and over again. In all likelihood the mysticism of the number thirteen resulted from the thirteen "moons" of the lunar year that was the same in the Aztec, Maya and Incan calendrical systems.

Aside from their calendrical system, that was far more complicated and involved than that of the Mayas, and their engineering skill and art in structural enterprises, their various crafts, their metallurgical work, their gem cutting, their weaving, and their remarkable paintings the Aztecs were not as advanced as their neighbors in Yucatán. Very largely they were steeped in superstition and believed thoroughly in omens, prophecy, astrology and divination as practiced by the priests who claimed the ability to foretell the future and the status of souls after death, all based on their study of the stars and on omens such as the condition of fruits, flowers, seeds, the flight of birds, certain bones, stones and many other objects.

The governmental and social organization of the Aztecs was unlike that of the Mayas and Incans. The reigning king or ruler was supreme and held sway over practically all parts of what now are the States of Vera Cruz, Guerrero and Mexico, as well as having nominal power over many other sections of the country. Although the Aztec monarch was theoretically supreme yet within the empire there were a number of small states and cities whose rulers were laws unto themselves and who, although paying tribute to the central Aztec government, were more or less independent. In fact the country was in a condition more or less resembling mediaeval Europe with its numerous feudal lords and barons, each all powerful within his own bailiwick but all owing allegiance to the king or emperor of the land.

Although the Aztec rulers were always members of the royal family, the succession was not hereditary and when an emperor died it was his eldest brother who ascended the throne. If there was no brother, then the next in line was the eldest nephew. However, as was the case with the majority of Indian tribes, a ruler might be chosen for his military prowess or his political or religious standing especially if the rightful heir proved to be incompetent or a weakling.

Aside from the supreme or "Great Lord" ruler, there were councillors who were analogous to our cabinet ministers, others devoted to military affairs and still others acting in a judicial capacity, for every city and province had its courts and judges who held both criminal and civil authority. Their decisions superseded those of the emperor, just as our Supreme Court's judgment is final. In addition to all these high officials, all of whom were members of the nobility, there were the lesser magistrates, the police and the military officials.

Almost as powerful as the ruler, in fact in some respects, more powerful, were the priests. They had complete charge of all education, which was a very important matter, the educational system being as well organized as our own and divided into two grades, primary and secondary. The boys were taught by the priests, the girls by the nuns, the primary grade being similar to our public schools education while the *Calmeac* or second grade might be compared to our college course. In this grade education consisted almost entirely of studying and deciphering codices and inscriptions, the symbols and signs used, and learning astronomy, and studying astrology, divination, religion and the higher sciences.

Although the Aztec priesthood held immense power and was a hierarchy, and despite their fanatical devotion to a most bloodthirsty religion, yet the priests devoted most of their time and power to instructing the people on religious matters, teaching them the sciences and endeavoring to benefit and better the conditions of the populace. Even the Spanish priests remarked on this and Sahagun wrote that the Aztec priests, cruel pagans though they were, "performed the duties clearly indicated by their religion."

The immense expenditure incurred by the upkeep of the Church was defrayed by land tenures with the revenues derived from them, the law of "first fruits" and a certain part of tribute collected from outlying sections. Any surplus over and above legitimate expenses was divided among the poor, the aged and the helpless.

At the head of the Church was the *Mexicatl Teohuatzon* or the "Mexican Lord of Matters Divine." He was second only to the emperor, was a member of the Council and held a great deal of secular as well as religious power. Next to him in rank was the Priest of the Plumed Serpent who held authority only over his own caste. Beneath these two chief dignitaries were the various *Tlenamacac* or secular priests, all robed in black and wearing long hair covered with mantilla-like cloths, while still lower in the priesthood were the *Lamacazton* or "Little Priests" who corresponded to the novices or lay brothers of the Catholic Church.

Unlike the priests in many places where the Church is almost as powerful or even more powerful than the State, the Aztec priests did not live in ease, luxury and idleness but led rigorous and austere lives. The demands of their religion were exacting and many and called for penitence, prayers and fasting. Even during the night they were obliged to rise often and engage in rituals to their gods and they frequently were obliged to indulge in self-sacrifice by drawing their own blood. Absolute cleanliness was a tenet of their religion and was rigorously enforced. Cruel, bloodthirsty, offering innumerable human sacrifices accompanied by fiendish rites, yet the Aztec priests were, according to their religious faith, the most zealous and holy of clerics and fully as fanatical in their beliefs as were the Spainsh padres.

Their rituals called for a certain amount of cannibalism in connection with the sacrifices, yet, on the other hand, there were confessions, baptisms and communion as well as kindness and aid rendered the poor, the aged and infirm. In fact the religion was in some respects far superior to that of the old Romans and Greeks and at the time of the arrival of the Spaniards it was rapidly becoming a worship of one supreme god known as TEZCATLIPOCA or "Air god" who was supposed to carry a polished shield in which he could see all the activities of mankind.

The Aztecs believed in the immortality of the soul and in eternity, but with epochs or eons dependent upon the sun. Every four "suns" marked one of these epochs when disaster was expected, the details of which were foretold and recorded.

As is generally and widely known, the victims of the sacrifices were killed by having their hearts torn from their bodies by the officiating priests which, bestial and cruel as it sounds, was about the quickest and most merciful of deaths—far more merciful in fact than hanging, or other means employed by civilized communities for ending a man's life.

However, the widely accepted tale of the victim of sacrifices being held in place upon the altar by means of a massive stone yoke or collar about his neck has no basis in fact. The stone collars or yokes are fairly common but there is no evidence that their purpose was to secure sacrificial victims. When used in connection with sacrifices their purpose was entirely symbolic, the form of the yoke representing the land of the dead in the conventionalized mouth of a mythical monster. However, the pre-Aztecs did use stone collars for holding victims on the altars but these were very different from the "yokes" (Fig. 11). For that matter it is unlikely that it was necessary to secure a sacrificial victim on the altar for those who were doomed to die were as firm believers in their religion and the need of human sacrifices as were the priests themselves. They felt that by their deaths they were winning immortality and divine favors and seldom were unwilling victims.

Fig. 11. Type of yoke used to hold down the sacrificial victims

With few exceptions the men, women and children who met their deaths on the Aztec altars were either prisoners of war or were captives from other tribes who were taken for the sole purpose of sacrifice by one of the strangest of all Aztec customs. This was their annual battle with the Tlascalans when warriors of the two races met on a prearranged battlefield and engaged in a struggle in which the contestants' aim was not to kill but to capture their opponents who were destined to be sacrificed. Weapons were not used, the warriors of either tribe seizing those of the other and endeavoring to carry them off until the "battle" was a confused, frenzied chaotic mass of struggling men pulling and tugging to either bear off or rescue the combatants.

The Tlascalans captured by the Aztecs were placed in cages and transported in triumph to Tenochtitlán while the Aztecs who were prisoners of the Tlascalans were carried off to the latters' city, in both cases doomed to die on the sacrificial altars of the temples.

When the captives reached Tenochtitlán they were given a

chance—although a very slim one—of winning their liberty and their lives. With one foot fastened to a huge block of stone, the captive was given a miniature shield and a wooden weapon and was attacked by a fully armed and equipped Aztec warrior. If by any miracle the handicapped prisoner succeeded in defeating half a dozen of his opponents in succession he was given his freedom, but if he failed and received the least wound he was doomed to sacrifice.

Although in their religious practices the Aztecs were cold-blooded, cruel and bloodthirsty yet in their everyday lives they were good natured, kindly, hospitable and passionately fond of music, flowers and pets, while their secular festivities were beautiful and peaceful.

They were, however, an ambitious and dominating race, clever and shrewd in trade, born conquerors and warriors and without mercy when it came to extracting tributes or enforcing laws. Religion was of such paramount importance that a large part of their lives, a great deal of their art and the bulk of their customs, work and ceremonies were inextricably mixed with their religious beliefs. Their folk lore also was mainly of a religious nature and dealt largely with deities, supernatural beings, monsters and mythical personages so it is almost impossible to separate fiction from fact in their traditions and history.

The religion of the Aztecs was very complicated and involved with a great number of gods, goddesses, lesser deities and sacred heroes. Quite frequently, also, many of these were known by two or more names and were regarded as being the gods or goddesses of more than one thing.

As a result of this confusion, scientists have found it necessary to classify many of the Aztec gods by numbers rather than by names. To enumerate and describe all of the Aztecs' deities would require an entire volume, but many were of so little importance— and very well may have been duplications of others—that descriptions of some of the more important and interesting of their deities will serve.

As mentioned above, the Aztecs at the time of the Spanish conquest were tending toward the worship of a single almighty and supreme god. The deity selected was Tezcatlipoca but he was not by any means the most important god of the Aztecs' mythology. This honor should go to the sun-god or "Sun Chief," TONATIAH, who was regarded as the source of life and was known also as *Teotl* meaning merely "God." Another name for this deity was "He by whom men live" or *Ipalneomohuani*. He was always in evidence in the background of the adoration of other deities and was insatiable in his demand for daily human sacrifices, and the hearts of all victims were invariably held up and offered to him first.

In order to obtain enough victims to satisfy this most bloodthirsty of all the Aztecs' deities a special corps of warriors were engaged solely in securing captives, and the soldier who took the largest number was regarded as a champion and felt sure of heavenly reward. For that matter all of these special duty warriors believed that after death they would still remain in the god's service and would share his spiritual life.

The greatest festival of the Sun god was celebrated by dressing

AZTEC

NASCA

SUN GODS

Fig. 12. Symbols of the Sun God in Mexico and Peru

and painting the sacrificial victims to represent the lesser deities and Tonatiah usually is shown licking up the blood of those sacrificed. He is commonly depicted with his tongue extended and with the head of a jaguar or puma on either side of his head. It is of interest to note that the sun god of the Nascan people of Peru was also shown with a protruding tongue and with face flanked by jaguar heads (Fig. 12).

The air god, Tezcatlipoca, is an excellent example of the deities with several names and attributes, for he was also known as the "Hungry Chieftain," *Nezahualpilli;* the "Enemy," *Yatozin;* the "Young Warrior," *Telpochtli;* the "Night Wind," *Yoalli Ehecatl* and the "Demander of Prayers," *Nonenque.* It was believed that, as the night wind, he sped along the roads searching for those who were near the ends of their lives, for he was regarded as the "Dealer of Death" as well as the "Giver of Life," and in order that he might rest there were stone benches placed amid the foliage beside the highways.

It was also believed that he had taught the Aztecs their arts and sciences and led them in the development of their civilization. He is customarily represented as a warrior carrying a spear and a mirror-like shield in which it was believed he could view all the activities of mankind, and as a symbol of his status as Demander of Prayers there is a gold ear surrounded by gold tongues fastened in his hair.

Among the many sacrifices made to this deity was that held during the fifth month of each year and known as the Oxcatl, when a youth was selected for his physical perfection from the prisoners destined for sacrifices. A year before the time when he would meet his death upon the altar he was given the name of the deity, attired like the god and was regarded by the people as the earthly representative of the spiritual air god.

He was regarded with the greatest reverence, was entertained, feasted and welcomed in the homes of the nobility and was provided with four beautiful virgins as companions. During the day he rested and enjoyed every luxury and at night, armed with spear and shield, he impersonated the deity by rushing along the roads and resting upon the stone benches I have mentioned. At the close of the year during which he had impersonated the god his girl companions bade him a tearful farewell and he was led up the steps of the temple pyramid and met death upon the altar.

The Aztec god of War, HUITZILOPOCHTLI, was another important and high ranking deity. He is credited with being the son of COATLIQUE, the goddess of the Earth or "Earth Mother" who is depicted wearing a skirt of rattlesnakes and with a death's head. His name means "Hummingbird to the left" and was given him because, according to Aztec mythology, he was born a fully armed warrior wearing a headdress and leg guards of hummingbirds' feathers.

XIPE was the god of sacrifices and was known as the "Flayed One"; he is represented wearing the skin of one of his victims. At the times of his festivals the priests of his cult flayed those to be sacrificed and wore the skins for a period of twenty days. Even the emperor took part in this sacrifice by covering his hands and feet with the skin stripped from the extremities of a victim and wearing a coat and crown of spoonbill feathers and a skirt of green feathers, the colors of the sacred Quetzal and also symbolic of Xipe who wore the symbols of heaven, earth and hell in the forms of the spoonbill, the blue cotinga and the jaguar.

The Aztec Rain god or TLALOC was almost identical with the Mayan Rain god, Chac-Mool, and who may have been adopted from the Aztecs or *vice versa*. In the Aztec mythology he was the husband of the "Emerald Lady" or CHALCHIHUITLICUE, while their children were thought to be the clouds or Tlalocs. The victims sacrificed to this rain god were maidens and children and if, while nearing the sacrificial altar, they wept, this was deemed a sign of copious rains to follow.

Quite appropriately the Emerald Lady was represented as a green frog and during the feast of *Etzalqualiztli* ("When bean-food was eaten") the priests devoted to this god plunged into a lake and moved about and croaked in imitation of frogs. Tlaloc and his "Emerald Lady" were supposed to dwell in the volcanoes of Popocatepetl and Teocuinani and on the summit of the latter was a temple dedicated to the rain god and containing a green stone image of Chac-Mool or Tlaloc.

Although the majority of the Aztec deities were bestial and cruel there were some of a very different type. Among these was XOCHIPILI, the "Flower-god-child," who is always represented as a lovely child adorned with flowers of which he was the god. ITZA-PAPALOTL or the Obsidian butterfly, was another of this class of beneficent and lovable deities.

Undoubtedly the most famous and widest known of all the Aztec gods was their "Plumed Serpent" or QUETZALCOATL although in many respects he was by no means their most important deity. He was not a cruel or bestial god, never demanding human sacrifices but calling upon his devotees to shed their own blood as a symbol of sacrifice. There are innumerable myths and legends in regard to this famous god. In most of these he is reputed to have been a bearded white man from overseas who arrived in a ship at the place where Vera Cruz now stands. But in one of the legends it relates that he first appeared in the form of the resplendent trogan or quetzal and, as a result, the quetzal became the sacred bird of both the Aztecs and Mayas.

However, recent researches and exhaustive studies tend to prove the truth of the mythical arrival by ship and it is such a highly important matter that we feel that a separate chapter should be devoted entirely to Quetzalcoatl.

In addition to worshiping their numerous deities, the Aztecs also adored *Citlalpol* or the "Great Star" which was the planet Venus. But when Venus became the morning star it was called *Tlauizcalpanecutli* or "Lord of the Dawn" and was believed to be a visual manifestation of Quetzalcoatl.

Each time when the planet appeared, sacrifices were made to it and as it rose in the heavens the people stopped up their chimneys to prevent evil spirits from entering by the light of the brilliant star.

The most striking and the best known of all the remains left by the ancient Mexicans' civilizations are their immense temple-mounds. Although ordinarily referred to as Aztec only a comparatively few were actually built by these people, the majority having been erected by races who long antedated the Nahuas. Among those built by the Aztecs, and the largest of all known *teocalli*, as these pyramids are called, was that of Huitzilopochtli, the god of war, erected in the heart of the Aztec capital of Tenochtitlán during the reigns of Montezuma I, Tizoc and Ahuitzotl. It was completed in 1487 by the latter. The walls surrounding the gigantic structure were covered with carvings of braided snakes and were known as the serpent walls or *coeipantli*. They were nearly a mile square and enclosed an immense court or plaza in the center of which rose the vast pyramid whose base was three hundred feet square and with its summit more than three hundred feet in height. It was constructed of rubble overlaid with cut stone with six terraces or platforms and the entire structure was covered with gypsum stucco. A flight of three hundred and forty stone steps led to the top where there were twin three-storied towers each fifty-six feet in height and containing the sacrificial altars of polished jasper, and carved figures of the War god. Within this temple holy virgins or nuns tended the sacred fires that were kept burning perpetually, for the Aztecs believed that if the fires died out it would mean the loss of their rule and power, and similar fires were kept alight in all their temples. In their capital alone there were over six hundred of these fires constantly burning in their braziers.

Surrounding the titanic pyramid of the War god there were over forty lesser temples, together with the Temple of Skulls or *Tzomptli* wherein were preserved the skulls of all those who had been sacrificed on the War god's altars. At the time of the arrival of the Spaniards this structure contained more than one hundred and thirty thousand skulls.

Today no traces of the vast pyramid remain visible above the surface of the ground. Relentlessly razed by the Spaniards, much of its stonework went into the building of the great Cathedral, the Palace and other structures.

But much of the War god's pyramid, the vast courtyard and the walls, lie buried beneath the broad Paseo de la Reforma, the Cathedral, and many public and private buildings. A short distance from the Zocolo, where a small vacant lot permitted excavations to be carried on, there is a fenced-in area where one may see portions of all that remains of this second greatest of ancient Mexican structures. Among the other temple pyramids of the Aztecs are that at Teopanzolco near Cuernavaca, and the magnificent structure at Tenayuca.

It is doubtful if any other race ever erected more numerous, more massive and more striking structures than did the ancient Mexicans. Regardless of their racial identity or the area of their culture every civilized group of the ancient Mexicans seemed obsessed with a mania for pyramid and temple building. In a way, however, it was perfectly natural and to be expected, for the teocalli were built to please and show respect to their gods, and wherever a city was founded the first and most important of all undertakings was to erect a temple to some deity. Moreover, while we do not know anything very definite in regard to the mythologies, religions, deities, numerical and calendrical systems of any of the ancient Mexicans other than the Toltecs and Aztecs, though in all probability all these matters were more or less alike, we find much the same teocalli throughout Mexico. To be sure they varied considerably in design, ornamentation and other details, but in a general way all were similar and only an experienced archaeologist who has specialized in the ancient Mexican civilizations can distinguish one from another. Moreover, it is probable that all had a common origin for extending over the greater portion of Mexico, and underlying all other remains, are traces of an extremely ancient archaic culture of which almost nothing is known.

We should be thankful that these ancient Mexicans built so massively and so well, for to destroy or raze such structures was, in most cases, too much of an undertaking even for the fanatical Spanish priests. But in a number of cases they compromised by building a Christian church on the top of a teocalli, as at Cholula, thus inadvertently following the pagans' custom of a temple on a pyramid, and doubtless believing that a Christian church erected where human beings had been sacrificed to pagan gods would take the curse off the place.

Pyramids of various sizes and types are scattered all over Mexico. Some have been thoroughly excavated and restored to practically their original condition, others have been explored only, while far more still remain as great mounds or hillocks of earth often overgrown with vegetation and giving no hint of what may be buried beneath.

Today many of the more notable and accessible remains have become Meccas for tourists and other visitors to Mexico and have proved archaeological treasure troves to the scientists. Among the most striking and best known are those at Teotihuacán, near Tezcoco. Here at Teotihuacán, once the holy city of the Nahuas, are the temples of the Sun and Moon and the magnificent temple of the Plumed Serpent god, Quetzalcoatl, all being attributed to the Teotihuacán culture. The temples of the Sun and Moon rise high above a level plain in a series of terraces. The latter is 137 feet

in height with its base over 400 feet square while the sun pyramid is 735 feet square at the base and towers to a height of 204
feet. From the base, flights of stone stairs led to the summits where,
on the Temple of the Sun, was an immense stone statue of the
Sun god with a great star of solid gold set into its breast.

At one time the "Pathway of the Dead" led from the Temple of
the Moon through a vast cemetery covering more than nine square
miles. Here, among the many thousands of graves, wonderful specimens of art and handiwork have been found. Among them are terra-
cotta figurines; incense burners, masks and other objects of
magnificent mosaic work; decorated human skulls; stone carvings,
objects cut from obsidian; gold, silver and copper ornaments and
utensils; carved gems and semiprecious stones; weapons and implements.

Not far from Tezcoco is the "Hill of Flowers" or Xochicalco
with its massive blocks of sculptured porphyry, many being over
twelve feet in length, weighing many tons and now considered of
the Toltecan culture.

But the most beautiful and imposing of all the Teotihuacán
pyramids is the great temple of Quetzalcoatl, the Plumed Serpent,
with its imposing grand stairway, and its broad stone terraces. Between each of these are rows of magnificently sculptured conventionalized heads of plumed serpents set into the elaborately carved
façade and projecting outward for several feet. This splendid structure is surrounded by an immense leveled area enclosed on all sides
by broad stone terraces and raised platforms. To my mind this is
the most imposing, most artistic, most magnificent and remarkable
of all the numberless temple pyramids in Mexico.

Even to mention all of the teocalli would require many pages
and an entire volume would be needed to describe them in detail.
Among the most noteworthy of the pyramids of Totonac origin
are those of Tajin and the beautifully sculptured remains of Papantla; and the strikingly lifelike carvings of human heads and of
animals and the buildings and splendid pottery in the State of
Vera Cruz.

There are also the mysterious stone yokes, and the strange flat-
nosed, broad-faced stone heads and the stone tombs of the La
Venta area. Finally and probably the most noteworthy and impor-

tant of all the ancient remains in Mexico are those of Mitla and Monte Albán near the city of Oajaca.

Unlike the Mayan buildings with their inward-sloping walls, the Mitla structures were built with straight vertical walls and were designed to support roofs. The construction is massive with the stone lintels often eighteen feet in length, and with the surfaces of the walls covered with a wealth of magnificent carvings, mainly in geometrical designs. The Palace of Columns with its long rows of immense monuments is famous, as is the Hall of Fretwork where the walls are a mass of deeply cut geometrical patterns.

Probably the most remarkable features of Mitla are the subterranean rooms and corridors. These are completely faced with stone and with every square inch of their surfaces most elaborately carved. It is believed that these formed the resting places of slain warriors and sacrificial victims. According to tradition, the more fanatical of the people practised a fearful form of self-sacrifice by being voluntarily cast into the subterranean charnal house where they wandered about amid festering cadavers until they died from thirst and starvation.

CHAPTER 6

Art and Life of the Ancient Mexicans

Long after Mitla had been explored, excavated and restored and had become a Mecca for those interested in the ancient Mexican civilizations, Monte Albán remained an unexplored, almost untouched group of formless ruins in the mountains near Oajaca, yet it was not only a veritable archaeological treasure house but was the most remarkable, the most amazing site in the whole of Mexico—if not in all America.

Here an entire mountain top had been cut down to form a vast level area or artificial plain with other leveled terraces totalling thousands of acres in extent hewn from the mountain side. Stupendous quantities of rock had been cut away and the rubble used to fill arroyos, small canyons and depressions. And on the plain and terraces the Zapotecs built their great city and erected their magnificent pyramid-temples and buried their dead in great stone tombs. It was the most stupendous, most remarkable feat of engineering ever accomplished by any pre-Columbian race in the New World. Building air strips on tropical islands or on the roughest terrain is child's play by comparison.

Even today it would be a tremendous undertaking; with power driven drills, high explosives, bulldozers and drag-lines and all of our modern up-to-date mechanical devices and resources it would take years to accomplish the feat. Can anyone actually believe, as archaeologists claim, that the colossal work was accomplished with crude stone implements and that the broken rock was transported in baskets carried on human heads? No one with an atom of common sense and a smattering of knowledge of engineering problems can actually believe that the ancient Zapotecs cut away hundreds of thousands of tons of rock, filled yawning ravines and deep fissures with rubble, leveled an area hundreds of acres in extent and built huge, imposing structures all with no knowledge of steel tools, no explosives, no wheeled vehicles and no beasts of burden. Even admitting, for the sake of argument, that such a feat were possible who can estimate or even conceive the length of time that would have been required for its accomplishment? Centuries, tens of centuries would have passed as the Zapotec laborers and artizans pecked away at the lava rock with crude stone tools, as the women and children garnered the chips and fragments, piled them in baskets and trudged across the miles of broken rock to dump their tiny loads in the yawning chasms.

If it were carried out in this way the work must have been started at a time far antedating any indications of highly cultured races so far found in Mexico, yet the oldest remains found at Monte Albán were those of the Zapotecs and Mixtecs who had reached a very high state of ancient American civilization.

Regardless of how, when or by whom the amazing engineering feat was accomplished, Monte Albán remained a number of groups of formless ruins on the great man-made plain until at last the Mexican archaeologists, led by Dr. Alfonso Caso, undertook the first systematic intensive excavatory work at the site. The results were almost as astonishing and remarkable as the place itself. Hidden beneath the accumulated detritus and earth of countless centuries were pyramids, temples and tombs totally unlike anything previously known.

To be sure, the pyramids of rubble faced with cut stone were not as high nor as gigantic as some at other localities in Mexico and Yucatán but their terraced walls covered immense areas and, leading to their summits, were giant stairways of stone steps one of which measures 130 feet in width, the widest stairway in America. Although lacking the ornate carvings and elaborate sculptures of some of the Maya and Mexican temple-mounds, those at Monte Albán are fully as imposing in their severe lines.

But by far the most interesting and the least expected discoveries were the numerous tombs deep within their stone mounds that sometimes were higher than the neighboring pyramids, and with their inner walls decorated with polychrome frescoes.

Never in the history of American archaeology has there been

such a treasure trove of specimens as these contained. There were scores of magnificent pottery vessels and figurines, objects carved from onyx and rock crystal; carved jade and jet; obsidian ear plugs and other objects; turquoise mosaics on wood; turquoise-decorated masks made from human skulls; strings upon strings of pearls and countless gold, silver and copper ornaments and jewelry, among them necklaces, earrings, brooches, nose ornaments of gold, finger rings, a golden head-band or crown with a feather of gold and an immense gold breastplate representing a warrior chief with elaborate headdress.

Perhaps most interesting of all, even if of less intrinsic value, were numbers of bones of deer and jaguar all completely covered with the most minute, delicate and elaborate carvings, and some with turquoise inlay. No one knows what purpose these served, but almost identical specimens have been found at Coclé, Panama, in Ecuador and even near Tal Tal, in Southern Chile. It has been suggested that they may have been used in weaving cloth for sacred garments.

Another unsolved puzzle at Monte Albán is the reason for the numerous relief carvings of malformed or crippled human beings. Some have twisted or withered arms or legs, others have malformed heads or bodies or other defects and they occur both as sculptures on walls and carved on stone slabs. It has been said that these sculptures belonged to an earlier cultural phase but were reused by later artisans in reconstructing the old structure, or in building a newer pyramid or platform. The position in which they were found by modern archaeologists seems to substantiate this fact.

Why did the ancient people who dwelt here prefer cripples in their carvings? As Dr. Caso says: "Was it to ridicule certain enemies or should we see in these sculptures a representation of the sick who came to a temple in which there was a god who performed miraculous cures? Could Monte Albán have been at one time a kind of Lourdes?"

Although the original structures themselves are of the Zapotec culture yet a great many of the tombs and the objects they contain are distinctly Mixtec.

Long after the city had been abandoned by the Zapotecs it was occupied, or at least used as a cemetery by the later Mixtecs who superimposed their culture on that of their predecessors. Today both the Zapotecs and Mixtecs inhabit the area about Oajaca. Originally each of the Mexican races or tribes inhabited its own particular area. Although a greater number of each tribe still inhabit the same area as did their ancestors in the days of Montezuma yet after the downfall of the Aztec Empire and the conquest of the country by the Spaniards, tribal boundaries were more or less cast aside. In addition there has been a sort of migratory movement from north to south, while to add to the confusion members of the different tribes have intermarried. As a result we find Huicholes from the northern part of Mexico, as well as Tarascans, even in the State of Oajaca.*

Originally each of the great pyramid-temples must have been in or near a densely populated area or a large city yet very few traces of the homes of the inhabitants remain. This is not surprising, for the majority of the houses of the ancient Mexicans were of perishable materials, wood, adobe and thatch, exactly like those of the Mexican Indians of today, and even many of the more pretentious homes were of adobe often covered with stucco. In many localities the foundations of such buildings remain although the edifices themselves have long since disappeared.

Although the temples and pyramids are the most spectacular remains of the ancient Mexican civilizations, yet there are many other relics that, to the archaeologist, are of tremendous importance.

Most famous of all is the Aztec calendar stone with its fascinating and remarkable history. This piece of stone carving is in the form of a huge disk weighing over twenty tons and twelve feet in diameter. It is cut from a single block of black porphyry and according to its date glyphs it was completed between 1487 and 1499 A.D. Originally placed in the great temple of Tenochtitlán it was buried under tons of debris when it was thrown down by the Spaniards as they razed the temple.

Not until 1560 was its resting place discovered and the Spanish bishop, fearing its pagan influence upon the Indians, ordered it buried. For over two hundred years it remained, forgotten and lost to memory, until in 1790 laborers excavating in the Plaza Mayor in Mexico City again unearthed the great stone carving. It was

* During the regime of President Porfirio Diaz, a great many of the hostile Yaquis, Huicholes and Apaches were deported to southern Mexico and Yucatán where their descendants remain, together with Indians of mixed tribal blood.

then built into the façade of the cathedral where it remained until 1885 when it was removed and placed in the Museo Nacional where it may now be seen.

Although called a calendar yet the immense stone disk is not only calendrical but in addition gives the Aztec version of the history of the world, tells of a prophecy and records the Aztec myths. The carved figures that at first sight appear intricate and largely ornamental actually consist of symbols and glyphs arranged about the central figure representing the Sun god, Tonatiah, with the symbol *Olin,* a day sign which signifies an earthquake. The portion of the stone dealing with history is divided into five suns or eras, four being of the past and one of the present. The latter is dominated by the existing sun symbol: Olin-Tonatiah, because, according to an Aztec prophecy, the earth is fated to be destroyed by an earthquake.

Arranged about the Olin symbol are the four past eras, each within a rectangle and designed to be read from right to left. The first of these is Ocelotl, the jaguar; the next Ehecatl or the wind; the third is Quiahuitl, or rain of fire while the last is Atl signifying water.

These when interpreted record that the first age or era was destroyed by a jaguar, the second age or "sun" was destroyed by a hurricane, the third by a rain of fire, and the fourth era by a flood. According to the symbols a man and woman managed to escape each destruction and lived to repopulate the earth. Beneath the tails of the two reptiles at the top of the stone there is the symbol 3-*Acatl* or "reed," to indicate that the existing or present era began in the year of the reed, while another symbol indicates that the present period will come to an end with a vast terrific earthquake on the day *Olin-4.* This date symbol is followed by three characters indicating the points of the compass. Outside of the historical portion of the stone there are the twenty day signs and surrounding all are two monsters face to face and with their tails at the top of the stone. These are probably the twin Xiucoatl or Turquoise snakes, the symbols of fire and water. Each of these reptiles holds in its jaws a human head. The jaws at the left hold the face of Xiutecutli, the god of fire and those at the right hold the face of Tonatiuh, while on the sides of the stone are sculptured figures of the Obsidian butterfly, Itzpaplotl.

In all probability our interpretation of the inscriptions on this stone fall far short of their meanings to the Aztecs, for signs and symbols to an Indian who understands them may reveal, in a sort of short-hand manner, long and detailed stories. We may feel sure that the Aztecs when studying their great calendar stone set in the temple wall read in the carved characters a full and detailed history of the past and an equally detailed story of the prophecy as to the future.

Other highly important and valuable objects left us by the ancient Mexicans are their codices. Many hundreds of the Aztec codices are in existence but the great majority deal mainly with tax or tribute accounts, and everyday matters, or were made after the Spanish conquest and in addition to the Aztec figures and symbols bear notations in Spanish and include paintings of the Spaniards. If we possessed a complete series of the more important pre-Spanish codices we probably would be able to trace the entire history of the Aztecs and the other Mexican cultures, together with all their migrations and wanderings, but unfortunately all but a few were either lost or were destroyed by the Spanish priests in their fanatical religious zeal.

Fig. 13. Portion of Mexican codex showing sacrifices to the "Flayed God"

Several of the more important original codices are preserved as well as a number of very accurate copies made by Mexican Indian artists who, from their memories and knowledge, painstakingly reproduced the originals that were destroyed by the conquerors. As these copies were interpreted by the artists they are known as interpretive codices. Three of these are known. One is the *Oxford Codex* in the Bodleian Library in England. This is historical and gives a list of the cities that were subject to Aztec rule. The second of these codices is in France and is known as the *Paris* or *Tellerio-Remensis Codex* and records a number of facts regarding the settlement of the Nahua city-states. The third of the interpretive codices is in the Vatican at Rome and is known as the *Vatican Codex* and is mainly calendrical and mythological. Among other matters a portion of this codex illustrates the Aztec conception of the soul's travels to the other world after death. First there is a picture of a shrouded corpse with the spirit issuing from the mouth. Then the soul is depicted with a wooden collar about its neck to signify that it is a prisoner, and led by an attendant clad in an ocelot skin to the presence of the deity Tezcatlipoca to be sentenced. The soul is next shown undergoing various tests to determine its right to enter the realm of Mictlan or world of the dead and is provided with bow and arrows for its protection.

First it passes between two high mountain peaks that may topple upon it at any instant. A most fearsome serpent bars the way and if this monster is overcome the soul must face a giant crocodile. Then it must travel across eight successive deserts and mountains while buffeted by a hurricane blowing with such force that it cuts away solid rock. After this trial the spirit battles with a demon named Izpuzteque and with a fiend called Nextepehua, and passing through clouds of hot ashes it finally reaches the gates of the "Lord of Hell" where it meets its spirit friends.

Once a person understands the principle or system of the Aztec codices it is not difficult to interpret them, especially the shorter ones such as the *Mendoza Codex* preserved in Oxford University, England. A portion of this codex telling of the education of a young girl is shown in Fig. 14. In the upper panel the mother (18) is handing her daughter (20) a cotton spindle. To indicate that the mother is talking, a tongue is depicted outside her mouth while the girl's daily ration of a single tortilla is shown (19). In

Fig. 14. Aztec codex showing a mother teaching her
daughter to weave

the next panel the mother (21), still talking, tells the girl (23) how to use the cotton spindle to spin thread and as a reward for her diligence her ration has been increased to a tortilla and a half (22).

In the bottom panel the girl (26) who has become quite proficient by this time, is shown weaving a blanket while her mother (24) continues to instruct her. To indicate that considerable time has passed, the girl is depicted with long hair while her ration of two tortillas (25) is indicated. Of course this is an example of a very simple codex, a sort of codex primer as one might say, and it is a very different matter to interpret a really advanced and complicated codex such as the *Codex Nuttalli,* portions of which are shown in Fig. 3.

To interpret such an elaborate codex dealing with the ceremonies attending the feast of the Flayed God (Xipe Totec) one must be familiar with the Aztec mythology, the meaning of details of costume and other accessories and the numerical and calendrical systems whose symbols appear in the form of circles and elipses with date glyphs. But almost anyone could readily understand that the pictures dealt with a ceremony and a sacrifice, for the intended victim is depicted chained to the altar while the priests and warriors, marching along with bared weapons, leave no question as to their homicidal intentions.

Almost, if not fully as important from an archaeological point of view, are the innumerable sculptures, the pottery, the metal work and weapons, utensils and other objects that by some miracle escaped the destructiveness and cupidity of the Spaniards, the passing centuries, the wear and tear of time and still remain intact or nearly so.

Very probably it was the sheer beauty of the Aztec mosaics, carved stoneware, gold and silver ornaments and semiprecious stones that caused so many of these specimens of the Indians' art to be preserved. As a result, the museums of the world, as well as many private collections, possess a remarkable number of these priceless relics of the ancient Mexicans.

Fortunately, also, the Mexican Government long ago realized the scientific importance of all objects pertaining to the pre-Spanish people of Mexico and in the Museo Nacional in Mexico City there is a marvelous collection of specimens of Aztec and Maya origins.

In many of their arts the Aztecs (to use a general term) far exceeded any other American people. Their feather work was magnificent and in order to insure an ample supply of bright colored feathers they kept countless gaudy-plumaged birds in immense aviaries. The priests, rulers, officials and royal armies wore clothing and mantles of gorgeous feathers and the details of these are clearly shown on many of the codices and sculptures.

Feathers were also used for mosaic work on shields and various other objects of wood, rawhide, etc., some of these being among the most remarkable examples of ancient American artistry. In their mosaic work these people surpassed all other races in the western hemisphere if not in the entire world. The greater part of this was in turquoise used to cover wooden shields, the hilts of sacrificial knives, carved wooden representations of various creatures used in ceremonies, vessels, plaques, human skulls, and even sculptured stone statues and idols.

One of the finest known examples of this turquoise mosaic work is a shield in the Museum of the American Indian, Heye Foundation, in New York City. Over fifteen thousand pieces of turquoise were used in covering the wooden shield with its elaborate ornamental design with human figures in the center. Incidentally, this magnificent example of mosaic work is of Zapotec and not of Aztec workmanship and was found at Monte Albán by the late Dr. Marshall Saville long before the Mexican Government realized what a treasure trove of specimens lay hidden in the huge tombs of this immeasurably ancient city.

In their carvings on wood, bone, and stone, the ancient Mexicans attained a skill and refinement never excelled by any other race, and no material was too refractory or too hard for the Mexican artizans. Agate, jade, obsidian, iron pyrite and rock crystal; topaz, amethyst and even sapphire, were cut, carved and polished in the forms of human beings, skulls, birds, reptiles, mammals, flowers, and other objects. Among the most remarkable examples of the Aztec lapidists' skill is an almost life size human skull carved from a single mass of glass-clear rock crystal that is in the British Museum. Every detail, even to the sutures, is so carefully and accurately reproduced that it seems incredible that it is an object made by human hands and not a genuine skull transformed by some alchemy of nature into the transparent stone. At the other extreme are the true gems, carved, polished and perforated, and many so tiny and with the carvings so minute that it seems impossible that the work could have been accomplished without a lens.

The epitome of these people's stone cutting was their work in obsidian or volcanic glass which is one of the hardest and most refractory of all minerals in addition to being far more brittle than any man-made glass. Yet the ancient Mexicans carved, cut and shaped this material with, apparently, as much ease as though it had been wood. Not only was it used for edged tools and weapons but in addition it was widely employed for ornaments, jewelry, receptacles and mirrors. Even huge ceremonial objects of ornate design and complex forms were carved from obsidian.

How these people—as well as the ancient inhabitants of Peru, cut and worked these many extremely hard minerals is an unsolved mystery. Only diamonds will cut sapphire and only diamond or sapphire will cut rock crystal, amethyst and other precious and semiprecious stones, and only hardened steel will cut such rocks as porphyry, diorite, arsenite, and peridotite, yet all of these were worked with apparent ease. Scientists would have us believe that all this ancient stone cutting and gem carving was accomplished by means of stone implements. But I defy any of these scientists, or any other human being for that matter, to duplicate the simplest of the ancient Americans' stone and gem cutting with any stone implement.

Even Indians, who possess far more patience and perseverance than white men, cannot carve diorite or arsenite or jasper with stone tools. I have tested this theory and I know. While excavating the ancient remains at Coclé in Panama (see Chapter 11) I selected a plain piece of diorite that had been cut and squared by the long-vanished people and upon the surface I outlined a simple geometrical design in chalk. Then, providing five of my Indian workers with several dozen stone implements taken from the graves, I told them to cut the design on the stone. For ten days they labored steadily. They completely wore out practically all of the stone implements yet they had not succeeded in producing any recognizable carving on the diorite.

Undoubtedly some of the ancient races, such as the Mayas, *did* carve rock with stone tools but they were cutting soft limestone that when first quarried may be cut with a saw but which becomes flinty hard after prolonged exposure to the air, or were working almost equally soft sandstone, which is a totally different proposition from diorite, porphyry, arsenite and similar igneous rocks, let alone quartz, obsidian and precious stones.

For weapons the Aztecs, as well as other tribes, used bows and arrows with beautifully made obsidian or stone heads. Lances, throwing-spears hurled by the throwing-stick or *atlatl;* maces and the Aztec sword or *maquahuitl.* These were of hard wood, usually carved and often decorated with mosaic work, and with both edges set with sharp rectangular obsidian "teeth" placed close together like the teeth of a saw. At close quarters it was a terrible weapon and it is of interest to note that its Aztec name, *maquahuitl,* became corrupted into the word "machete," the universally used implement of Latin America and the West Indies.

As metals were scarce among the ancient Mexicans little was used except for jewelry and ornaments. Copper was prized more than silver or gold and small copper bells and other objects were used as money. As the Aztecs were a militant, warlike people armament and weapons were of great, I might say vital, importance and some of the finest specimens of their handiwork and art are among the fighting gear that has been preserved.

For protection the soldiers wore armor of quilted and padded cotton cloth and strips of cane as well as helmets or casques, and carried shields of thick rawhide and wood. So efficient was the cotton armor that the Spaniards soon adopted it in place of their heavy cumbersome steel armor, for they found that the quilted cotton armor would stop an arrow or a spear thrust even better than steel.

As the ancient Mexicans did not possess tin and hence could not make bronze, even if they knew how, and as copper was not only scarce but soft, few if any metal weapons were used. Their stone and obsidian-tipped arrows and spears and their jagged-edged swords were fully as effective as metal-tipped weapons of similar style when battling with their fellow countrymen, but when it came to fighting the invading Spaniards it was a different matter. They did not even possess the sling, which was used so effectively by the ancient Peruvians, or the terrible spike-headed bronze maces of the Incan races. In fact their lack of really effective weapons was an important factor in their conquest.

Although the handiwork of the ancient Mexicans give us a fairly good idea of their attainments, their craftsmanship and their occupations it is the first-hand accounts of the Conquest, as recorded by Bernal Diaz and others, that enable us to visualize the everyday life of the people, their customs, dress and occupations.

As I have mentioned, the Mexicans were and still are passionately fond of flowers and many of our most prized ornamental plants originated in Mexico and were hybridized and cultivated by the Aztecs and others for centuries before the arrival of the Spaniards. They were also fond of music and used drums, flutes, horns and other instruments, and modern adaptations of ancient Aztec operas and their music are widely enjoyed by admirers of good music today.

The majority of the people were little better than slaves and were compelled to labor strenuously, either in the fields or at their various trades such as quarrying, pottery making, mining, building, metal-working, stone cutting, weaving, paper-making or feather work. There were also the vendors of fruits, vegetables, flowers and innumerable other articles in the big open markets that were in every city and village. And of course there were the servants, the street cleaners, porters, gardeners, and those of innumerable other trades and professions. In fact the occupations of the masses in ancient Mexico were not very different from those of today.

Mainly the people wore simple garments of hand-woven cotton often decorated with embroidery or appliqué. Each tribe had its own distinctive form of dress and its own decorative designs and this custom still persists, especially among the women. And just as the Mexican Indians of the present time feel lost without the inevitable *serape* or poncho to protect them from cold and inclement weather, and wear palm leaf waterproofs when it rains, so in the days of Montezuma the *serape* was an essential part of the Indians' wardrobe and palm leaf coats were donned when it rained.

The upper classes or aristocracy led very different lives, lives of ease, luxury and laziness. They dined on turkey, venison, rich pastries, peppery tamales, enchiladas, tacos and maize, served on dishes of gold or silver and drank *pulque* or *tequila* made from the sap of the maguey plant or rich, vanilla-flavored chocolate, and smoking was universal. Their costumes were rich and magnificent, they wore ornaments of precious metals and precious stones and they dwelt in stone houses, many of which might be classed as mansions if not as palaces. Of course Montezuma outshone them all. Within the large patio of his palace opposite the great temple he maintained a menagerie and botanical garden. Here were kept living specimens of all the birds and mammals found in Mexico that would withstand captivity, and here were the ornamental, medicinal and economically important plants of the country.*

For everyday use the monarch wore simple but richly ornamented garments but on official or ceremonial occasions he outshone Solomon in all his glory. His three-piece costume consisted of a shirt or tunic, a skirt and a mantle or cloak all completely covered with gaudy feathers (often the iridescent feathers of thousands of humming birds) either arranged in intricate designs or in plain masses of color. Golden jewelry, carved jade and ornaments of precious stones covered his chest, arms, and legs. He carried a ceremonial shield of feather mosaic and an obsidian-bladed dagger with a hilt of carved jade and turquoise inlay, and upon his head wore a most elaborate headdress of gold and feathers topped by long, graceful green plumes of the sacred quetzal bird. Green, red and white were the colors of the sacred bird; green, red and white were the colors used for ceremonial garments and utensils, and today green, red and white are the colors of the Mexican flag.

It has been stated by certain of the "belittlin'" type of archaeologists that the life, dress and houses of the Mexican aristocracy were grossly exaggerated by the Spanish chroniclers. That no traces of anything that could be called a "palace" have ever been found, that Montezuma dwelt in an ordinary house of adobe similar to the houses of the Pueblo of Taos, but probably not as well built. That there were no such costumes as those the Spaniards described and that the entire description of life in the Mexican capital at the time of the Conquest was highly overrated and colored by the imaginations of the Spanish chroniclers to please their sovereign and aggrandize their personal achievements. Such statements are not only ridiculous but utterly erroneous. Everyone at all familiar with Mexican history knows or should know that the National Palace with its attendant buildings, including the Museo Nacional, now stand on the site of the palace of the Aztecs' monarchs and the huge

* The first American bison ever seen by Europeans were those Cortez and his men saw in Montezuma's menagerie in Mexico.

gardens, and that Cortez himself took possession of it, occupied it as his residence and headquarters and added to it. In its reconstruction little was left of the original palace of the Aztec rulers but portions of the alterations made by Cortez are still in evidence. If there are no traces of the palatial homes of the Aztecan élite outside of the boundaries of the National Palace walls it is not surprising, for any traces that may have remained have long since been buried beneath the paved highways and towering skyscrapers of Mexico City of today. If the Aztec nobility and well-to-do did not use dishes and utensils of gold and silver who *did* use the hundreds of these that have been found? And it merely shows a woeful lack of knowledge for anyone to discredit the accuracy of the Spaniards' descriptions of Aztec costumes and customs. Sculptures, paintings, pottery, frescoes, all depict these with great detail. Moreover, the feather costume worn by Montezuma is carefully preserved in the Royal Museum at Brussels, Belgium.

Along the streets of the Aztec capital there were shops wherein were displayed innumerable articles, new to the Spaniards, and others where clever artizans carried on their trades of mosaic making, gem cutting, making gold and silver ornaments or painting pottery. But the most intriguing thing to the Spaniards were the barber shops. It may seem strange that Indians should have barber shops for it is a popular idea that Indians have no beards. This is not the case, however, for a great many tribes have quite heavy beards. In Mexico today it is not at all unusual to see full-blooded Indians with heavy bushy beards and Montezuma himself wore a beard as did the Inca of Peru. Even among our own North American Indians there are many who have beards that if allowed to grow would be quite luxuriant.

Many of the Navahos have moustaches as do many of the present-day "civilized" Indians of other tribes. Even in the past, men of the Delawares and some of the Iriquois and Chippewas, as well as Pawnees and a number of other tribes, allowed their moustaches and even their whiskers to grow. As far as known, however, the Aztecs were the only ones to have tonsorial artists. And they must have been rather proficient at their trade for although they used razors of obsidian they were patronized by the Spaniards who declared they were equal to the barbers of Seville or Cadiz.

Also displayed in the markets of the Aztec capital were strange fowls, vegetables and fruits some of which were destined to alter living conditions throughout the world. For untold centuries the Mexicans had domesticated the wild turkeys, the muscovy and tree ducks and had cultivated maize, beans, cacao, vanilla, potatoes, peppers, tomatoes, pineapples, squashes, pumpkin and many other vegetables and fruits entirely new and unknown to the conquerors. Fortunately the Dons were not too bent on looting, proselyting and destroying to overlook the new and delectable foods of the new land although they did not take kindly to the strange hairless Mexican dogs that the natives prized for food.

When at last the Spaniards returned to Spain they took with them stores of the vegetables, plant seeds and domesticated birds. Perhaps the greatest, most important result of the conquest of Mexico was the introduction of American food plants to the Old World. Cortez and his men had destroyed a civilization and had disrupted an empire but in the doing of it he benefited the entire world.

CHAPTER 7

Predecessors of the Aztecs

As I have already explained, the Aztecs' civilization was not the only one in Mexico nor did it extend over the entire area of the country. Neither was Mexico an uninhabited area when they arrived as some accounts of the Aztecs would lead us to believe.

On the contrary there were fully as many if not more different Indian tribes at the time of the Aztecs' southerly migration than at the present time. Many of these, such as the Yaquis, Kikapoos, Seris, Huicholes and others in the more northerly area were primitive savages with no truly high culture. But farther south there were scores of races such as the Tarascans, Mixtecs, Tlascalans, Otomis, Zapotecs, Toltecs and others whose cultures or civilizations had attained great heights centuries before the Aztecs settled in the Valley of Mexico. Some of these civilizations were still thriving at that time, while others had passed away and had been forgotten for hundreds of years, although members of the races still existed in considerable numbers.

And when the wandering Nahuas or Aztecs finally selected the site for their capital, where Mexico City now stands, the area was quite thickly inhabited by survivors of the Toltecs whose civilization long antedated that of the Aztecs and whose temple-pyramids and other remains are among the most numerous and finest in all Mexico. In fact, according to tradition, the Aztecs asked the Toltecs for permission to settle in the valley. Yet, on the other hand, they claimed to be descendants of the Toltecs.

Unfortunately, however, the Aztecs' legends of the Toltecs are so interwoven with myths, allegories, symbolism, deifications and imagination that it is impossible to determine how much is fact and how much is fiction. For that matter these traditions may be merely allegorical histories of their own race or they may have been invented and elaborated to explain the existence of the much older civilization that they found.

Ixtlilxochitl, an Aztec chronicler who wrote a short time after the Spanish conquest, gives two versions of the legend. According to one of these the Toltecs reached Tlapallan or the Country of Bright Colors, near the sea after voyaging southward from their original homes which they had deserted in the year 1-Tecpatl or about A.D. 387. After passing Xalisco they landed near Huatulco and then traveled to Tochtepec and thence to Tollantzinco.

The second legend is similar but tells of an uprising of chiefs against the ruler of Tlapallan which compelled them to flee or be banished. According to the legend this took place about A.D. 438 so there is a variation of only about fifty years between the two traditions.

The legend then states that after eight years of rather aimless wanderings in the vicinity of their homeland the fugitive chiefs and their followers reached a place called Tlapallantanzinco where they remained for three years before starting on a century of wanderings.

Both these legends agree that the city of Tollan near the present city of Tula was established by the Toltecs about A.D. 566 having been guided to the spot by the necromancer Hueymatzin or Great Hand. The spot was called the "Place of Fruits" owing to its fertility and six years were devoted to building the city with its palaces and temples.

However, according to Dr. Manuel Gamio, a mistake has been made in the identification of the city built by the Toltecs at the Place of the Fruits and that, in reality, it was Teotihuacán and not Tula. However that may be the tale states that in the seventh year they elected a ruler named Chalchiuh-Tlatonac or Shining Precious Stone, who ruled for fifty-two years and under whose regime the community progressed greatly. This first dynasty continued to about A.D. 994 when Huemac ascended the throne. For a time he ruled honestly and wisely, but eventually he became corrupt and dishonest which resulted in a revolution with omens foretelling a great calamity.

Then the mystical sorcerer Toveyo appeared, and beating his

magic drum drew the people to him. Forcing them to dance, he gradually led them to the verge of a precipice where they were dashed into the canyon below and were turned to stone. Toveyo also used his magic to destroy a bridge crowded with people so that thousands perished while, to add to the calamities, volcanoes burst into violent eruption. Then in an effort to appease the angry gods, the Tollan rulers ordered wholesale sacrifices. But when the first victim was stretched on the altar the priest was horrified to discover that he had neither blood nor heart. Also a terrible stench arose from the body causing pestilence that destroyed thousands.

As if this were not enough Huemac was attacked by the Tlalocs or gods of Rain who spared him and departed when he bribed them with all his riches and abdicated the throne. Before they left, the Tlalocs foretold six years of plagues. Droughts, floods, frosts, heat, locusts and other pests followed until nine-tenths of the people were destroyed.

By this time Huemac had reformed and endeavored to establish his illegitimate son, Acxitl, as ruler. The Toltecs rebelled at this but their leaders were bribed and for a time Acxitl ruled well. However, it was a case of like father like son, and when events showed he had inherited his father's characteristics the people again revolted and led by Huchitzin attacked the city aided by the Chichimecs.

When at last a council of wise men met at the sacred city they were attacked by a giant who appeared in various forms, and who killed most of the men, declaring that the gods were disgusted and that all were doomed. Again Huehuetzin and the Chichimecs attacked the city and finally after a three year war the survivors fled and took refuge in the marshes of Lake Tezcoco and the Toltec civilization came to an end.

If, as the legends state, the Toltecs' first dynasty ended about A.D. 994 and they ceased to exist as an entity about A.D. 1100 or about 200 years before the Aztecs arrived, it would seem an impossibility for the Aztecs—or any other race for that matter—to have developed such a civilization and to have attained such heights as the Spaniards found, all within two centuries. Either they had been at Tenochtitlán far longer than their traditions and codices relate or else there has been some great error in interpreting the dates recorded.

Otherwise we must give these Mexican Indians credit for having been far more progressive and industrious than the Europeans of those days. It took centuries for the European artizans and engineers to erect cathedrals despite the fact that they possessed highly efficient steel implements and facilities which the Aztecs lacked, yet no European cathedral can begin to compare with the vast pyramids and temples of the Aztecs either in the quantities of stone used in their construction or in the richness and amount of stone sculptures and carvings.

But the Aztecs had not only constructed dozens of these but had been offering sacrifices on their altars for more than one hundred years before Cortez arrived on the scene. In addition they had conquered numerous races, had built a huge capital city, had constructed splendid causeways across Lake Tezcoco, had perfected calendrical and numerical systems and had developed a highly advanced civilization all in the space of two hundred years or less.

We cannot seriously question the length of time that the Aztecs had been at Tenochtitlán at the time of the conquest, for they kept accurate records of their various kings or rulers that were as follows:

The	first	was	:	Acampichtli who ruled for twenty-one years
"	second	"	:	Huitzilhuitl " " " " - " "
"	third	"	:	Chimalpopoca " " " ten "
"	fourth	"	:	Itzcoatl " " " thirteen "
"	fifth	"	:	Montezuma I " " " eleven "
"	sixth	"	:	Axayacatl I " " " twelve "
"	seventh	"	:	Tizoc " " " five "
"	eighth	"	:	Ahuitzotl " " " sixteen "
"	ninth	"	:	Montezuma I " " " "

The only plausible and logical explanation of the Aztecs' seemingly impossible rapid advancement is that they brought their civilization with them, that they already possessed their fully developed and highly complicated religion, their amazing astronomical knowledge, their numerical and calendrical systems, their arts, crafts and practically everything else, all inherited from the Toltecs who they claimed were their ancestors. In fact the first Aztec ruler, Acampichitli, was a Toltec and any Aztec who had Toltec blood in his veins was inordinately proud of the fact.

Perhaps their legends of the Toltecs' history are fanciful versions of their own wanderings or they may be of Toltec rather than Aztec origin.

However, we believe, as do several well-known archaeologists, that the ancestors of the ancient Mexicans came from northern Peru, in the vicinity of Callejon de Huaylas, Ancash and Junin. This opinion is based on the following established facts: On many of the carved stone figures of archaic type from the Department of Ancash and vicinity there are double-headed serpents, some with symbolic fire emanating from their mouths, conventionalized stars on their bodies and other distinctive features identifying them as the Xiucoatl or "Blue Fire Snake" or "Blue Fire Dragon" of the Mexicans, found depicted on carved stone chests, painted pottery and other objects. The Mexican-Maya-Xius had a powerful Serpent Priest clan, and called their empire Ishbaba or Xibalba, "Kingdom of the Great Snake," while the double-headed serpent of the Aztecs was covered with blue turquoise mosaic work.

In the ancient Hualla language Ancash means blue, while the Ancash word Sapallan (very similar to Tlapallan) means "first" or "original." Also on many of the figures from the Ancash-Junin area of Peru there are eagles or hawks and large, symbolic hands similar to those in Toltec and Aztec art, while on the diadems or headdresses of some of these carved stone figures there are two circles exactly like those on the headdress of the Aztec sun-god Tonatiah as carved on the famous Calendar Stone (Fig. 15).

Finally, near Vernal, Utah, there are many carvings and paintings upon the cliffs that are unlike any others so far found in North America. Some of these show men and women with garments and headdresses similar to those shown on carvings and pottery of the pre-Incan era of the area we now know as Bolivia, and of Tiahuanacan cultural style. Among the other figures shown in the Vernal carvings are two women carrying a mummy mask between them, a custom that was followed by certain pre-Incan races as an appeal to their deities in time of serious trouble. There is also the figure of a captive or slave painted black or dark brown, denoting that his skin was much darker than his captors'. He is wearing a breech cloth and may be a local guide or interpreter. He is securely tethered to a stake driven into the ground.

The dominating figure, obviously a chief or "king" wears clothing and jewelry as well as a crown and carries in his hand a mosaic-decorated shield painted in alternate stripes of red and white, identical with those shown on Mexican carvings, painted pottery, etc. (Plate VIII, 1).

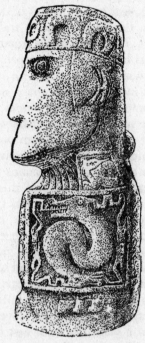

Fig. 15

If, as we and others believe, the ancestors of the Toltecs and their descendants came from Peru it would not discredit the Aztecs' legends of their own and the Toltecs' migrations southward into Mexico. In fact, if anything, it would substantiate them. Voyaging up the west coast of Central America and Mexico some of the Peruvians may have remained in Honduras, Guatemala and Yucatán (for in all probability there were many of these exploratory expeditions) while others entered Mexico. Eventually they would have reached the Gulf of California and the mouth of the Rio Colorado. By journeying up this river they could have reached the area of Chaco Canyon and scouting or exploring parties might well have penetrated to Vernal, Utah, for the Green River near Vernal is a tributary of the Rio Colorado.

There are also indications of the presence of these ancient people near Kanab, Utah, not far from the Arizona border. Here, rising above a large level area that obviously was at one time marshland, and where many rocks bear carved figures of ducks, there are seven distinctive mountains. Leading up one of these is a vast stairway cut in the igneous rock. Not far from the summit is a conspicuously white peak, and, at its base, there is an opening or tunnel mouth about 17 by 14 feet which was sealed with stones and a form of cement composed of mud and wiry grass stems, very obviously from a marsh or swamp. Within the tunnel that extends several hundred feet into the mountain were charcoal, the bones of deer and rabbits and other evidences of human occupancy.

All about the vicinity are caves and narrow arroyos or canyons, and in some of these are crumbling remains of very ancient cliff dwellers' houses. In almost every respect this might well be the legendary *Chico-Moztoc* or "Place of Seven Caves," for the word may be translated as either "Place of Caves" or "Canyons."

As I have already mentioned, the Aztec legend names their original home as *Aztlan* or "Place of the Reeds," which may well have been the ancient marsh I have mentioned but which is now a desert. That it was once a marshy area is unquestionable. Not only are there the duck figures cut in the rocks but in the bluish clay of the old marsh bed there are stems and even leaves of sedges or reeds. Finally, at the base of a giant monolith east of the Johnson Canyon, some miles from Kanab, an amateur archaeologist discovered a number of obsidian disks or "coins." They vary from the size of dimes to quarter dollars and bear slightly raised hieroglyphs on both sides (Plate VIII, 7-8).

A scientist of the Smithsonian Institution, when shown these "coins" stated: "We have never found a coin like these in the United States before, but we have found identical coins in the Valley of the Nile near the Egyptian pyramids."

According to Mrs. Verrill, who has made a very exhaustive study of the Sumerian archaeology and history, the symbols on these Utah coins are: "Of the type found in Hittite glyphs and in the archaic so-called Sumerian script. This script was employed by the earliest dynasties of Egypt and also in the pre-dynastic period."

There are a dozen or more logical explanations of why the ancestors of the ancient Mexicans should have left the Utah areas and migrated southward. Raids by savage Indians, climatic changes such as droughts and a series of unusually severe winters, floods, the exhaustion of soil fertility, the drying up of the swampy land, intertribal wars such as mentioned in the traditions of the Aztecs and Toltecs—any of these or a combination of several would account for the exodus. Whether the remains in the Spiro Burial Mound, Spiro, Oklahoma, were left there by the southerly migrating people from Tlapallan or whether they belonged to another group of these ancient Mexicans is impossible to say, but the presence of numerous engraved sea shells from the Gulf of Mexico lead us to believe that they were brought in by another group of early American ancestors of the Toltec-Aztec race (Fig. 16).

Fig. 16

Until quite recently archaeologists believed that the most ancient civilization in Mexico was that of the Toltecs, but the results of the excavations at Monte Albán altered this opinion and the Zapotec culture was considered the oldest, with that of the Mixtecs preceding the Toltec. Then remains of the Totonac (Tajin) culture in the State of Vera Cruz and the mysterious puzzling stone-work unearthed at La Venta in Tabasco, inclined the scientists to place the Totonac or Tajin culture as older than that of the Zapotecs, in fact, the most ancient in Mexico with the La Venta remains still an inexplicable mystery.

That there was contact between the ancient civilizations of South and Central America is beyond question. The numerical and calendrical systems of the Peruvians, the Mayas and the Mexicans were almost identical—even to the five days added to the 360 day year. Many features of the religion as well as the deities were very much alike and there are far too many other resemblances to cast them aside as merely coincidental.

In a shell heap on a river bank in Panama I dug up a black earthen water jar of unmistakable Chimu (Peruvian) origin. Sea shells from the Gulf of Mexico are frequently found in pre-Incan graves in Peru and numerous decorative designs on Peruvian and Middle American pottery are identical. Also, the Toltecs recorded much of their history by means of knotted strings very similar to the "quipos" of the Incan races. Here it is of interest to note that the Guaymis of Panama, whose head chief is always known as Montezuma, as well as the Shayshans of the Panama-Costa Rica border, not only keep tribal records but send long, involved messages by means of knotted vari-colored strings.

Among the remains of the Totonacs is a wealth of magnificently sculptured stone work such as that at the temple-pyramid of Tajin at Papantla. This is a many-terraced pyramid faced with cut stone and is provided with a balustraded stairway. The terraces have over-hanging cornices and false windows consisting of deep niches very similar to those in many of the ancient buildings at Cuzco, Peru. On the other hand, the exceedingly ornate cornices lend an Oriental effect to the imposing structures. The façades of the terraces are elaborately sculptured and in places the cornices are supported by beautifully and perfectly cut cylindrical columns elaborately carved. These columns are made up of numerous sections supported by a central stone core or shaft.

In addition to the temple there are several other fine edifices at Papantla. Among these is the ball game court whose walls are covered with high relief carvings apparently illustrating the various stages of a royal funeral, for the symbolical God of Death, in the form of a priest dressed to resemble a hawk or an eagle, is prominent in each of the panel-like carvings. In one scene the corpse is shown reposing on an ornate couch while priests prepare it for burial and in another the funeral sacrifice is shown with one priest holding the arms of a prisoner while another priest plunges a knife into the captive's heart.

Masters of stone cutting, the Totonacs left many fine examples of their art. There are lifelike figures of various animals, human figures and heads, deities and truly magnificent stone "yokes" or "collars." It would be very difficult to find anywhere—not excepting the Louvre or any museum in Europe—more perfectly wrought, life-like and striking pieces of sculpture than the ceremonial axe, the "closed yoke" with the owl's head, the jolly-faced, smiling woman's portrait or the pottery head of the devil-may-care, adventurous-looking chap, who, like many of the Totonacs whose portraits are preserved in pottery and stone, wore a beard (Plate VI, 9).

Even more ancient than those of the Totonacs are the mysterious unique stone objects found near La Venta and San Lorenzo, and tentatively designated as Olmec. Here, among other unique objects is a hand carved stone sarcophagus of large size and the shape of the top edge seems to suggest that it originally had a well fitted lid or cover. There are numerous cave dwellings containing pottery, stone sculptures and other artifacts, and innumerable stone idols and other carved stone objects have been found. Most noteworthy of all is a gigantic stone head nine feet in height with eyes two feet in length, and a mouth three feet across and weighing many tons, yet analysis of the rock from which it was carved proves that it was transported overland from the mountains more than sixty miles away in a bee line.

Like all of the stone and pottery heads found in this area the great stone head has thick lips and a broad flat nose of Negroid type, totally unlike the features of any known American race past or present. And like the other stone heads it wears a tightly-fitting cap or helmet similar to the helmets worn by our football players.

Another remarkable piece of sculpture from this area was a heroic size figure with a huge serpent on its lap, while the prize of all was a ten ton human figure supposedly representing some deity or priest of the long vanished, forgotten race. As in all the representations of human beings the imposing central figure with its ornate headdress has the typical flat nose and thickened lips.

Among the other noteworthy remains in the La Venta district are numerous stone table-like altars partially carved with deep tunnel or cave-like openings at the base and with the stone figure of a man emerging from the opening and carrying a miniature human being. Although these have been called women carrying children yet the small figures are not in the least babyish or child-like in their anatomical details but appear to represent dwarfs (Plate VII).

Among many ancient races, both in the New World and the Old World, dwarfs or pygmies were regarded with more or less superstitious reverence and were kept by the rulers, priests and members of the nobility, just as the court jesters—also usually dwarfs—were considered essential members of the courts of mediaeval Europe. According to the present day Mayas of northern Yucatán they have a tradition that the world was first inhabited by dwarfs, the "Adjuster men" or *Saiyam-Uinicob,* who, the Mayas believe, built the great cities now in ruins. The tradition is that the work was done before the sun was created and when the sun first rose the dwarfs were turned into stones that are the images of today.

Even more interesting is the fact that dwarfs or abnormally small persons are quite common among the living Indians of Tabasco. These miniature Indians are about four to four and a half feet in height with rather dark skins, broad flat noses and rather thick lips, very similar to those shown in the La Venta sculptures. One of these, a woman whom I knew, was the living replica of a La Venta stone head and her children—all dwarfs—were very similar. In their actions and behavior they are very much like the Bushmen or Hottentots of Africa and are inordinately fond of jokes, playing tricks and conversing in pantomime. Also they are exceedingly active. Perhaps they are reversions to an ancestral type of an undersized, broad nosed race that once occupied the La Venta area or, on the other hand, they may be freaks that always have occurred among the Indians who regarded them with more or less superstition and perpetuated their characteristics in stone. If there was a race or a community of such dwarfs, as there must have been, it might explain the tiny doorways and rooms with ceilings too low to permit an ordinary man to stand erect, the legend pertaining to the "House of the Dwarfs" at Uxmal, and the so-called Temple of the Virgins of the Sun at Pachacamak in Peru.

Whoever the La Venta dwarfs were it is very evident that they were sacrificed by decapitation, which would explain the many headless stone images and the bodiless stone heads. Carved stone panels from pillars at the temple at Palenque show figures of priests carrying the headless bodies of dwarfs in their arms in exactly the same manner as the figures represented as emerging from the stone cells at La Venta. Both male and female dwarfs are shown on these panels and the anatomical details prove they do not represent children. Also, in nearly every case the dwarfs have malformed feet. Other panels show the priests holding dwarfs, with heads intact, up to Kukulcan as if offering them to the deity. It is a significant fact, and another link in the chain connecting the Old World cultures with those of America, that in the island of Malta numerous stone figures of headless dwarfs, both male and female, have been found scattered about mushroom-shaped stone tables like those at La Venta. Also, the feet of these Malta dwarf statues are malformed or crippled, similar to the mysterious reproductions of cripples found at Monte Albán. Perhaps the dwarfs' feet were purposely crippled by their captors in order to prevent them from running away.

Probably the most outstanding and remarkable feature of the La Venta cultural remains is the abundance of jade objects. Not only is much of the jade of extremely high quality and fully equal to the most precious jades of the Orient, but this very hard refractory stone apparently presented no difficulties to the ancient La Venta artizans, for as Dr. Stirling states: "It was treated as though it were some sort of plastic material." Dishes, plates, spoons, bowls, celts and axes; figurines of human beings and animals of innumerable forms were beautifully carved from the rich green mineral which must have been obtainable in abundance despite the fact that no deposit of true jade has yet been found in America.

In addition to jade these ancient people carved quartz, amethyst, turquoise, malachite and obsidian, as well as iron pyrite, with equal skill and facility. In one spot the archaeologists of Dr. Stirling's expedition uncovered a stone cist or tomb seventeen feet in length, six feet in depth and five feet in width which once had been the coffin of some great ruler or high priest. No vestige of cloth, skin, flesh, feathers or even bones remained, but on the sandy bottom of the cubicle were the utensils and ornaments that once had been upon the body, and plainly marking its position at the time of burial.

Where an impressive feather headdress had once been there were the ornaments of carved jade, turquoise, rock crystal and other semiprecious stones that had adorned it. There were ducks' heads, animal figures, pendants and a dozen other forms of ornaments.

Two jade ear-plugs, engraved and polished, were where the ears had been. There was a double necklace of sixty-two ovate jade beads with the jade head of a turtle at each end, and scattered about the area that had not been covered were thirty-seven stone axe heads, seven to ten inches in length, twenty-eight of which were jade. Altogether the stone chest contained three hundred and forty specimens of inestimable archaeological value and interest of which three hundred were carved from the highest quality jade—by far the greatest number of jade objects ever found at one site in America.

According to Dr. Stirling, the La Venta culture dates back to about 450 B.C. and came to an abrupt end about 600 A.D. Judging by the conditions found by the archaeologists it would appear that at that time the flat-nosed people were destroyed by an alien race who not only wiped out the others but devoted an enormous amount of time and energy to defacing and destroying their idols, stonework, monuments and anything else they could do away with. It would seem probable these invaders were from Palenque for in the Temple of the Jaguars there is a stucco panel showing the same type of figure wearing the "Phrygian" cap exactly like that shown on the pottery portrait head from San Lorenzo. A similar portrait appears on a ceremonial axe of Totonac origin. Also the dates agree. Dr. Stirling places the end of the flat-nosed people's culture as about 600 A.D. and archaeologists have dated the Palenque remains as about 600 A.D. also.

Whatever the truth may be there is no question that the most ancient of the Mexican higher cultures was that of the fat-faced, thick-lipped, flat-nosed people of the La Venta area in the State of Tabasco.

CHAPTER 8

The Plumed Serpent

Fig. 17

The most famous, most spectacular and in some respects the most important of all the ancient Mexican and Mayan deities was the Plumed Serpent known to the Mayas as KUKULCAN and to the Mexicans as QUETZALCOATL. He was worshiped by every race in Mexico and much of Central America and he was more frequently and universally depicted on carvings, pottery and frescoes than any other deity. In fact there is scarcely a sculptured wall or monument, a fresco or a carved stone in Mexico or Yucatán that does not bear a representation of some form of the Plumed Serpent god and numerous temple pyramids were dedicated to him, the most famous being that of Chichen Itzá in Yucatán and the temple at Teotihuacán in Mexico. Although often, I might say usually, depicted in highly conventionalized symbolical forms having little or no resemblance to a human being (Fig. 17) there were innumerable sculptures, stone images and pottery figurines, as well as painted frescoes that are of portrait type. And in all of these the Plumed Serpent is shown as a bearded individual, often with a humped back varying from an incipient curvature to a fully developed deformity.* All of the Mayan and Mexican traditions of the Plumed Serpent describe him as a bearded white man wearing garments decorated with black and white crosses, and with one or two exceptions all the legends state that he came from overseas. Two voyages are noted. One tradition tells us that he landed on the West Coast of Mexico with the second largest group of immigrants to arrive in early times, and the second tradition tells of his arrival from overseas in a white winged ship and that he and his companions landed at the port that now is Vera Cruz.

In a great many, I might say most, of the sculptured and painted figures of this deity his association with the sea is indicated. In almost all of the representations, even those that are most highly conventionalized, he is shown with a sea-shell of the genus Pterocera or Lambis (commonly called a "Scorpion shell") suspended by a cord or string of beads about his neck (Figs. 1, 2). Also, at the temple of Quetzalcoatl at Teotihuacán, the sculptured frieze beneath the outjutting plumed serpent heads show sea shells amid wavy lines intended to represent water. So well and accurately carved are these shells that despite the erosion and wear and tear of countless centuries the shells are readily identified. Mainly they

* It is a most significant fact that all known representations of the human Plumed Serpent have the typical, high bridged, slightly aquiline Aryan nose. Nowhere is there a figure of the bearded Kukulcan or Quetzalcoatl with the heavy curved beak nose of the Mayan deities or the noses typical of the native Mexican and Peruvian races. Like our cartoonists, Indian artists invariably select some outstanding or unusual feature to identify a person, and we may feel quite certain that the original Plumed Serpent did have the Aryan or "Gaur" nose so universal on representations of the Sumerian rulers found in the Old World.

are gastropods of the genus *Fasciolaria* but there are also *Phalium* as well as bivalve shells and several nautilus (Plate IV).

As I have said, practically all the legends of the Plumed Serpent agree that he came in a ship from the east. One tradition, however, states that he first appeared in the form of the quetzal or the resplendent trogan and while in this form he was captured in the net of a hunter named Hueymatzin who was a hero-god. Because of this the quetzal became the sacred bird of the Mexicans and Mayas and Quetzalcoatl is always shown adorned with the long, fern-like green feathers of this trogan.

As the bird has a scarlet breast and a white band across the chest the representations of the Plumed Serpent when done in color are invariably red, white and green which became the national colors of Mexico.

However, in the light of recent discoveries and researches, it seems highly probable that the "plumes" shown in some of the effigies and pictures of this god are not feathers but leaves of maize (Plate II, 3). According to tradition it was Quetzalcoatl (Kukulcan of the Mayas) who brought maize to America and he was in certain instances represented as a Corn god. It is neither unlikely nor illogical that the feathers of the quetzal became attributes of the Plumed Serpent because of their resemblance to the leaves of maize.*

In addition to being regarded as the corn god the Plumed Serpent had many names. As the god of Air he was known to the Aztecs as *Ehecatl* and was also called *Yolcuat* or the "Rattlesnake"; *Tohil* or the "Rumbler"; as *Nanihehecatl* or "Lord of Four Winds" and as *Tlauizcalpantecutli* the "Lord of Light of Dawn" (Venus). As symbols of these several attributes he is usually shown surrounded by whirls or wind symbols and accompanied by rattlesnakes, while his head is the second of the Aztecs' twenty day signs: *Ehecatl* or "wind."

Although the legends of his arrival nearly all agree, there is much confusion when it comes to the manner of his departure. One legend states that he cast himself on a funeral pyre and that his

* This would appear to be borne out by the words of the ancient Aztec chant to the Rain god: "Thou, my God, descended has thy water, come is thy water. Already has it changed itself to green quetzal feathers; already has it become green; already has it become summer; already has the famine (drought) left us."

ashes ascended and were transformed to birds while his heart became the morning star. This version also relates that he vanished for four days, then wandered for eight days in the underworld when he was resurrected and went to heaven as a god. Another version is that he became disgusted with the perversion of the Aztecs' religion and their wholesale sacrifices and departed on a magic raft made of braided serpents. A third legend tells how he was overcome by Tezcatlipoca, the god of Darkness, who descended on a spider web and offered Quetzalcoatl a draught supposed to produce immortality but in reality caused such an irresistible homesickness that it compelled him to sail away. There are a number of other versions of the last days of Quetzalcoatl or Kulkulcan but these offered here are probably the most popular and best known.

In many ways, however, all agree that Quetzalcoatl, before he disappeared, prophesied that long after his departure bearded white men would arrive from overseas and would overthrow the Aztecs and enforce another religion, but that eventually he would return and reestablish the Aztecs and their faith. As the first part of this prophecy was fulfilled by the arrival of Cortez and his conquest of Mexico, there are countless Mexican Indians today who are still expecting their Plumed Serpent god to reappear and who still surreptitiously make offerings to him in the ancient temples of Quetzalcoatl.

Both the Mayas and the Mexicans credited the Plumed Serpent as having taught their ancestors their many arts and crafts and for the introduction of their calendrical and numerical systems as well as teaching them agriculture. He was, according to all accounts, a far less cruel and bloodthirsty deity than most of the Mexicans' gods and did not demand human sacrifices but preferred self sacrifices by his devotees and priests who pierced their ears and tongues to draw the blood that was smeared upon the mouths of the idols.

Although many scientists may scoff at the idea that the Plumed Serpent actually arrived in Mexico in a ship from overseas, yet there are innumerable facts and much incontrovertible evidence to prove the truth of the tradition.

In the first place, the Mexicans were not at all surprised at the arrival of the Spaniards who—by coincidence—landed at the site of Vera Cruz, for they had long been expecting the return of Quetzalcoatl or his sons. None of the ancient traditions mention the date of

the Plumed Serpent's arrival but it must have been at a very remote time if, as the legends state, he taught the people their various
arts and introduced their numerical and calendrical systems. This
fact has often been brought out as an argument in rebuttal of the
Old World origin of Quetzalcoatl, the "all-American team" declaring that at such a far distant time there were no vessels capable
of voyaging from the Old World to America. But in that they are
entirely mistaken. As early as 3100 B.C. the Sumerians, Dravidians,
and Phoenicians had large, well-built, well-rigged sea-going ships
far more seaworthy than those of Columbus and at the time of the
Third Dynasty of Egypt, King Snefru sent a fleet of forty ships to
a Syrian port for cedar wood, and the known length of one of these
was one hundred and seventy or more feet. Tin was mined in England, *"the Tin-land country which lies beyond the Upper Sea"*
(Mediterranean) at the time of Sargon of Agade, about 2500 B.C.
and ships engaging in this trade were most certainly of a sea-worthy
nature (see Chapter 2, Fig. 1). Also, it is recorded on many of the
ancient "Sumerian" tablets that their kings had voyaged overseas
to the "Land Beyond the Western Sea" or to the "Sunset Land,"
where they had established colonies and had erected monuments
and "built a holding." Among these Sumerian rulers who had
voyaged to the "Land Beyond the Western Sea" was Narām-sin,
a son of King Menes, who had set forth on an exploratory and
colonizing expedition some time before 2000 B.C.

There is an abundance of most convincing evidence that Narām-
sin was the Plumed Serpent. Sumerian carvings and other representations of this personage show him with a beard, with a peculiar
type of helmet and with his headdress decorated with three uni-
formly sized disks (Plate VIII, 3).

At Lake Tezcoco, at a depth of fifteen feet below the surface of
the mud, a ceremonial stone mace head was dug up and is now in
the Chicago Natural History Museum, Chicago (Plate VIII, 2).
This is unique and unlike any other carved stone object ever found
in America but is almost identical in shape with stone mace heads
found in the Near East known to have belonged to Narām-sin and
his grandfather, King Sargon of Agade, while existing portraits of
Narām-sin, one from Kurdistan and one from Egypt, have almost
identical features and helmet or headdress (Plate VIII, 3). Anyone comparing the Mexican specimen with those shown in Nos.

1 and 3 will instantly see the striking similarity between the Mexican portrait mace head and Near Eastern portraits in bas-relief that are known to represent Narām-sin. The beard and features are the same. The helmets with the chin covers are identical, even to the links or disks under the chin, as are the segmented or quilted top of the helmet and the twisted rope-like decoration encircling the lower edge. It is utterly inconceivable and beyond reason to believe that any ancient Aztec, Toltec or other Mexican artizan could have conceived such a human being as is so obviously accurately carved on the mace head. Even admitting that bearded men were common and frequently are depicted in sculptures and paintings of the ancient Mexicans, the beards were never of the type shown on the mace head.

No such helmets were ever known to or used by the American races and it is beyond all limits of coincidence for two sculptors of equal ability in two widely separated hemispheres to have hit upon the twisted rope-like band, the chin strap and other details of the mace head portrait from America and the bas-relief portraits from Asia and Africa. The only logical and sane explanation of its presence there is that it belonged to Narām-sin or some of his companions who were at Tenochtitlán several thousand years ago.*

Even more convincing is the remarkable stone pendant found in August, 1936, in Gallo Canyon, near an ancient Pueblo ruin in New Mexico by Dr. Charles F. Elvers, former curator of archaeology and anthropology for the Maryland Academy of Sciences at Baltimore. The pendant or amulet is of very hard dark gray stone of pear shape, about three inches in length, with a perforation at the upper or narrow end and has incised carvings on both sides (see Plate VIII, 5). On one side there is the figure of a man holding a crooked or serpent-like staff in his right hand and apparently climbing up a slope while looking over his right shoulder. There is a crown on his head but no garments are indicated. On the other side of the pendant is an inscription composed of an ele-

---

* On the carved stone frame of a mirror found in south-east Vera Cruz (Totonac culture), there is the head of a bearded man identical in many details with the mace head from Lake Tezcoco. There is the same quilted or padded helmet, the same type of chin strap, the same rope-like band about the helmet rim, the same ear coverings and the same collar composed of rectangular sections (Plate VIII, 4).

phant head, a triangle, a cross, a circle and two six-pointed stars. These are all symbols or glyphs used in the archaic Sumerian Linear Script to express the name of Narām-sin who existed about 2000 B.C. or earlier. In other words it was his signature and may be explained as follows: The elephant head expressed the phonetic *amma* which was a part of Narām-sin's epithets. In the Sumerian language the elephant was known as *amsi*, the "toothed wild bull." The ovoid enclosing the circle expressed the phonetic *nar* or *ner*. The cross within a square meant *Para* or "Pharaoh," while the twin stars meant a "Descendant of Divine Origin, Ruling By Divine Right." Translated, the inscription would read: "The Under-king-Companion (viceroy) Nar- or Nera, the Gut (the Goth) Am (Fig. 18).*

As corroboratory evidence of the Old World origin of this amulet is the stela preserved in the Louvre in Paris. This famous stone carving commemorates one of Narām-sin's conquests and shows him standing on a mountain slope, holding a staff or spear in his right hand, wearing a horned headdress and looking somewhat to the right. The features are not in profile. Above the mountain top near the apex of the stela are the twin many-rayed stars (Plate VIII, 6). In short the design on the amulet from New Mexico is a somewhat crude, yet exact miniature replica of the famous stela, even to the general shape of the two stones. In the light of all this the only conclusion is that the stone pendant from New Mexico was a badge or credential of Narām-sin worn by one of his high-ranking officers or officials, a sort of passport as it were, and analogous to the signet ring seals of potentates and others. How it reached the spot where

* The source material for the identification of the characters shown on the amulet are as follows:

1—"Seals from the Indus Valley" by Sir John Marshall
2—For *NAR* or *NER*: *Dictionary of Assyrian Languages* by W. Muss-Arnolt, Berlin, 1905
  "Classified List of Sumerian Ideographs" by Brunnow, Leyden, 1889.
  "Bismaya" by E. J. Banks, N. Y., 1912.
  "Egyptian Hieroglyphs" by E. W. Budge, 1920
3—*AM* or *AM-SI*: "Seltens Assurische Ideogramme" by B. Meisner, 1910
  "Dictionary of Assyrian Language" by W. Muss-Arnolt, Berlin, 1905
4—*GUT*: "Classified List of Sumerian Ideographs" by R. Brunnow, Leyden, 1889.
5—*BARA*: *"Bismaya"* by E. J. Banks, N. Y., 1912.
  "Classified List Of Sumerian Ideographs" by Brunnow, Leyden, 1889.

it was found is impossible to say, but if its story were known it doubtless would prove a most fascinating and romantic tale.

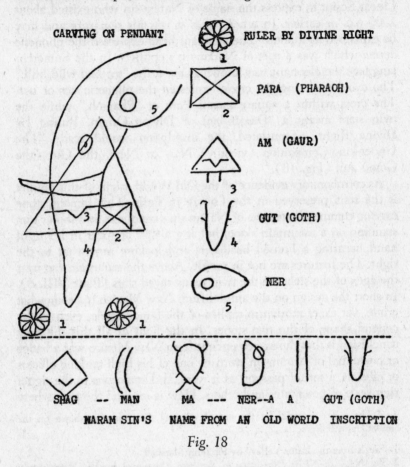

Fig. 18

In all probability it was worn by a representative of Narām-sin who, while on an expedition of exploration and trade, reached the ancient Pueblo near Gallo Springs. He may have lost the talisman by accident or he may have been killed by hostile natives. Neither must we forget that according to the Mexican traditions, Quetzalcoatl left Cholula in Mexico bound for Tlapallan (The Land of Bright Colors). If this was Arizona, Utah, or northwestern New Mexico, and he ascended the Rio Grande, he would have passed through or very close to the area where the amulet was found. That, however, is a matter of speculation, but there can be no speculation as to the origin of the amulet itself.

Finally and perhaps the most important and the most convincing of all evidences of Narām-sin's identity as the Plumed Serpent, there are the wonderfully preserved Santa Rita frescoes in British Honduras. These show in bright colors a series of figures, all of the same personage, but at different ages, attired in most involved and stylized garments and accoutrements and surrounded by calendrical glyphs of unmistakable Mayan type which leave no question of the personage being the Plumed Serpent or Kukulcan of the Mayas.

It always has been taken for granted that the many odd ornaments, decorations, etc., which cover the figures of the god were merely decorative, but Mrs. Verrill, who has made a very deep and exhaustive study of the ancient Sumerians, the genealogies of their kings, their records inscribed in the archaic Sumerian script and their history, recognized, in the apparently ornamental details of the Santa Rita figures, a number of characters of the Sumerian Linear Script.* When these had been separated from the less important portions of the costumes and accessories and were arranged in their proper sequences, they revealed quite a complete story of the figures and appear to leave no reasonable doubt as to the true identity of the Plumed Serpent of these frescoes. This is clearly shown in Plate I which gives the various Sumerian glyphs and their interpretations. As there were no prepositions, articles or conjunctions in the ancient Sumerian written language these must be filled in. When this is done we find the characters reveal the following:

"The Under-companion (viceroy), Under-commander (rear admiral) to King Menes; Priest Gan (or devotee of sun fire worship) in the Temple of the Sun; one who holds the scepter of Pharaoh in Sumerian owned and controlled areas. The personage at the right

---

* It is not surprising that our most eminent archaeologists had failed to notice the Sumerian characters on these frescoes. Students of American archaeology seldom if ever possess any great knowledge of the archaeology, theology, cultural backgrounds and records of the races of the Mediterranean, Mesopotamian and neighboring regions, and I doubt if any of our scientists, who are specialists in American archaeology, can recognize, much less decipher, any phase of the archaic Sumerian Script.

is shown arriving from the ocean indicated by conventionalized waves beneath his feet. He is wearing his insignia of office and personal credentials. In this figure he is depicted as more youthful and beardless. The third or left hand figures depict him wearing a beard, apparently much older and inflicted with a severe curvature of the lower part of the spine" (Plate I, 6).

These facts indicate that he was a young man when he arrived and remained for some time in the land. In the central figure he is shown at rest and seated on a low throne. He is here shown talking about his native land, and his maternal and paternal ancestors, and according to true script states that he is a Son of the Sun and has travelled around the world and declares himself pharaoh under dual rule. He also describes tilled and irrigated lands and their crops. These are indicated by the symbols for tilled lands to indicate crops and to show that these crops were for human consumption the glyphs are painted where the stomach would be. Crossed lines at his back, where he sits on his throne indicate that the family seat or home-land has drainage ditches or irrigation canals.

The left hand figure shows the much older personage departing and about to return to his homeland for the time has come when he must ascend the throne as a full emperor or pharaoh. Each of the Gaur symbols seems to indicate five kings or rulers of the royal family and as there are eight of these the personage on the fresco would be the fortieth Sumerian-Aryan ruler, or Narām-sin.

This account agrees perfectly with existing archaic records. Narām-sin *did* sail for the "Land of the Setting Sun." During his absence King Menes, his father, died in "Urani Land at the Lake of the Peak," and Narām-sin was called home to become the ruler of vast Asiatic areas and the "two Egypts" that had been united under one rule by his father.

According to some archaeologists, the Plumed Serpent did not appear in Yucatán until quite recently—about 600 A.D. and came from Mexico as previously mentioned. There also are traditions of Kukulcan having first reached Central America via the Pacific Ocean. The logical explanation would be that there were several Plumed Serpents or Kukulcans or Quetzalcoatls, which is neither surprising nor unreasonable for it was not unusual for priests, who were of the noble class, rulers, or high officials, to assume the names of their ancestors, deities or famous men who had preceded them.

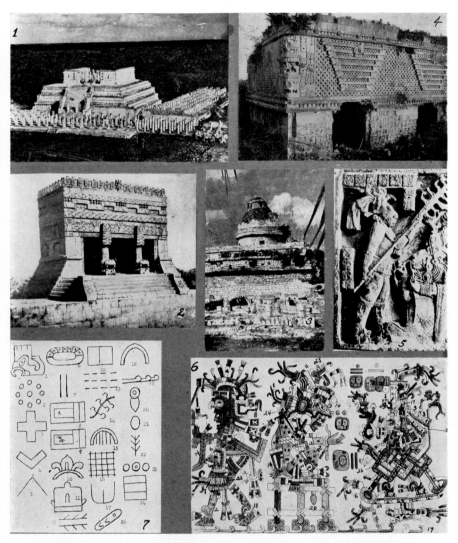

PLATE I (Chapter 4)

1 Temple of the Warriors. Chichen Itza. Yucatán. *(Inst. Nacional, Mexico)*
2 Temple of the Ball Court. (Restored), Chichen Itza. *(Amer. Museum of Nat. History)*
3 The Caracol or Observatory. Chichen Itza.
4 Portion of the "Nunnery." Uxmal, Yucatán. *(Amer. Museum Nat. History)*
5 Carved stone lintel. Menche, Yucatán. *(British Museum)*
6 Frescoe of Kukulkan. Santa Rita, Br. Honduras. The small numerals indicate symbols in Sumerian symbolic script.
7 Sumerian characters from Santa Rita frescoes.

PLATE II (Chapter 5)

 1 Temple of Tenochtitlan. City of Mexico. Reconstruction by Señor Ignacio Marquina.
 2 Stone carving, Sun God. Mexico. Note headdress similar to that of modern Zapotec women.
 3 Stone carving, plumed serpent wrapped in maize leaves. Mexico.
 4 Stone figure of a woman. Mexico.
 5 Rattlesnake carved from green stone. Aztec culture. Mexico.
 6 Stone figure of an Aztec deity. Mexico.
 7 Sculptured stone head. Mexico. *(Museo Nacional)*
 8 Temple of the sun. Teotihuacan, Mexico. *(Inst. Nacional, Mexico)*
 9 Detail of carving. Papantla. Totonac (Tajin) culture. *(Inst. Nacional)*
10 Porcelain elephant. South of Cuernavaca, Mexico. *(Dr. Mundy)*
11 Pottery wheeled toy. Valley of Mexico.
12 Chac-mool, the Rain God. Mexico. *(Museo Nacional, Mexico)*
13 Aztec spear-thrower or atlatl. *(British Museum)*

PLATE III (Chapter 6)

1 Human skull carved from rock crystal. Aztec. *(British Museum)*
2 Mask of turquoise mosaic. Mexico. *(Museum of Amer. Indian, N.Y.)*
3 Double-headed serpent of turquoise mosaic. Mexico. *(British Museum)*
4 Sacrificial knife with mosaic haft. Mexico. *(British Museum)*
5 Aztec calendar stone. Mexico City.
6 Carved stone chest. Aztec culture. Mexico.

PLATE IV (Chapter 7)

1 Monte Albán before excavating. Mexico.
2 Temple of Quetzalcoatl. Teotihuacan, Mexico.
3 Carved stone serpent head. Temple of Quetzalcoatl. Mexico.
4 Sea shell (Fasciolaria) from tomb at Monte Albán. Mexico.
5 Wall of temple of Quetzalcoatl showing sculptured sea shells and waves.
6 Wooden shield with turquoise mosaic. Monte Albán. (*Mus. of Amer. Indian, N.Y.*)
7 A corridor at Mitla. Mexico.
8 Stairway of temple. Xochicalco, Mexico.
9 Detail of carvings. Xochicalco temple, Mexico.

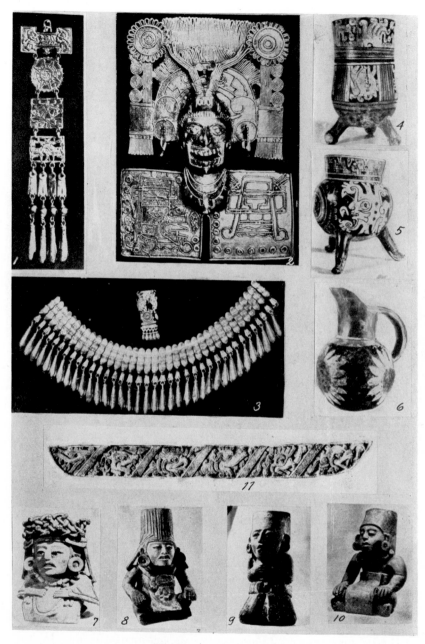

PLATE V (Chapter 7)

1, 2, 3 Gold ornaments from Monte Albán tombs. Mixtec culture. *Inst. Nacional, Mexico)*

4, 5, 6 Pottery from Monte Albán tombs.

7, 8, 9, 10 Figurines from Monte Albán. Zapotec and Mixtec cultures.

11 Carved bone utensil. Monte Albán. *(Inst. Nacional)*

PLATE VI (Chapter 7)

1 Stucco bas-relief. King on Jaguar throne. Palenque, Mexico.
2 Stone axe head; deity with horned helmet. La Venta, Mexico. *(Inst. Nacional, Mexico)*
3 Stone crypt with figure emerging carrying a dwarf. La Venta Area, Mexico (After Stirling)
4 Gigantic stone head. La Venta, Mexico. *(Inst. Nacional, Mexico)*
5 Stone yoke, *not* used to hold sacrificial victims on altar. La Venta area, Mexico.
6 Temple at Palenque. Chiapas, Mexico. *(Inst. Nacional, Mexico)*
7 Stone carving showing man and woman carrying male and female dwarfs. *(Smithsonian Inst.)*
8 Temple of Tejin, Totonac culture. *(Inst. Nacional, Mexico)*
9 Pottery head of bearded man, probably Kukulkan. San Lorenzo, Mexico. *(Museo Nacional, Mexico)*

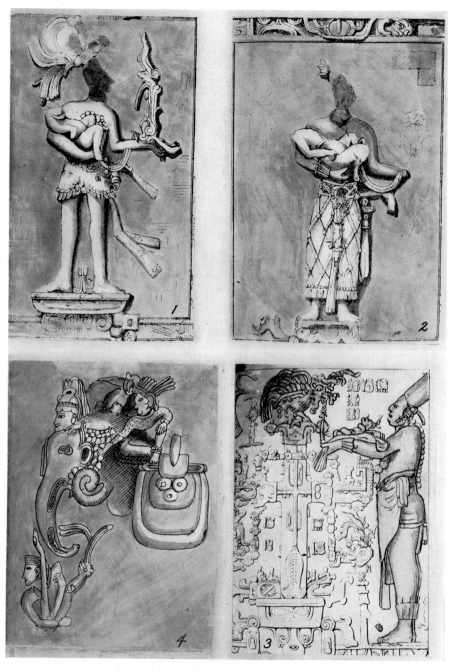

PLATE VII (Chapter 7)

1 Stucco bas-relief showing priest carrying female dwarf. Palenque Temple.
2 Stucco bas-relief showing priestess with male dwarf. Note the dwarf is headless and has malformed feet. (Palenque).
3 Stucco bas-relief, Palenque Temple, priest offering dwarf as sacrifice to Kukulcan.
4 Elephant on stele at Copan, Honduras. Early Maya.

PLATE VIII (Chapter 8)

1 Rock carvings, Vernal, Utah, showing warrior-king with Aztec type shield and dress; a captive bound to a rock; and warriors.

2 Ceremonial mace-head. Lake Texcoco, Mexico. *(Chicago Mus. Nat. Hist.)*

3 Rock carving of Naram-sin from Kurdistan. *(Ottoman Museum)*

4 Mirror-back from Tobasco, Mexico, showing portrait of a bearded man with helmet, earrings, etc., like those on Figs. 2 and 3.

5 Pendant-amulet of stone from New Mexico bearing name symbols of Naram-sin on one side and figure on the other.

6 Monument in Louvre, Paris, showing Naram-sin standing on a mountain with warriors and prisoners below.

7-8 Obsidian "coins" found near Kanab, Utah.

Just as the Inca Panaka-Socsoc assumed the name of the pre-Incan god, Wira Kocha and became Wira-Kocha-Inca.

Also it was not at all unusual for certain famous names or appellations to be handed down. Thus, in Peru, there were four Incas named Yupanqui and even in modern times we find this duplication of names among rulers and exalted personages, as for example the several Kings Louis of France, the various Williams, Georges, Henrys, etc. of England, and the Popes named Pius. If these men were not designated by numbers and were mentioned in history by their Christian names only, how could anyone be certain which King Henry was famed for his matrimonial and gastronomical feats or which William was the "Conqueror" or even the dates of their various reigns? Among the American Indian tribes this custom of assuming the name of some former famed personage is quite common. Although among the Aztecs, Montezuma was merely the name of a monarch, yet among the Guaymis of northern Panama the head chief is always called Montezuma which is their equivalent of "king."

Considering all this it is quite probable that in addition to the first Kukulcan or Quetzalcoatl, who we believe was Narām-sin, there were various other high priests of the Plumed Serpent cult, and perhaps even great warriors or members of the nobility or wise men, who were known as Kukulcan or Quetzalcoatl. Finally, if, as we and others believe, voyagers from Peru reached Yucatán and Mexico, what more natural than that the natives should have regarded the leaders as the Plumed Serpent returning as he had promised in the dim and distant past?

CHAPTER 9

Foods the Ancient Americans Gave Us

In a previous chapter I have mentioned that when Cortez and his followers reached Mexico they found many edible plants and fruits that were unknown to Europeans. It was the same in Peru and from both countries, as well as from the West Indies, the invaders carried seeds, tubers, roots and plants back to Spain, thereby benefiting the Old World inestimably.

Of all our food plants, our fruits and our nuts, over eighty per cent are indigenous to America and were cultivated by the ancient Americans. Even the most primitive tribes had their fields and gardens where they cultivated maize, beans, squashes, and pumpkins; melons of various kinds and, in the warmer areas, sweet potatoes, tomatoes, peppers, and other food plants. The more cultured and the civilized races—the Incans, Mayas, and the Mexicans, had great areas of well-tilled land, provided with irrigation ditches in areas where rains were few, and raised vast quantities of vegetable crops.

It would require an entire volume to name and describe all of the strictly American food plants, fruits, nuts, tubers, grains, etc., that were known to and used by the ancient Americans. Prominent among them are the various snap beans, lima beans, squashes, pumpkins, water melons, peppers, egg plants, tomatoes, white and sweet potatoes, manioc or cassava, pineapples, strawberries, avocados, arrowroot, sapodillas, cashews, cacao, custard apples, cheyotes, cranberries, papayas, grenadillas, guavas, Jerusalem artichokes, peanuts, pecan nuts, hickory nuts, butternuts, Brazil nuts, persimmons, maguey, Surinam cherries, blackberries, blueberries, crabapples, many of the grapes, raspberries, palm cabbage, pimento, vanilla, tonka beans and maize, or Indian corn.

Many of these had been cultivated, hybridized and developed into endless varieties countless centuries before Columbus set sail from Palos, and many had been so long cultivated by the ancient Americans that their original wild ancestors had completely disappeared, or were so unlike the cultivated forms that they are unrecognizable, with the result that no one knows the identities of the parent plants and where they originated.

However, Peru has been credited with being the home of the majority of the American food plants such as the squashes and pumpkins, melons, lima and other beans, tomatoes, white and sweet potatoes, peppers, peanuts, and others, while most botanists agree that Central America and Mexico were the original homes of the cacao, vanilla, avocado and some other food plants, while the pineapple, arrowroot, pimento, yautias, and some others were West Indian.

That all or most of these American food plants had been cultivated by the natives for thousands of years is proved by the fact that they are all depicted on the most ancient carvings in stone and on pottery and that many, such as peanuts, beans, lima beans, squash seeds and melon seeds, sweet potatoes, etc., are found buried with the mummies in the most ancient pre-Incan graves in Peru.

Moreover, long before the arrival of the Spaniards, these food plants of the Incans, Mayas, and Mexicans had spread from Chile to Canada and from the Atlantic to the Pacific and were cultivated and formed the principal food supplies of the Indians of South, Central and North America. But for some strange and inexplicable reason, the common white potato had never been introduced farther north than the area of our extreme south-western states and was unknown to the Indians of the Atlantic and New England states areas until brought to America by the British colonists. Carried to Spain by the conquerors, the lowly "spud" had been cultivated over a considerable part of Europe and finally reached the British isles whence it came back to the land of its origin—a long roundabout journey of nearly one hundred years.

Of all the American food plants the most important and valuable, as well as the most widely cultivated, was maize or Indian corn. In every part of the New World, wherever the climate was suitable, maize was the staple crop of the ancient Americans, as it is today. In fact it is difficult to understand how the Indians could have existed without maize.

The civilizations of the Mayas and Mexicans were founded upon corn. In Mexico the inevitable and indispensable "frijoles" or beans were a most important crop but what are frijoles without tortillas! Tortillas are made of ground maize, and many, many times more acres of Mexican land were devoted to raising corn than to all other crops combined.

It was even more important, in fact vital, to the Mayas, for the very existence of the people and their civilization depended upon maize. In fact many archaeologists believe that exhaustion of the soil and the inability of the Mayas to raise enough maize to feed the populace was what led to the abandonment of many cities and the decline of the Mayan civilization.

In South America maize was almost as important a crop as in Yucatán, Mexico, and North America, but the Incan races had a much greater variety of food plants than had their more northern neighbors.

Peanuts, which have become distributed all over the world and are one of the world's most important and valuable crops, formed a large part of the Peruvians' diet in pre-Spanish times as they do today. They had dozens of varieties of white potatoes that do not succeed well in tropical countries and innumerable varieties of sweet potatoes, squashes and other food plants.

That they had been cultivating, hybridizing and improving corn for two thousand years or more is proven by the corn cobs, often with kernels intact, found in the most ancient pre-Incan graves. Moreover, they had every distinct variety of maize that is known to us today. They had popping corn, sweet corn, flint corn, feed corn, red corn, yellow corn, and black corn, and several varieties we do not have such as the "moti" corn with kernels as large as chestnuts that are roasted and eaten like the nuts, as well as the stubby, dwarf, hard-kernelled variety of the high Andes that withstands frost.

Until quite recently botanists and archaeologists were of two schools when it came to the origin of maize. Some believed, with every good reason, that it originated in Peru, while others were equally firm in their belief that it was developed from some unknown wild grass in the highlands of Central America or Mexico. As there were no wild grasses known that could have been the ancestors of maize the theory was promulgated that maize had been developed from a wild plant named teosinte. But competent botanists declared that teosinte could not have been the parent plant but was, perhaps, a hybrid of maize and some other plant.

On the other hand those who believed that maize originated in Peru based their claims on the fact that the oldest known evidences of maize were the dried-up ears in ancient graves and the representations of maize on ancient stone carvings and pottery. Then, in the bat caves of Arizona, an archaeologist unearthed corn cobs that by the carbon test gave their age as about 1500 to 2000 B.C. To be sure, the specimens found in the lowest stratification of the cave's floor were miserable apologies for maize, being tiny ears of "pod corn" but by a careful study of specimens found in the various strata up to the topmost layer, a steady improvement was found, with the best a fairly good although runty ear of flint corn.

The controversy had now narrowed down to whether the Peruvian or the Arizona maize was the most ancient. Then evidence was unearthed that led the most eminent botanists to question the American origin of maize.

In a letter to me, Dr. George Carter of the Isiah Bowman School of Geography at Johns Hopkins University, wrote as follows: "I am inclined to think—just as a free hand guess—that corn was introduced to America, probably from southeastern Asia across the Pacific about 2000 B.C. and that this corn was somewhat like the earliest corn in Peruvian graves." In another letter he stated: "I think that maize is as likely to be of Asiatic or African origin as of American origin." Dr. Carter also wrote that there were plants in northern India that were of a type that might have been the ancestors of maize.

These more recent ideas as to the origin of maize have been given additional support as the result of my having sent both Dr. Anderson and Dr. Carter some remarkable mutations of the Black Mexican variety of corn I raised in my garden. In these, which appeared to be reversions to the ancestral form, there were distinct kernels, as well as "silk" on the tassels or male flowers, while the miniature "ears" on the stalk had no protective covering. By carefully watching my corn, I found quite a number of other mutations until eventually I obtained a complete series showing every gradation from the tassels bearing well-developed kernels and silk and with no ears on the stalk, to those with both fairly well-developed stalk-borne ears and tassels with kernels and silk among the male flowers (Plate IX). Whether or not such reversions to the ancestral form occur among other varieties of corn I cannot say, but as far as I have been able to ascertain none have been recorded. However, the chances are all against it for the majority of the varieties of maize now cultivated are complex hybrids. The Black Mexican, however, (which despite its name is a Peruvian variety), has been little if at all hybridized for countless centuries. This is proven by the fact that ears of well-preserved Black Mexican corn found in ancient Peruvian graves are indistinguishable from the Black Mexican of today, hence this variety is not only one of the most ancient but is probably the purest of all and therefore nearer the original wild plant than any other known maize.

Judging by the specimens I collected and that are shown in the photograph, the original maize—or its parent—was a grass which bore a "head" or tassel with grains or kernels and a silk "beard" not very different from the heads of barley or wheat. How or by what means the seed kernels were induced to leave the "head" and to form separate seed clusters covered with a protective covering of specialized leaves, we do not know and probably never will know, but it doubtless required centuries of careful cultivation and selection to achieve the desired result. On the other hand, it may have been the result of a "sport" or freak. Somewhere at some time in the distant past a stalk of the grass may have borne an ear on its stalk with a tassel free of seeds. If the primitive farmer noticed this and realized the improvement and planted the seeds it may not have required a very great period of time to have produced maize as we know it.

Whether or not maize was brought to America from the Old World has not definitely been proved, but there is considerable evidence to support the theory. On a carved stone panel from the wall of the Hall of Nations in the palace of the Assyrian king, Ashur-nasir-pal at Calah (Nimrud), and dating from about 800 B.C. there is the figure of a deity standing beside a group of tall corn-like plants with jointed stalks and maize-like leaves and with stylized cobs and conventionalized tassels.

The figure is depicted holding a small hand bag or basket in his left hand while in his right hand he grasps an unmistakable ear of maize (Plate IX, 3).

As each of the panels was carved to represent some distinctive feature or activity of the nation to which it was dedicated, this particular panel might be that of Mexico, Central America or South America. On the other hand it may have been dedicated to India or some other country. However, a circular piece of embroidery from the same palace and of the same date, shows two deities facing a well-drawn stalk of maize while about the outer edge of the specimen there are a number of recognizable ears of maize (Fig. 19).

Fig 19

In addition to these there are the symbols denoting mountains and the "setting sun" glyph or in other words: "Land of mountains of the setting (western) sun." Among several beaten gold vessels from a mound in lower Egypt and dating from about 1000 B.C., and now in the Cairo Museum, there is one jar modeled to represent an ear of maize, another decorated with the maize flowers or tassels and with the Goat Crop-God for a handle, while a footed goblet shows the husks of the ears. Moreover, one of these jars bears the symbol of the "Land of western sunset mountains" (Plate IX, 4-5).

Finally in the East Indian classic, the *Râmâyana* it is stated that dishes of corn "boiled in the husks" were served to guests at a great feast. It is difficult to imagine anyone dining on either wheat barley or rice "boiled in the husks," so the "corn" must have been maize.

In view of all these evidences of maize having been known to the Asiatics and Egyptians centuries before the Christian era, and considering the fact that maize was unknown to people of the Old World at the time of Columbus, it would seem probable that maize was carried from America to Asia by the earliest Sumerian voyagers, but in its new home, where the people were unfamiliar with its proper cultivation and hybridization, it deteriorated and died out, whereas, in America, where the Indians were familiar with the proper care of the corn, it increased and improved.*

In addition to the innumerable food plants, fruits, nuts, and other vegetable products given to us by the ancient Americans, we must not forget the turkey and the Muscovy ducks, both of which had been domesticated and bred to an infinite number of varieties ages before the time of Columbus. Moreover, our own barn yard turkeys are descendants of the Mexican turkey, for no one has succeeded in thoroughly domesticating the wild North American species.

Also we owe an enormous debt to the ancient Americans for the many medicinal plants they gave us. Most of our most valuable, widely used, most efficacious and indispensable medicines and drugs are of American origin and were widely cultivated and used by the Indians of North, South and Central America many centuries before the conquest. Among these are cocaine (from the Coca plant of Peru); quinine and calisaya, sarsaparilla, impecachuana, rhubarb, aconite, wintergreen and sassafras (sources of salicylic acid and aspirin), liverwort, arnica, boneset, gold thread, ginseng, mandrake, viburnum, tansy, yarrow, and a host of others, as well as tobacco.

That the people of the Old World ever managed to survive with-

* In a letter from Dr. George F. Carter of Johns Hopkins University, he writes: "You will be interested to know that pineapples and Anona are portrayed in murals at Pompeii."

out some of these medicines that are now in daily universal use is little less than a miracle. And how they must have suffered with injuries and illnesses without sedatives, pain killers, and local anaesthetics that were all in use by the ancient Americans. No one possibly can estimate the benefits that have resulted from the discovery and use of American medicinal plants and their derivatives, but undoubtedly, during the centuries that have passed since the Spanish Conquest, medicines and drugs of the ancient Americans have saved more lives than all the Indians ever slain by the white men.

CHAPTER 10

The Mysterious Sun Dogs

Among the remains left by the Incans, the Mayas, the Aztecs, and the Toltecs, there are innumerable carvings, paintings and figures on ceramic ware, as well as woven in textiles, showing the sacred "Sun dogs" or Wari-Wilkas as they were called by the ancient Peruvians.

Many of these representations are obviously excellent likenesses, others are highly conventionalized, but all show the outstanding and distinctive characteristics of the quadruped. These are large, sharp claws and offset thumb-like toes, a long narrow tongue, out-jutting lower jaw, retracted lips showing long, sharp fang-like teeth, a mask-like marking on the face and a long tail with slightly prehensible tip. And all show the distinctive "sun spot" on the breast.

Some of the best of these pictures were engraved on sea shells found in the Spiro Burial Mound at Spiro, Oklahoma (Plate X, No. 4). A great many have been found about Vera Cruz, Mexico, and at Chichen Itzá in Yucatán (Plate X, Nos. 8, 9). Others are on pottery and stone from Chan Chan, Ancash and Chavin in Peru (Plate X, Nos. 5, 7) while still others have been found at the extremely ancient city of Tiahuanaco, Bolivia. One on a drum from Mexico shows two "Sun dogs" armed with axes guarding the Sun god (Plate X, 6) and an engraving from the Spiro Mound also shows the creatures acting as guardians of the Sun god. A very fine representation is carved on the chest of a stone figure of a man from Chichen Itzá (Plate X, 8). In all probability he was a keeper or priest of a cult built around the animals which were regarded as sacred.

On an idol of the Sun god at Tiahuanaco there are sculptured figures of a group of priests, each with a "Sun dog" on his chest and wearing the same type of headdress as the figure from Chichen Itzá and bearing in their hands, staffs with the head of a Wari Wilka at one end.

On a sculptured frieze from the Temple of the Warriors at Chichen Itzá there are several "Sun dogs" surrounded by men (Plate X, 9) who may have been priests, while a sculpture shows one of the creatures curled up with its hind foot in its mouth.

That such creatures actually existed and were not purely mythological or imaginary is obvious, yet no scientist has ever been able to even guess at the identity of the animal which it has been assumed is extinct. Judging from its size in comparison with human figures associated with it, the animal must have been five or six feet in length.*

It has all the appearance of a ferocious beast and the Incan word "Wari" means brave or ferocious. It is also known that at Tiahuanaco the Wari Wilkas were kept in deep smooth-sided stone-lined pits or dens where fragments of bones have been found; as an identical pit has been found near Vera Cruz, Mexico, it is assumed that the Aztecs and probably the Mayas followed the same practice.

Personally I have always believed that the "Sun dogs" still existed in some remote little known area in South or Central America. From time to time new and previously unknown mammals, reptiles and birds are discovered in the tropical jungles. The so-called wild dogs of the Guianas were believed to be purely figments of the Indians' imaginations until they actually were found and specimens obtained by zoologists, and if an animal, even of large size, was noctural in its habits and dwelt in holes in trees and was not abundant the chances of finding one would be less than one in millions.

My belief that the Wari Wilkas still existed was based mainly on the stories of the Indians of South and Central America.

* One of the "authorities" of the American Museum of Natural History states that *all* depictions of the Wari Wilkas represent cats. It is obvious, however, that many of these paintings, sculptures, etc., are accurate likenesses of the animal I obtained in Chiapas and most certainly do not depict felines. No species of "cat" has a somewhat prehensile tail, a long, anteater-like tongue, prognathous lower jaw and retracted lip, offset thumblike toes, and neither do felines squat on their haunches and hold food in their front paws in the manner of a squirrel.

Throughout the area the jungle-dwelling Indians tell tales of a most ferocious and dangerous but luckily very rare creature known as the "Warrawana" or to the English-speaking Carib tribes, the "Warru-tiger." In all of the various dialects of these aborigines the word *warru* or *warra* means brave or ferocious and is practically identical with the Quechua (Incan) *Wari*. According to the Indians the animal reaches a length of about five feet, it is described as having short legs, a long body, a large head with powerful jaws, huge, knife-like teeth, large sharp claws and a long tail. According to the Indians' tales it is nocturnal and preys upon other quadrupeds and birds and especially the trumpet bird which is known as the Warracabra or Warra food and for this reason the animal is often referred to as the Warracabra Tiger.

The Indians declare that it is absolutely fearless, will unhesitatingly attack any creature it meets including man, and that it moves, springs, strikes with its hooked claws, and slashes with the terrible teeth with incredible speed and agility, and they all firmly believe that it is a more or less supernatural creature inhabited by a devil.

During the many years I lived among the Indians of South and Central America and explored the little known jungles I never saw a Warracabra tiger and never met an Indian who claimed to have come upon one personally, but I always had hopes that sooner or later I might be lucky—or unlucky—enough to find one.

At last, when my jungle exploring days were over and I was living in the little town of Ixtepec in southern Mexico, a Lacandon Indian from Chiapas brought me a living specimen of an animal which I instantly recognized as the long lost, supposedly extinct sacred Sun dog of the ancient Americans.

To be sure, it was a young animal, barely two feet in length but it had all of the characteristics shown in the immeasurably old sculptures and paintings. There were the hooked sharp claws, the offset toes, the large head, the undershot lower jaw, the retracted lips, the large knife-like canine teeth. Its face bore a dusky mask-like marking and the tip of its tail was slightly prehensile while upon its light-colored breast was a large golden yellow "sunspot." There was no doubt left in my mind. I actually had a living Wari Wilka, a live Warracabra Tiger, the only known specimen of a supposedly long extinct semi-mythical animal. And I very soon

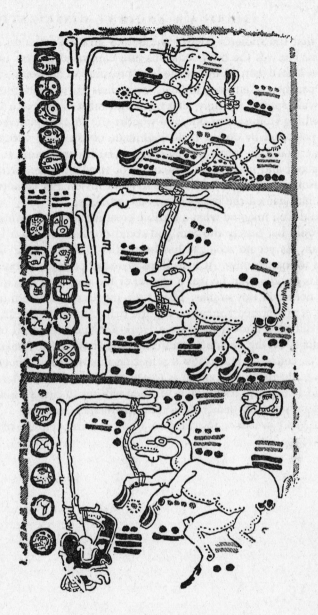

Fig. 20. Portion of a Maya codex

found that the Indians' tales of the beast's savagery were no exaggeration. He was the most ferocious and dangerous animal for his size that I have seen. Without the least provocation he would spring like a panther at anyone, his toes with their curved needle-sharp claws wide spread, his ugly jaws open and razor-edged teeth bared and slashing from side to side. No wonder the Indians believed the beasts possessed by devils. If an inanimate object came within his reach he would fly into a maniacal rage, tearing and biting it, tossing it about and making his paroxysms of fury the more terrifying by fearsome deep throated snarls and loud hisses. No wonder the Incans had named the beasts Wari—or ferocious.

I could well imagine what a terrible creature a fully grown specimen would be. Surely the Sun god could not have found a better guardian. As yet no zoologist has been able to identify the "Monster" as we named him. At first, from my description and drawings, scientists decided that he was a species of the very rare Bassaricyon for his dentition was similar. Then they suggested that he must be a freak, a malformed Kinkajou. But the dentition of that creature is totally different and—if he were a freak Kinkajou, then all of the "Sun dogs" of the ancient Americans must have been freaks also which of course is practically a scientific impossibility. About the best that the zoologists can do is to say that in case the "Monster" dies and I will send them the skull they will *try* to classify him. So for the present the demoniacal creature remains unique, a "Sun dog" or Wari Wilka or Warracabra Tiger and the epitomé of fury incarnate.

CHAPTER 11

The Puzzling Culture of Coclé

Could we but know the stories of these past civilizations, we would no doubt find they had most tragic and most romantic histories. Unfortunately, their stories are usually buried with their long-dead people, and only now and then do we find evidences that enable us to guess as to their fate. Such is the case with the Coclé culture which I discovered in Panama in 1924.*

Although I refer to it as a "culture," yet it is so far beyond other mere cultures in many ways that it may almost be considered a civilization. In many respects it is essentially different from all other known American cultures; in other respects it shows remarkably striking similarities with such cultures and civilizations as the Nicoya, the Maya and the pre-Incan. Although nothing definite is known as to its history, its age, the race it represents or anything regarding it—other than what we can surmise from the objects and artifacts uncovered and from a study of the remains, yet there are good reasons for considering it one of the most ancient of known advanced cultures in Central or South America.

This assumption is based partly upon the decomposition which

* Mr. Lothrop has stated that the Coclé culture had been well known to archaeologists for many years before I called attention to the site. However, upon receipt of my first specimens from the area, Mr. George G. Heye wrote me as follows: "Congratulations. The specimens are unlike anything ever previously known. You have written a new chapter in the history of Central American archaeology." In a letter from the late Prof. Marshall Saville he wrote: "There is no question that the material you are sending us from Coclé represent a previously unknown and very ancient culture. In many respects both the stone artifacts and the pottery differ materially from anything hitherto unearthed in America."

has taken place in much of the stonework; partly upon the depth of the alluvial and other deposits which have accumulated since the culture ceased to exist, and partly upon the fact that many of the remains have been covered with volcanic ash from an adjacent volcano where geological evidence gives us a fairly adequate idea of the time which has elapsed since it was last in eruption. Leaving out the question of the decomposition of diorite and other rocks at this locality, a question not as yet determined, we have the best evidence of extreme antiquity in the alluvial and other deposits. From four to twelve feet of soil have accumulated since the abandonment of the site by the unknown cultured race which left these mute remains. That alone bespeaks an enormous period of time, for while we have no definite data as to the annual rate of deposit in the locality we can form some idea of the ages that must have passed since the prehistoric people first worshiped and offered sacrifices before their idols at this spot. We know that the site has not been occupied or in use since the arrival of Europeans, and hence the thin superficial layer of mold that covers the uppermost potsherds and remains must represent the debris of at least four hundred years.

Brush fires have probably destroyed a portion of the decaying vegetation which accumulated upon the surface, and some probably has been carried away by heavy rains. But even if we allow fifty per cent destroyed annually in this way, the accumulation would not have exceeded two or three inches in a century. At this rate it would require four hundred years to deposit a foot of soil, and an accumulation of ten feet would indicate that some four thousand years have passed since the first monuments were erected. I say "first" for it is evident that the site was occupied and used through hundreds, probably thousands, of years, for in many spots there are remains buried twice the depth of others, while some are exposed at the surface of the earth. But in every case the accumulation of soil about them is several feet in depth.

The district where these remains were found, and where I carried on excavations for six months, is a level alluvial plain or llano lying between the Pacific Coast and the mountains, a district cut by many streams and rivers, broken by occasional knolls or small hills, and, with the exception of the river bottom-lands, sterile and wholly unfit for agriculture. It is therefore remarkable that a vast teeming population should have occupied this territory, especially as the prehistoric denizens of the area were obviously preeminently agricultural. The only explanation is that in the days when the prehistoric race dwelt here the country was fertile, and that the tufa and ashes from the volcano's eruption transformed it to a barren, almost desert land.

Towering above the plains at the feet of the cordilleras is the volcano Guacamayo. The broken-down crater is still raw and burned, the mountain still rumbles and emits steam and hot water from its fumeroles, and over a great portion of the llanos there is a layer of volcanic ash which has not yet thoroughly decomposed to form soil.

During the rainy season the entire district from sea-coast to foot-hills, is transformed into a veritable swamp, the streams overflowing their banks and flooding the llanos, while during the dry months the plains become baked, the streams vanish or dwindle to mud-holes, the scanty vegetation withers, and the district becomes a parched desert country.

My statement that this area was once inhabited by a vast and teeming population is based on several obvious facts: first, the immense number of burials, ceremonial monuments, village sites and mounds; second, the incredible number of potsherds, stone artifacts and other manufactured objects scattered over a wide area, and often forming deposits several feet in depth; third, the enormous size and great number of stone stelae, monuments and idols which could have been moved and erected only by thousands of hands working in unison; finally, the remains of the culture have already been found over an area of approximately five hundred square miles. By this I do not mean that every square mile of the immense area is covered with remains, but over this entire area remains of the same prehistoric race occur, sometimes widely separated, at other times thickly covering hundreds of acres. Among the remains are kitchen middens, refuse piles, village sites, burials, ceremonial or temple sites and mounds. In places, along some of the rivers, village sites extend for miles, and the strata of discarded stone artifacts and potsherds are from five to twenty feet thick. In other spots burials are so numerous that it is practically impossible to dig anywhere, over an area of many acres, without disclosing a grave.

Ceremonial monuments of stone are numerous, and there are hundreds of low rounded mounds full of pottery and stone implements, which were probably once surmounted by temples or buildings of some sort. By far the most extensive remains, the spot which ' so far has yielded the finest and most astonishing objects, and the nucleus of the whole culture, is a huge temple or ceremonial site which may well be called the "Temple of a Thousand Idols." The remains of this vast prehistoric place of worship cover a level area between two rivers, an area more than one hundred acres in extent, although only a small portion—about ten acres—has been cleared of jungle and partly excavated. This portion, however, appears to be the most important part of the whole, and was probably the central and most sacred part.

Although when first visited the site was overgrown with dense thorny brush and only the summits of stone columns were visible here and there, the clearing of the jungle and preliminary excavations soon revealed the arrangement and details of the place.

Running north and south, and east and west are rows of immense, hand-cut stone monuments or phallic columns placed in an almost geometrically perfect quadrangle. In the northern row there were thirty-one of these, spaced from eight to twelve feet apart and extending due east and west. One hundred feet east of these and one hundred feet south, were two immense basalt columns over fifteen feet in height and nearly thirty inches square, both of which had broken off and fallen to one side.

One hundred and fifty feet south of these, and running due north and south, were twenty-seven columns. Two hundred and fifty feet south of these, and directly in line with them, were two more huge columns like those already mentioned. Three hundred feet west of these was a semi-circular row of smaller columns, twenty-five in number. Three hundred feet north of these and three hundred and fifty feet from the first row of thirty-one columns, were twenty-one others running north and south. Thus the three rows of stone monuments, with the two corner groups, formed a quadrangle approximately three hundred by seven hundred feet in area, an open court bounded by the great, tooled phallic columns of hard basalt, many of them elaborately sculptured, which, when the site was in use, had been gaily painted, for traces of the pigment were still visible upon them. This in itself denoted a surprising culture and spoke eloquently of the herculean labor of the prehistoric inhabitants who had cut, carved, transported and erected the massive monoliths.

But as work progressed and new discoveries were made the wonders of the place increased. The columns in themselves were astonishing objects. Many of them were fifteen to twenty feet in length, from sixteen to thirty inches square, cut and tooled to rectangular, octagonal, pentagonal, cylindrical or elliptical form, and sometimes covered with symbolic sculptures and glyphs which appear to be characters with some unknown meaning.

No stone of the same sort existed near the site, and later investigations revealed the quarry on a hill several miles distant and on the farther side of a large river. To have cut and quarried these stones—even though in the rough they were natural cleavages of basalt—to have transported them overland for miles, to have ferried them across the stream, seemed an almost superhuman feat. To accomplish the same results with modern devices and equipment would be no small undertaking and would require months of labor.

Yet the prehistoric people who cut and dragged the huge columns to this long-buried place of worship must have been limited to hand labor, to ropes and possibly rollers, to the crudest of tools. Even though thousands toiled and labored, years, decades, perhaps centuries, must have been required to transport the hundreds of monoliths, often weighing many tons, from the distant quarry to the temple. One marvels at the sublime faith, the sincerity, the belief in their deities that led these ancient people to this task and that kept them at it for month after month, year after year, until their temple was completed.

At times, too, their efforts must have seemed almost hopeless. Many of the finest columns were cracked or broken in transit and still lie where they were abandoned by the wayside. And after the great stones were safely at their destination the work was only begun. Even the smaller columns were so heavy that eight or ten of my husky peons found it difficult to lift or move them, and we can scarcely conceive how or by what means the forgotten builders of the temple raised these immense monoliths to perpendicular positions and secured them firmly in place to form the straight rows of monuments that, in most cases, still stand.

Even more remarkable, more interesting, and indicative of even

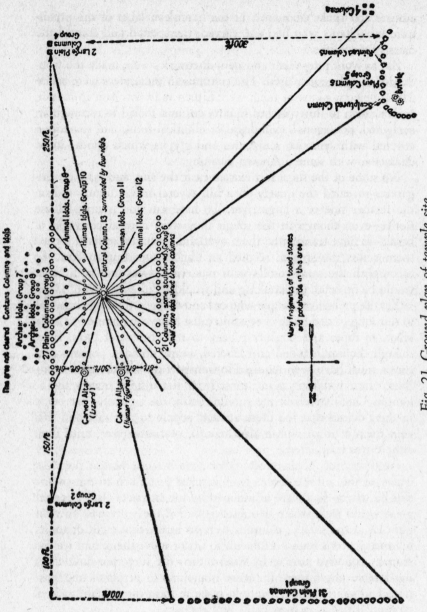

Fig. 21. Ground plan of temple site

more inexplicable labor, are the innumerable stone images which were brought to light by the excavatory work. These, like the columns, were arranged in regular rows running north and south, and in all cases with the faces toward the east.

East of the group of twenty-seven columns were two rows of these stone images. Six feet west of the same row of columns was a second line of idols, mainly of animal forms. Six feet west of these was a row of idols of human forms. Thirty feet west of these was still another row of human figures, and six feet west of these was another row of animal figures. It was evident that originally the idols had been evenly spaced about six feet apart, but through the ages many had fallen, others had sagged to one side or the other, many were broken and their fragments scattered, while all which had been partly exposed above the surface of the earth had been broken off and eroded.

In the exact center of the area, and buried under fifteen feet of soil, was a great stone column nearly twenty feet in length, over two feet square, and most accurately cut and tooled. The lower portion still stood firmly perpendicular, but the upper portion had been broken in three places and the three sections were widely separated (Fig. 21).

At the base of this central monolith were four stone figures—one a man, another a woman and child, another a jaguar and the fourth a bird—probably symbolic of the four cardinal points of the compass. Standing here by this central column with its stone idols, one quickly grasped the ground-plan of the entire site, for the idols and columns had been so placed and spaced as to form radiating lines with the central column as a nucleus, no doubt symbolizing the sun and its rays. At the base of this central monument, as well as at the bases of all the other columns, were large stones or boulders of semitransparent quartz or red or yellow jasper, artificially cut and polished and flattened on the upper side. Evidently these had served the dual purpose of sacrificial altars and supports for the columns or idols, for some were elaborately sculptured about the circumference and one was magnificently carved with a raised edge worked into the figure of a giant lizard or alligator. Moreover, on several were found remains of human skeletons—teeth and bits of calcined bone—among half-silicified charcoal.

Many of the idols or stone figures of this culture are marvelous examples of prehistoric stone carving. In size they vary from a few inches to seven feet in height, and among them are representations of human beings, birds, reptiles and practically every quadruped of the country. Some show men seated upon thrones formed of coiled serpents, upon chairs or stools held up by smaller human figures, or standing upon conventionalized animals. Several show the peculiar hunchback figure that I have mentioned as cropping up throughout Central and South America, and one shows a Siamese-twin figure connected back to back. On one a jaguar or puma is shown with its front paws resting on a wounded man, while another bears the figure of a jaguar holding a dwarf or child in its jaws. One human figure is represented with one hand stroking a long chin-beard which is strikingly reminiscent of an Assyrian figure.

As a rule the human figures are shown with one hand upon the stomach and the other on the breast, an attitude typical of Tiahuan-aco figures, but others have the hands resting upon the knees. Strangely enough, not a single carved or sculptured figure is repre-sented with a vestige of clothing, the nearest approach to garments being a cord with an amulet shown about the neck of one of the largest and finest idols. But in every case the figures have carefully carved and elaborate headdresses of a peculiar type. We may assume that the race used no garments, although the presence of spindle-weights indicates that they knew how to spin and probably how to weave.

In character of workmanship the idols vary greatly and show not only a perfect chain of development in the art of stone sculpture, but prove the tremendous lapse of time which must have passed between the beginning and the end of the temple. Those figures at the lowest level are crude, archaic and badly decomposed, while those nearest the surface are splendidly cut, elaborate in detail and are in perfect condition. In every case the figures or sculptured por-tions surmount pedestals or columns, either cylindrical or square, slightly tapered toward the base, and beautifully tooled.

The most astonishing of the idols is one bearing a figure which is so strikingly and obviously elephantine that it cannot be ex-plained away by any of the ordinary theories of being a convention-alized or exaggerated tapir, ant-eater or macaw. Not only does this figure show a trunk, but in addition it has the big leaf-like ears and the forward-bending knees of the hind legs peculiar to elephants.

Moreover, it shows a load or burden strapped upon its back. It is inconceivable that any man could have imagined a creature with the flapping ears and peculiar hind knees of an elephant, or that any human being could have conventionalized a tapir to this extent. To my mind there is no doubt that the people who built this temple and reached such heights of culture in Panama in prehistoric times had either seen elephants, had domesticated some species of mastodon, or were in direct and frequent communication with the Orient and had heard descriptions of elephants from visitors from Asia. Until a better explanation is offered I see no other way of explaining the presence of this figure.*

One of the most remarkable features of this ancient culture is the vast quantity of pottery that occurs everywhere. The burials are filled with it; closely packed masses several feet in thickness surround every column and idol, and over hundreds of acres it is impossible to lift a shovelful of earth without turning up potsherds. This accumulation of pottery shows, like the stone figures, the development of the culture and its great age.

The lowest—from ten to twenty feet beneath the present surface

* Elephant figures in ancient American art and sculptures that were formerly discredited by the archaeologists are now quite generally accepted as such. The finding of mastodon bones in association with human remains in Ecuador and elsewhere proved that the ancient Americans were familiar with the pachyderms. At Copan, Honduras, the ancient Maya capital, there is a famous stela near the apex of which are beautifully carved figures of twin elephants, one facing the right, the other the left. Both have netted trappings on the heads and both have men seated upon their backs. In a mound about seventy-five feet in height near Quehutla in the vicinity of Cuernavaca, Mexico, Dr. H. A. Monday in 1940, unearthed a porcelain elephant figure bearing a seated human being on the back. The elephant was at a depth of about eight feet below the surface. Competent authorities and archaeologists have identified the figurine as of Persian or East Indian origin of the late sixth or early seventh century A.D. At the same spot two other elephant figures were discovered. One was of carved stone, the other of pottery. Both appear to be rather crude attempts to copy the porcelain figure from the Orient. It has been suggested that in all probability this figurine was brought to Mexico by some of the early Chinese voyagers who are known to have visited Mexico between 500 and 700 A.D.

In addition to elephant figures, carved stone lions have been found in both Mexico and at Tiahuanaco in Bolivia. They are very similar and both the Mexican and Tiahuanacan lions are shown with manes. If there was no contact with the Old World how did the ancient Americans know that lions have manes? (See Plates XXII, 11-12).

of the earth—is of a crude, plain type, with little embellishment and usually decorated, if at all, with simple incised designs or rudely modeled ornaments in the forms of animal or human heads. Above this, and especially near the surface, the pottery is of a quality and beauty unexcelled in prehistoric American ceramic art. Indeed the beauty, the coloring, the motifs of this Coclé pottery are the most surprising features of the culture. One has but to glance at the specimens obtained to realize to what a high degree of perfection the ceramic art had been developed by these ancient people. Some pieces might have well come from Mexico, others are strikingly similar to examples from Ecuador, Peru and Bolivia, but by far the greater portion are wholly distinct in every way from anything hitherto known to archaeologists.

Forms representing conventionalized birds, reptiles, quadrupeds and human beings are very common. Others are of the "portrait" type so abundant in Incan and pre-Incan pottery, and there are numerous figurines of birds, quadrupeds and human beings. In shape and size the vessels range all the way from tiny cups and bowls to large plates, pots and immense burial urns. Practically every krown form is represented, and in addition there are several types peculiar to the culture. One is a square or rectangular form, another is a globular-bodied vessel with long, gracefully tapered neck like a carafe, while still a third is a teapot-like jar with spout and handle.

With very few exceptions, the vessels have annular bases, and in every case (even the very largest ones two feet or more in diameter) all are so perfectly true that it seems impossible they could have been formed without the aid of a potter's wheel. In a number of instances the designs painted upon the pottery are most remarkable and apparently represent prehistoric creatures. One in particular might well be intended for a pterodactyl or flying lizard, and in some respects shows the characteristics of the famous "plumed serpent" of ancient Mexico.

This plumed serpent motif reappears frequently and in many forms, but as a rule the representations of animals are very accurately drawn and are easily recognizable. Regardless of the motif used or the central or predominant figure depicted, the pottery of this remarkable culture is distinguished by the use of a scroll of a peculiar and elaborate type. Sometimes the scroll itself appears as a decorative design, in other cases it is used in combination with other patterns, and often figures of men or animals are made up of scrolls cleverly wrought and combined to give the desired effect of a conventionalized figure.

But the outstanding features of the ceramics as a whole are the predominance of polychrome ware and the colors employed. Not only do the ordinary colors, such as black, white, brown, ocher and red appear in endless combinations, but in addition, there are brilliant blues, purples, soft lavendar, pink, orange and other shades. Green, however, was not used, and was probably a taboo or evil color, for green pigments are common in the neighborhood.

Numerous stone metates were secured, but none was of the ornate type abundant in other portions of Panama and Central America, while the vast quantities of stone implements, weapons and other stone utensils were of the crudest, most primitive type. Comparing the wonderful pottery and splendid stonework with the almost unrecognizable stone implements, one finds it difficult to believe that they could have been produced by the same people. Most of the stone implements are almost Chellean in type, often merely chunks of stone slightly chipped or hammered into rude form, and the arrow and spear-heads are badly made, rough and crooked. Apparently, however, the race was improving in the art of making stone implements, for now and then axes, chisels, etc., were found which are fairly well shaped and have been rubbed to a smooth surface. Still fewer were secured which were beautifully made, but several bodkin-like and chisel-like tools are remarkable examples of workmanship.

It seems almost preposterous to believe that a race which had developed stone sculpture to such a high degree should not equally have developed stone implements, if, according to accepted theory, the prehistoric artisans depended upon stone tools. To have thus cut and sculptured the huge stone blocks into the forms of human beings and animals such as those at the Coclé temple site, would have required a lifetime for each.

Unfortunately, the greater portion of all the pottery found had been intentionally broken—"killed" or sacrificed, as is the custom of many living tribes during ceremonial or religious rites or when interring the dead. Although, as I have said, potsherds, stone implements and broken stone utensils are scattered over a wide area, they are particularly abundant at the temple site and especially about the columns and idols. In many cases the earthenware vessels have apertures made by stones thrown at them; frequently the stones are found in the midst of the shattered vessels, and practically all the columns and idols bear smears of color made by the clay vessels thrown against them.

In many spots the fragments of pottery and broken metates and implements are so densely packed and so numerous that they form fully eighty per cent of the soil deposit, and so firmly have they become cemented together by induration that they form a brick-like mass six to ten feet in depth.

The burial customs varied greatly. In some cases the dead had been placed in huge urns in clay-lined graves within which a fire was built, thus cremating the body and at the same time baking the clay walls and floor of the grave to brick-like hardness. There were also secondary burials where skeletons, evidently disinterred from other graves, were buried. In the rear of the semicircular row of columns southwest of the "temple" two of these secondary burials were found. The bones had long since disappeared but their impressions in the packed clay, and a few teeth, revealed their arrangement, showing that the bones had been placed in neat piles with no regard to their natural positions, with the skulls facing east. One of these burials was on a legless metate, the other on a flat-topped stone and each was surrounded by a number of miniature pottery vessels, stone implements, etc. Near these were traces of human bones mingled with charcoal, resting on a flattened quartz boulder at the foot of a stone column bearing the incised figure of a man with an oversized head and wearing a feather headdress. Whether the remains were those of children or dwarfs we do not know, but the miniature metate and the apparently adult teeth, as well as the crowned figure, would indicate that they were dwarfs.

Where there were urn burials they were almost completely covered with fragments of pottery vessels, miniature figures, etc. Obviously the friends and relatives of the deceased stood about as the body was being cremated and made offerings to their deities by casting their finest possessions into the flames.

By far the most interesting and most remarkable burials of all were at some distance from the "temple" and beside the Rio Grande. There can be no doubt great changes have taken place in the area during the centuries since the bodies of chieftains or "kings" had been buried here. Not only had the river altered its course until numbers of these graves had been exposed and washed away as the bank receded, but the entire area must have sunk for a number of feet as the graves were flooded for nearly half their depth, and it is not logical to think that the bodies of the dead, together with their wealth of possessions, were interred in water several feet in depth. Moreover, it would have been a practical impossibility to have dug these graves, often twenty feet in depth, in mud and water.

At the temple site very few ornaments were found. There were a few clay ear plugs, some labrets or lip-pins of a polished black material and some earthenware and agate beads. No gold objects were found other than a beautifully cut and polished nose ring of bloodstone with two ends, where they clasped the septum of the nose, finished with perfectly fitted gold caps.

Fig. 22. Carved whale tooth, Coclé

For many years the natives had been obtaining gold objects from the graves whose contents were exposed by the erosion of the river bank, for practically every grave contained an abundance of gold ornaments and utensils, cut and polished beads of agate and other stones, magnificent pottery and the beautifully engraved bones of deer and manatees and the carved teeth of sperm whales. No other graves of any ancient American race, not even those at Monte Alban in Mexico, contained such a wealth of gold objects. There were golden chains, some of the most minute links, others of gold beads with pendants; gold collars, pyrite mirrors set in gold frames, gold masks and caps, breastplates, arm bands and gauntlets, gold headdress ornaments, ear plugs, labrets and other objects of crystal, emeralds and semiprecious stones.

Apart from their intrinsic value these were of much less interest than the carved bones which, in many respects, were almost identical with those from Monte Albán (Plate V, 11). Mainly they are of manatee bone which is as fine grained and even harder than ivory. Not only is the carving very beautifully done, but in some cases the designs were inlaid with gold. The sperm whale teeth are rather crudely but effectively carved to form pendants to necklaces.

Some of these graves contained evidences of wives or attendants of the chief having been put to death and buried with him, for in a grave opened by Dr. Samuel Lothrop beside the Rio Grande there were a number of skeletons with evidences that the deceased had been sacrificed.

It is interesting to note that Dr. Lothrop places the age of the Coclé culture as from 1330 to 1520 A.D. In other words, according to him, the oldest remains are only a little more than 600 years old and the area was still inhabited by the Coclé people at the time of the Spanish Conquest. Perhaps there were Indians still living in Coclé at that time. In fact there are numbers of Indians still dwelling in villages among the mountains of Coclé, and it may be possible that the remains unearthed by friend Lothrop were not by any means ancient.

Very probably, centuries after the temple site had been abandoned, the remnants of the cultured race still dwelt near the banks of the Rio Grande. But how does Dr. Lothrop explain the flooded graves and the alterations of the land and rivers that have taken place since the dead were buried? Does he or any other scientist actually believe that from ten to twenty feet of alluvial deposit could have formed at the temple site, or that diorite could have decomposed to the extent that it had, all within the space of six centuries?

As a matter of fact Dr. Lothrop never investigated or excavated the temple site. He would not even permit members of his party to visit the area where I had worked, and hence he had no first-hand knowledge of the conditions there and could not judge of the age of the culture. Why he so sedulously avoided the spot is a mystery that even members of his party cannot explain.

Is it possible that he felt the results of such an investigation would have been inimical to his preconceived ideas of the age of the site and the Coclé culture?

With the present-day radioactive carbon test it would be a simple matter to establish the ages of both the temple site and the riverside burials, for at both there is ample material for such tests.

Although this temple site was no doubt the most important place of ceremonials and worship of the people, yet it is evident that ceremonials and sacrifices, as well as offerings of utensils, etc., were not confined to this one spot. At many places over the area once occupied by this prehistoric race there are similar but smaller rows of stone monuments with their characteristic altars, a few idols and the same accumulation of sacrificed or "killed" utensils on a smaller scale. In other words, the main temple corresponded to a great cathedral and the smaller sites were the equivalents of our village churches and chapels.

It would be vastly interesting to know just how these people lived, what were their customs, habits, beliefs; what sort of dwellings they used, and what was their personal appearance. We can determine very little about such matters, although we can form fairly accurate opinions regarding them. We can safely assume that they were nude, that they were not given to much personal adornment, and that they were intensely religious and very industrious. Undoubtedly they were agricultural and peace-loving, for there are few weapons of warfare or the chase among the ruins. But the presence of fishnet sinkers, a few spear and arrowheads, an occasional animal or fish bone and numerous perforated chama shells prove that they hunted and fished to some extent.

They knew how to spin cotton, and it is clear that they made use of thread, cord and rope, for all these are represented in carvings or ceramics, while several of the pottery vessels have handles of rope form. Moreover, these were not merely twisted to represent rope, but were actually made up of three strands laid exactly like modern rope.

Probably they had hammocks, and as no remains of stone dwellings have been found we can feel reasonably sure that they dwelt in wooden or cane houses with thatched roofs which were far better adapted to the climate and country than stone houses would have been.

From the arrangement of the temple we can feel sure they were sun-worshipers, and from the number and character of the idols or effigies we can feel equally positive that they held many creatures sacred, that they revered certain human beings, that they had many deities, and that they believed in the plumed serpent god. The fact that they "killed" or sacrificed their pottery would indicate that they believed that in this manner they prevented evil spirits from entering or abiding in them. Something of the same general character is practiced by the Guaymi Indians of northern Panama today. During their ceremonials these Indians have numbers of small clay images representing animal and human forms and imaginary beings. These are not idols, but serve as proxies for such individuals as cannot be present in person, for "good-spirit-creatures," and for kindly-disposed deities. At the close of the ceremony these are broken or "sacrificed" and cast into a sacred fire to prevent evil spirits taking possession of the effigies.

If we substitute a stone column or a stone idol for the sacred fire (although probably sacred fires and possibly sacrifices were in progress at the bases of the columns at the time) we can readily understand why the prehistoric denizens of Coclé destroyed pottery, implements, and other objects during ceremonials.

Or it may have been that the people considered the sacrifice of valued possessions fully as efficacious as the sacrifice of human beings or animals. No doubt food was also sacrificed at the same time, for sea-shells, fish bones and animal bones are abundant among the broken pottery. As the temple or ceremonial place was unquestionably used for many centuries it is not surprising that such vast masses of the sacrificed pottery should have accumulated about the sacred idols and columns.

As to the personal appearance of these unknown people, we can scarcely do more than guess, although, judging from the fidelity with which they depicted other forms, we have no reason to think that their drawings and sculptures of human beings were not fully as accurate. If such were the case, then we can easily picture their physical appearance. Judged from this standpoint, they were tall, well formed, muscular. Their heads were of the round type, rather broad, with artificially flattened craniums in some cases, and with features that are unlike those of any known American race.

Nowhere do we find the heavy beak-like nose of the Aztec and Mayan carvings. Nowhere are there the strongly aquiline noses of the Incan and pre-Incan races. Nowhere the oblique eyes of the Mongolian. The nose depicted is always well bridged, straight or slightly aquiline, and the nostrils are narrow. The eyes are full and straight, the lips rather full and thick, the chin is receding, and the eyes are set far apart. Whether they were light- or dark-skinned we cannot say, but we may feel sure that they wore their hair long, braided or twisted into a sort of queue at the back, and either braided into elaborate form upon the head or else covered with a cap-like, close-fitting and highly ornamental headdress.

Why, it may well be asked, did the inhabitants of these villages and the worshipers at the temple disappear? What drove off or wiped out the teeming population so completely that no descendants have been left, that no traditions or records have remained to tell us who they were or whence they came? What was the catastrophe that destroyed the race and its advanced culture? Unlike the majority of similar questions which confront us when studying the remains of pre-historic American civilizations, and which are still unexplained mysteries, the answer in this case is simple. Only by the theory of a severe, a most terrific series of earthquakes and an accompanying volcanic eruption can we account for the condition of the ruins and remains.

Nothing but an earthquake could have tossed the immense stone columns and images about. By no other means could these have been broken and the pieces thrown so far in various directions. In many cases the largest stone monuments are snapped squarely off, while the upper portions are thrown to one side and frequently end for end, or with the middle portion farther from the base than the top.

In many instances, too, the largest idols are found turned end for end, with the base of the pedestal uppermost, while others have been broken and the heads of the figures are found fully one hundred feet from the bodies. Still more eloquent of the terrific earth movements is the fact that the strata of hard tenacious clay or "bed-soil" on which the idols and columns were set has been lifted and moved so that in places it presents a wave-like surface.

Moreover, in many places, a thin layer of volcanic ash covers the remains at the burial and village sites, and in one spot I obtained several entire vessels and many potsherds from beneath a layer of ash more than nine feet in thickness. This had obviously been hot when deposited, for it had been burned firmly onto the pottery.

Hence we can feel more than reasonably certain that the destruction of the culture was the result of an eruption of Guacamayo volcano which, as I have said, is barely six miles from the temple site. Such an eruption must have been accompanied by tremendous earth tremors and upheavals which probably did more damage than the falling ashes and red-hot mud. It is not difficult to imagine the terrorized people, who escaped from the first of the catastrophe, rushing madly from their razed homes to their temple. We can picture them striving to placate their gods by wholesale sacrifices, by the mad destruction of their most prized possessions at the feet of their idols. We can visualize their utter despair as the tremors shook the earth, the ground rose and fell, and the sacred monuments and images were broken and thrown down.*

Possibly every member of the race was destroyed by the blasting heat, the poisonous gases and the blinding dust emitted by the volcano. But the chances are that many escaped, for at the temple site there are no indications that ashes or dust fell upon that spot. Undoubtedly, also, those who may have survived, finding their gods powerless to help them, took refuge in flight. No doubt they had canoes upon the near-by rivers, and some probably pushed off in these while others may have fled by foot to north or south. Scattered far and wide, they may have reverted to primitive savagery and have completely forgotten their past cultures and their identity as they mingled with other races.

* It is a rather remarkable fact, that the Aztecs' legend or myth of the Toltecs contains an account of a violent volcanic eruption near the city of Tollan which caused the Tollan rulers to order wholesale sacrifices in order to placate the gods. Although similar eruptions have no doubt occurred and have destroyed prehistoric settlements in many places, the ancient Nahua legend and the actual occurrence at Coclé are remarkably similar. It is not beyond the bounds of possibility or reason that the story was based on the eruption at Coclé. At all events it proves that a devastating eruption would have brought about the wholesale sacrifices which we know occurred at the Coclé site.

PLATE IX (Chapter 9)

1, 2 Mutations of black Mexican corn showing reversion to the ancestral type with
   kernels on tassels, etc.

3 Bas-relief in palace of Nimrod, Hall of Nations, Assyria, showing deity picking an
   ear of corn.

4, 5 Gold vessels from lower Egypt showing rows of maize kernels (Fig. 4) and
   tassels of maize (Fig. 5). Also goat crop-god as handle.

PLATE X (Chapter 10)

1 The "Monster" taken alive in Chiapas, Mexico. Drawn from life by the author. Note lower jaw, face marking, toes, etc.

2 The animal photographed from life.

3 Carving of "Wari-wilka" from Tiahuanaco, Bolivia. Note the resemblance to animal from Mexico.

4 A "Sun Dog" engraved on sea shell. Spiro Mound, Oklahoma. Note facial markings, offset toes, bared teeth, sun spot, etc.

5 Painting of "Wari-wilka" from Chan-Chan, Peru. The head at tip of tail indicates "life" or that it is prehensile.

6 Wooden drum from Mexico showing a Wari-wilka armed with axe and guarding the sun.

7 Painting of a Sun-Dog from Chavin, Peru, showing same characteristics as the live animal from Mexico.

8 Stone carving of "Keeper of the Wari-wilkas" from ball court at Chichen Itza, Yucatan. Compare with Fig. 1.

9 Wari-wilkas on frieze in temple of warriors, Chichen Itza.

PLATE XI (Chapter 11)

1 Sculptured stone column and small stone idols. Cocle, Panama.
2 Altar of red jasper with sculptured glyphs. Cocle.
3 Ceremonial metate (or altar) with alligator figure. Cocle.
4 Stone columns. One on left with elephantine figure. Cocle.
5 Stone figure, Archaic type. Cocle.
6 Stone column with seated figure. Cocle.
7 Carved stone column marking a grave. Cocle.
8 Section of column showing area of decomposition (light area). Cocle.
9 Gold breast ornament.

PLATE XII (Chapter 11)

1 Row of stone columns partly excavated. Cocle, Panama.
2 Altar stones at bases of columns. Cocle.
3 Columns showing depth of accumulated soil. Cocle.
4 Columns with sculptured figures. Cocle.
5 Rear view of figure (Plate XI, Fig. 6).
6 Urn burial at base of central monolith. Cocle.
7 Section of oven burial. Cocle.

PLATE XIII (Chapter 11)

Pottery vessels from the Temple Site, Cocle, Panama.

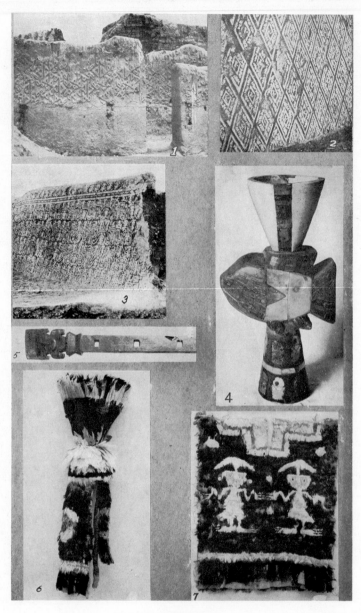

PLATE XIV (Chapter 14)

1 Gateway in wall. Chan Chan, Peru.
2 Decorated wall at Chan Chan.
3 Portion of decorated wall at Chan Chan.
4 Ceremonial cup of mother-of-pearl, bitumen, bone and red shell. Chan Chan.
5 Loom post of carved hard wood. Lambayeque, Peru.
6 Headdress of blue, black and yellow feathers on cloth. Chan Chan.
7 Tunic of blue, black and yellow feathers on cloth. Chan Chan.

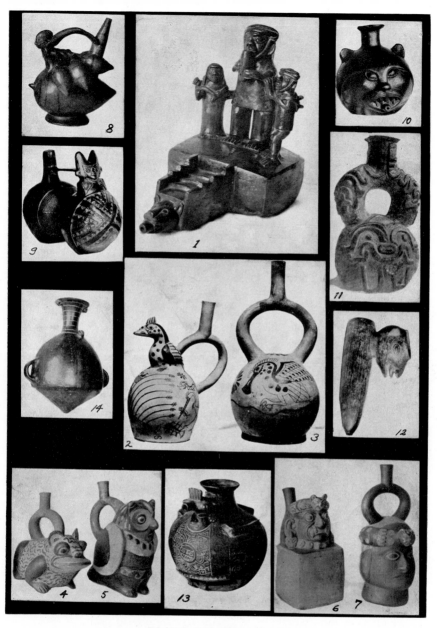

PLATE XV (Chapter 14)

1 Pacha or ceremonial drinking vessel showing three blind beggars. From grave
  at Lambayeque, Peru.
2-3-4-5-6-7 Pottery from graves at Chan-Chan, Peru.
8-9 Pottery vessels from graves at Lambayeque, Peru.
10-11-12 Pottery vessels from Chavin, Peru.
13 Pottery jar from grave at Recuey, Peru.
14 Arabel or water jar, Incan culture. Cuzco, Peru.

PLATE XVI (Chapter 15)

1 House of an official (restoration) at Cajamarca, Peru.
2 Ruined wall showing sculptured head insert, Cajamarca type, Peru.
3 Crystal boat hand-mace with owl at one end and feline at the other. Spiro Mound,
  Oklahoma. *(Museum of American Indian, N.Y.)*
4 Plaque from Lagash (Persian gulf) showing owl and lion emblems of the city.
5 Niches in wall at summit of Temple-Mound. Pachakamak, Peru.
6 Looking outward from summit of temple, Pachakamak.
7 The so-called "House of Virgins" at Pachakamak.
8 Portion of the ancient Incan road near Huarichiri, Peru.

CHAPTER 12

El Dorado

Unquestionably the most romantic, most spectacular and most famous of all treasure hunts in the history of the world was the search for El Dorado, the Gilded Man, and the Golden City of Manoa.

So greatly did the search appeal to the public that El Dorado became the accepted synonym for any great treasure and is still in common use today.

Even if the search for the Gilded Man and his Golden City of Manoa was unsuccessful it resulted in far greater treasure than was ever accredited to El Dorado and the Golden City, for it led to the discovery and exploration of vast areas in South and Central America. It was the lure of the Gilded Man that was responsible for the expeditions of Sir Walter Raleigh, his discovery and exploration of the Guianas and, incidentally, to the loss of his knightly head by orders of the ungrateful Queen Elizabeth. Even doughty Captain John Smith had a fling at the romantic search and the numbers of Spanish, French, Portuguese and other treasure hunters who combed the unexplored jungles of the New World in their efforts to find the Gilded Man are legion.

Although the Golden City of Manoa was fabulous and existed only in the imaginations of the treasure hunters, the Gilded Man actually existed in the person of the ruler of the Chibchas of Colombia. Each year at the time of Chibchas' greatest ceremonial the ruler's body was smeared with honey and was sprinkled with gold dust. Upon a ceremonial barge, accompanied by the priests, he embarked on the great lake of Guatavita that filled the crater of an extinct volcano, and, bathing in the sacred waters, washed off his golden covering while offerings of gold, silver and platinum objects, precious stones, stone images and sacred vessels were cast into the lake by the priests. Unquestionably, as this custom had endured for centuries before the arrival of the Spaniards, a vast treasure, a veritable El Dorado, was hidden beneath the waters in the ancient crater. Several attempts have been made to recover the vast accumulated treasure but none has been wholly successful. At one time the lake was partially drained by means of a tunnel and numerous articles of gold and platinum were recovered, but the bulk of the treasure has sunk for hundreds of feet into the seemingly bottomless mud of the crater and is far beyond reach by drainage, pumping or dredging, and there it will probably remain forever.

Just who the Chibchas were, their racial affinities, their origin and their history are all hidden in the dim and distant past, and we have very little accurate information regarding their customs, their lives, their attainments or their government, although they were still in existence at the time of the Spanish conquest of what is now Colombia.

Their territory was the high Andean region of Colombia, and they were ruled, at the time of the conquest, by two kings or rather regents. One of these was the Zippa whose capital was in the vicinity of the present city of Bogota; the other was the Zoque whose capital was at Tunja. As was the rule with the Aztecs, the eldest brother of the regent, or if there was no brother the eldest nephew, succeeded to the throne, instead of the son of the ruler himself. This rule would indicate that the descent was by the matrilineal line, as is the case with many Indian tribes of the past and present. As among the Incas, monogamy was enforced and the rulers married their sisters.

The social organization was very complete, and there was a strictly observed code of laws with unusual and often severe penalties provided for nearly every offense or crime. An unfaithful wife was compelled to eat red peppers or be killed. If she chose the former punishment, and survived the ordeal, she was forgiven and her husband was forced to apologize to her. Men who showed fear or were adjudged cowards were forced to dress and act like women, and to do women's work. Blasphemy and many other offenses were punishable by death, and crimes or misdeeds which

injured another resulted in the offender being compelled to serve
as the slave of the injured party.

The Chibchas' houses were built of adobe with conical roofs
of reed mats, and were placed in groups within high-walled en-
closures guarded by watch towers occupied by armed men. Honey
formed a large part of their food, and they carried on an extensive
trade in cereals which they exchanged for salt with the coastal
tribes.

Their religion was a modified sun-worship. The Chibcha priests
inherited their office from their maternal uncles who had to be of
noble lineage. Their training was rigorous; fasting and impeccable
living was demanded during their twelve years as novitiates, but
at the end of their ordeals they were honored by fêtes and other
forms of entertainments.

According to their mythology the moon was the wife of BOCHICA,
the Sun god. As she was a most disagreeable sort of being, and was
forever trying to destroy men, she was permitted to appear only
during the night. Bochica, the Sun god, was a semihuman divinity,
and the myths regarding him bear a most striking and remarkable
similarity to the Aztec legends of Quetzalcoatl and the Mayan
myths of Kukulcan.

· Human sacrifices were practised, the victims being trained and
prepared for their fate for several years in advance. The Chibchas
also held certain mountains and bodies of water sacred, and greatly
venerated Lake Guatavita.

According to old Spanish accounts, the Chibcha dead were embalmed with resin and other preservatives, and together with all
the possessions of the deceased, were buried in wooden coffins covered with sheets of gold. A number of Chibcha burials have been
found in recent years and the wealth of golden ornaments and
utensils that have been obtained prove that the Spanish conquerors'
tales of the Chibchas' riches were not exaggerations.

Gold beads, armlets, chains, necklaces, ear and nose ornaments;
heavy solid gold heads to ceremonial staffs and maces; magnificent
lace-like collars of wrought gold; breastplates, arm-bands, crowns
and coronets, belts and images, are among the precious objects
found. There are massive, beautiful golden breastplates a foot or
more in diameter, and a belt or girdle three feet in length and seven
inches in width composed of one hundred and thirty-eight solid

gold bars, each four inches in length. The majority of these were obtained from excavations in the mountains of Antioquia, Colombia, and are now in the Museum of the University of Pennsylvania in Philadelphia. As Dr. Farabee stated: "This is the greatest discovery of buried treasure that has taken place in South America since the days of the Conquest."

Despite the magnificence and intrinsic value of these golden objects the entire collection is a drop in the bucket compared to the vast quantities of golden utensils and ornaments looted from the Chibchas by the early Spaniards. On his first expedition into Colombia, Pedro Heredia obtained golden objects to the value of $3,000,000 as well as a single gold idol that weighed one hundred and twenty-five pounds. Vadillo returned from his trip with gold objects worth $90,000, and Quesada secured gold objects to a value of more than $2,000,000 as well as hundreds of magnificent emeralds, not to mention innumerable objects of platinum which were discarded by the Spaniards who regarded platinum as worthless metal. Undoubtedly, for every pound of gold obtained by torture and murder by the conquerors, many pounds remained hidden or in tombs. So intense and merciless were the Spaniards in their search for gold that the Chibchas were completely exterminated.

In their arts the Chibchas had reached a very high development. They wove excellent cloth and textiles of cotton and fibers; they made magnificent pottery; they constructed excellent roads and large temples. They were past masters at working gold, silver and even platinum, and they possessed a knowledge of some unknown and lost process of plating objects with precious metals which was only equaled by the Chimus.

Although they never erected great stone buildings nor built large stone cities, as did the Aztecs, Mayas and Peruvians, and never approached those races in the extent and beauty of their stone sculptures, they were expert stone-workers and erected many well-carved stone columns or monuments.

Possibly they were of the same race as, or related to, the Manabis who occupied the Pacific coast district of northern Ecuador. But no early cultural remains pertaining to the Chibchas have been found, and from what evidence we have it would appear that the Manabis were a distinct race with a culture differing materially from that of any other ancient people of South or Central America. So little is really known of this race and its accomplishments that it is impossible to say whether they actually attained to a civilized state. The only remains they left were their remarkable stone sculptures, their pottery and their gold objects. No traces of their houses, buildings, temples or other structures have been discovered. It is assumed that they dwelt in flimsy cane and thatched houses, and that these have long since vanished. Their pottery is unusual and distinctive, the typical form being a baseless, elliptical-bodied jar with narrow mouth.

Scattered over the area occupied by the race are numerous slabs and monoliths of stone elaborately carved and sculptured in low bas-relief, as well as many very remarkable stone seats or thrones. These vary in size from small affairs to immense chairs weighing half a ton or more. But all are alike in shape, being similar in form to the ancient Roman chairs, and with the bases elaborately sculptured. Even though these are made from a fairly soft volcanic rock, yet to hew and carve the material into the form desired must have entailed incredible labor and skill and a vast amount of time.

If only a few specimens of these stone thrones had been found it would not be so amazing, but their number is astonishing. Why any race should have made so many chairs, what purpose they served, why they were left scattered about hit-and-miss, are among the greatest mysteries of ancient American races.*

However, it was in their metal work that the Manabis accomplished the most astounding results. Not only did they manufacture beautiful objects of gold of ordinary size, but they produced ornaments of gold of microscopic dimensions. In the Museum of the American Indian, Heye Foundation, in New York are many tiny particles of gold which appear to be natural grains or small nuggets. But when viewed through a magnifying-glass they are revealed as most perfectly and beautifully wrought beads. Many are elaborately engraved or chased, others are built up of several almost invisible pieces welded or soldered together, and all are pierced. It

---

* Within the past few years some of the stone thrones have been found with traces of human remains adhering to the seats. This has led to the reasonable conclusion that the bodies of deceased rulers or members of the priesthood or nobility, were fastened in a seated position on the thrones, perhaps sheltered by buildings of wood and thatch, and left to time and the elements.

seems impossible that such minute objects, many smaller than the head of a common pin, could have been produced by human beings without the aid of a lens. The only solution seems to be that the Manabis actually made use of crude lenses fashioned from crystal, or else they had eyes that possessed the power to see microscopic objects and more adept and delicate fingers than any other race of men.

Despite the high attainment in art, engineering, astronomy and government which were reached by the Aztecs, the Incas, the Mayas and others, in a way these unknown, forgotten races of South America were more remarkable, and were unquestionably far more ancient. From the Chibcha district in Colombia to northern Chile, numerous races rose to a civilized state, vanished and were forgotten centuries before the first Montezuma or the first Inca saw the light of day.

Indeed this area, much of which is today arid desert or even more sterile mountains, and which is so austere, so uninviting and so bare of the very essentials of existence, appears to have been the center of ancient civilizations for an immense period of time; the spot wherein the ancient Americans developed the most numerous and most diverse civilizations, and wherein the mysterious races of the dim past reached the highest attainments in social organization, in engineering and in many other lines.

Some of these races existed at the time of the establishment of the Incan Empire, and were conquered and made an integral part of the Incan confederation. The largest and most important of these was the Kingdom of the Grand Chimu whose capital was Chan Chan.

Sketch map of Peru showing principal cultural sites

CHAPTER 13

What We Have Learned of the Chimus

Until comparatively recently the visitor to Chan Chan could trace the outlines of the various buildings, the tanks and baths and reservoirs and could reconstruct in his mind's eye the magnificent palaces and temples. And until 1925 the truly wonderful complicated and beautiful designs in bas-relief, that covered numberless walls, were almost intact, as well as portions of the colored frescoes on the façades. But the unprecedented rains that fell in 1925 played sad havoc with the ruins of Chan Chan. Although the district is normally rainless, yet at various periods within historic times fairly heavy rains have fallen along Peru's arid coast due to meterological conditions resulting from an alteration in the Humboldt Current. Such rains also fell during the days of the Chimus, for floods are recorded on their pottery. In 1701, 1720 and 1891 rains did much to destroy portions of the frescoes, the painted walls, the adobe sculptures and the lesser buildings. On February 14, 1619 a severe earthquake destroyed every house in Trujillo and in 1687, 1725 and 1739 there were almost equally heavy earthquakes. The massive walls of Chan Chan withstood the shocks but each time portions of the buildings of the city were shaken down. The heavy and prolonged rains of 1925 were the last straw. The walls that for centuries had resisted former floods and earthquakes crumbled and were reduced to mud, the bas-reliefs and sculptured decorations were almost wholly obliterated and scarcely a trace of the ornate decorations remained. In addition to the earthquakes and the rains, vandals have added to the destruction. In their search for treasure they undermined walls and buildings, dug in the great plaza and the courtyards and even wrecked baths and reservoirs.

Considering all this it is not surprising that at the present time Chan Chan is little more than a hodge-podge of ruins, a mass of rubble and debris.

Rising above the barren plain round and about the ancient city, there are countless mounds or *huacas*, each composed of thousands of small cubicles or tombs containing the sun-dried mummies of the Chimu dead. Although many hundreds of these have been opened and the contents removed there are many more hundreds that still remain sealed up and intact. These huacas have not only yielded millions of dollars worth of gold, silver and precious stones but have been a veritable treasure house for archaeologists. Although comparatively few contain objects of intrinsic value, every one contains pottery, textiles, implements, tools, weapons, carved wooden objects, ornate headdresses or other artifacts.

From these, scientists have obtained a very comprehensive knowledge of the Chimu civilization, the lives and industries of the people, their costumes and customs, their agriculture and many other matters. Also, we now know that the Chimus' culture, ancient as it was, had been preceded by an equally advanced if not superior culture known as the Moujik.

Of all the ancient people of Peru the Chimus and the Moujiks—for it is next to impossible to differentiate between them—were the most expert potters. Although they fashioned innumerable pots, pitchers, plates, bowls and other utilitarian forms of pottery the greater number were exceedingly ornamental and were molded in the forms of vegetables, birds, fish, mammals, reptiles and human beings. Neither was their pottery of any one type or color. They used black, red, buff and white pottery and when the vessels were not modeled in natural forms they were very beautifully and accurately painted with scenes showing the people engaged in their occupations, arts and industries or with veritable menageries of animals, some easily recognizable and others weird, perhaps mythical or imaginary creatures or forms that have long been extinct.

Many of their pottery pieces were made in baked clay molds so that the vessels could be duplicated over and over again. But the most remarkable examples of their pottery are the so-called "portrait jars" which have no equal anywhere. These were vessels of various shapes bearing heads, faces or entire figures of men and women as perfectly modeled and as true to life as any sculptures known to man. Every type and every possible emotion was depicted upon these. Unquestionably most of them were modeled from life and were intended as portraits or busts of actual persons while others were as obviously cartoons or caricatures, but even these were carried out with a fidelity that is actually astounding. Not only do these vessels serve to give us a very comprehensive and accurate idea of the personal appearance of the people, but in addition they illustrate exactly how they dressed, the garments they wore, their ornaments and decorations, the musical instruments they used, how they lived, cooked, ate, cultivated the earth, fished, hunted, fought and played. In fact they form a complete pictorial record of the entire organization, the occupations, lives and customs of the race. Some are even modeled in the form of dwellings with one wall omitted to show the interiors where there are life-like figures of the occupants engaged in their daily tasks and occupations.

Just why the Chimus should have made so many of these portrait and effigy jars and why they should have produced such an infinite variety of forms is a mystery. It has been suggested that they were ceremonial and perhaps some of them were. For instance one common form depicting a man with exaggerated nose and accompanied by an ear of maize, was their Corn god and it was common practice to bury such jars in the fields when planting in the belief that they would insure a bountiful crop. It has also been suggested that these vessels may have served as records, that they were, in effect, similar to hieroglyphic symbols in pottery form and that, by some unknown arrangement, they were used in much the same manner as a child uses alphabet books. According to this theory each form denoted a symbol signifying some thought or idea. It is easy to understand how such a system of recording important events might well have been carried out. For example if it was desired to record a year in which locusts destroyed crops and a famine followed, a jar representing an ear of maize could be placed beside a pot in the form of a locust, and next to this could be placed a human figure greatly emaciated and showing every sign of being on the point of death by starvation. Other symbolic vessels could be added to indicate the year, the month and even the day. With their endless array of forms and variations of pottery and the incalculable number of combinations made possible by these, any message, idea, event or other matter could have been recorded and easily understood by the Chimus. It seems to be a very reasonable theory and explains the reason for so many duplicates of the pottery motifs. The one great objection to it is the fact that no one has ever found these imitative vessels arranged in any orderly manner, neither has anyone yet been able to suggest any intelligible interpretations of such groups of pottery as have been found.

In addition to the Chimus' portrait vessels and those representing natural forms, there are many showing, with all the gruesome details, cadavers, skeletons, death's heads, amputated limbs, malformations, wounds, tortures, sacrifices and death throes. Others show surgeons engaged in performing both minor and major operations, for despite the crude instruments available and the probable lack of anesthetics and antiseptics the Chimu surgeons performed many operations that would have been a credit to the medical profession of today. Not only the Chimus but other pre-Incan surgeons amputated limbs, trepanned skulls, removed eyes, performed major abdominal operations, removed injured or diseased internal organs and filled, crowned and bridged teeth. We know from the condition of skeletons and skulls that a great many of these most serious operations were entirely successful. Judging from the number of trepanned skulls that have been found we might well feel that the Incan surgeons considered trepanning a sort of universal cure-all. But we must bear in mind that head wounds were unquestionably the commonest type of injuries received by men whose weapons were mainly axes, clubs, maces and slings. As many of the trepanned skulls have the bone healed about the edges of the incisions, and as others have a silver or gold plate covering the opening in the skull and with its edges overgrown with new bone, it is obvious that the patients survived and lived for years. Moreover, many of those who survived had undergone far more extensive trepanning than many of those who failed to recover, and in more than a few instances sections of the skull had been removed at various times. One cranium from Parakas had three trepanned areas, one about two inches in diameter at the back of the head, and on either side of the skull large sections over three inches in length and two inches in width had been removed leaving only a narrow ridge of bone on the top of the skull. All three openings had been covered with silver plates and the newly formed bone about the edges proved conclusively that the man had lived for years after the greater portion of his cranium had been removed.

Artificial limbs and hands were not unknown to these ancient Peruvians. There are pottery vessels showing men wearing artificial legs and arms and on a few specimens there are accurately modeled figures of a man in the act of removing an artificial hand from the stump of his forearm.

A great many of the Chimu vessels are of the so-called erotic type. In these every known form of social and solitary vice is portrayed with a fidelity and frankness that would put our most questionable sex plays and novels to shame and which outdo any medical work. The purpose of these is a mystery. Some claim that they were merely obscene and prove the makers were a morally degenerate race. Others believe that they were records of actualities and were added to the other forms of pottery in order to make the records complete. There are other authorities who claim with equal reason that they were used in an educational manner and served as pathological exhibits for the suppression of vice. There are still others who believe they were of a ceremonial character and were used in sex worship, or had a symbolical meaning used in expressing ideas in connection with other vessels when arranged in proper chronological order.

As a general rule, when we find a race excelling in some one art or occupation we find the people deficient in some other art or industry but the Chimus appear to have been masters of all trades. Their textiles, especially their laces, were marvelous examples of weaving and their mosaic and mother-of-pearl work was exquisite. Many specimens of these are truly wonderful examples of this highly developed art. There are vases, cups, ceremonial utensils, ear plugs, breast plates, wooden utensils, objects made of clay and of bone that are highly and most artistically embellished with mosaic inlay of mother-of-pearl, the red Spondylus shell, colored stone and precious metals. Many of their robes and ponchos of magnificent textiles are completely covered with ornaments of gold, silver, mother-of-pearl and sections of bright colored sea shells arranged in charming patterns so as to give the effect of a mosaic cloth.

They were also highly skilled wood carvers and there is scarcely a wooden object that is not handsomely carved. Even the uprights to their hand looms are thus decorated as are the implements used in tilling the ground, the hafts of their tools and weapons. In a great many cases the exceedingly hard, fine grained wood has been hollowed out through narrow slits and with several perfectly spherical wooden balls within the opening. They had developed a unique method of weaving feathers into cloth thus producing feather robes, tunics, head coverings, etc., that are gorgeous in colors and designs, and although they never sculptured stone yet they invented a process of adobe sculpture which was not known to any other race.

But it was in their metal work that they attained the highest skill. Not only did they smelt copper, gold, silver and even platinum and from these metals formed innumerable utensils, ornaments, weapons, tools, images, bells and musical instruments, but they had even discovered a method of metal plating.

From the tombs and graves at Chan Chan and elsewhere within the Chimu area have come many articles of copper and silver plated with gold. So perfectly and evenly is the plating done that they have all the appearances of having been electroplated. However, as we know that these people could not have possessed any knowledge of electricity, it is obvious that they knew of some other process of coating one metal with another.

If, as has been suggested, it was accomplished by some chemical process, this seems almost as incredible as the electrolytic process would have been. It might have been done by dipping the objects in molten metal but in that case a delicate thin copper or silver object would be instantly melted and combined with the gold. Another theory is that the Chimus employed some unknown adhesive or lacquer which was sprinkled with gold dust and burnished. But there are no signs that the surfaces have been burnished and no traces of any underlying preparation.

Some authorities have claimed that the plating was accomplished by rubbing the objects with a mixture of mercury and gold. But such mercurial plating does not endure for long as anyone knows who has tried any one of the preparations so widely advertised as a means of replating cutlery and jewelry. The only plausible explanation would seem to be that the plating was accomplished by fuming. Molten gold gives off fumes when treated in certain ways and fumes might have been created which would deposit a metallic coating on another metal. But if this was the Chimus' method it is most certainly a lost art.

Even in their ordinary metal work the Chimus exhibited the greatest skill and a most artistic taste. Metals were cast, embossed, etched, engraved, pressed, hammered, spun or built up into innumerable forms by welding and soldering. In fact every means of working metals known to modern artisans was employed by the Chimus. Among their most noteworthy metal objects were tall, slender beautifully proportioned vases of gold or silver wrought in open fretwork designs of flowers, birds and other natural objects combined in harmonious and graceful motifs. There were large pots and bowls of massive gold beautifully chased and embossed, gold plates and plaques, and gold feathers almost as soft as the plumes of a bird.

Like all ancient Peruvians the Chimus did not consider gold of any intrinsic value. It was prized only because of its color, its ductility and its enduring qualities. Where or how they obtained such vast quantities of gold is a puzzle, for gold is not known to occur in the districts they occupied. In all probability it was obtained in the form of tribute or barter from tribes inhabiting gold bearing areas.

The mystery surrounding many of the Chimus' arts and culture is no greater than the mystery of the race itself. We really know very little about them, their origin or history. We know that they used the Mochica or Yunga language which is still spoken by some of their descendants.

And if we are to believe their traditions they came from some land to the north. We also know that, as I have already mentioned, the Chimu civilization was superimposed on the older Moujik culture and recent excavations seem to prove that the immeasurably ancient Moujiks were antedated by still another highly cultured race. As to Chimu history prior to the Incan domination we know they had a highly organized government with its court, its nobility, its aristocracy and its priesthood. According to their traditions there had been twelve kings until the monarchial government was abolished and the people established a republic. This continued for a very long period and was apparently a success until a powerful feudal chieftain of the Chicama Valley led a revolt and with his clansmen overthrew the government and proclaimed himself the

Chimu-Kapak or emperor. Under his reign the Chimus' dominions were vastly increased as outlying tribes were conquered and placed under Chimu governors, just as in later years the Inca Yupanqui conquered the Chimus and reduced them to mere cogs in the wheel of the vast Incan Empire of Tihuantisuyo.

But it is not difficult to revisualize Chan Chan as it was when the city was the capital of the Chimu kingdom. The wealth of artifacts, implements, garments, weapons, utensils and the accurately made pottery depicting every phase of Chimu life enables us to mentally picture Chan Chan and its people as it was centuries before the Spanish conquest.

CHAPTER 14

The Capital of the Grand Chimu

In its heyday, Chan Chan, the capital of the Kingdom of the Grand Chimu, covered an area of eleven square miles and had a population estimated at a quarter of a million inhabitants.

It was built upon a plain within easy reach of the sea with which it was connected by canals with docks at the city itself. Surrounding the city were immense walls of a cement-like mixture of clay and gravel, their surfaces everywhere ornate with bas-relief designs of intricate patterns in brilliant colors. In addition, many were decorated with enormous frescoes forming a veritable pictorial record of Chimu life, history and important events.* Within the walls, that were pierced by ornate gateways, were straight paved streets shaded by palms and flowering trees and beside each street was an irrigation ditch fed by a great aqueduct that brought the water across mountains and deserts from the distant Moche River. Flanking the streets were countless houses, often several stories in height, and their steeply-pitched roofs were of heavy timbers covered with reed thatch and capped by baked clay tiles. In order to support the weight, the walls were thickest at the base, and the doors and windows were wider at the bottom than the top and were closed by reed mats or the tanned hides of deer and sea lions. Within, the houses were divided into numerous rooms separated by beautifully woven cotton draperies and many had porches or balconies with railings hung with multi-colored rugs. They were well and com-

---

* There are remains of two cultures or more at Chan Chan. The most important are the Moujik or Mochica and the Chimu. However, as only an expert can distinguish between them, I have referred to the Chan Chan pottery, graves and other remains as Chimu.

fortably furnished with wooden stools and benches, low tables and beds. Some were supplied with running water and there were even indoor toilets. Although meagerly furnished as judged by our standards, yet they had everything really essential. In the kitchens were clay stoves and ovens, metates for grinding corn, cooking utensils and even some cutlery. The wooden stools and low tables were carved and the beds were covered with blankets and robes of vicuña hides or the breasts of pelicans. There were hand looms, the various implements and materials for spinning, weaving and pottery making. In fact the Chan Chan homes were far more comfortable, more sanitary and better designed than were those of Europe centuries later.

Looming high above the residences and built upon mounds of rubble, rose the public buildings, the palaces and temples. These were magnificent affairs, richly and ornately decorated with figures of animals, birds, deities and mythological creatures in bas-relief and with friezes of painted frescoes. Several of the temples, as well as the palace of the Grand Chimu, covered an area of several hundred thousand square feet.

Within them were innumerable rooms, passages and galleries with all the walls and in many cases the ceilings richly decorated with frescoes and bas-reliefs and in one great gallery were scores of niches, each containing the richly dressed and gold laden mummy of some royal personage or priest. The throne room of the palace was forty-five feet square with its walls completely overlaid with beaten gold plates. Beyond this, and in the center of the city, was the great plaza with its avenues and shade trees, its gardens of flowering plants, its fruit trees laden with cherimoyas, avocados, duraznos and other luscious fruits; with limpid pools and with public baths. To guard against possible dearth of water there were enormous tanks or reservoirs. One of these was six hundred yards in length by fifty yards in width and nearly twenty feet in depth while another was five hundred feet long, nearly two hundred feet wide and sixty feet deep. About the plaza and separated from the other buildings by high walls were the homes of the élite—built like the others but more ornate, provided with enclosed courtyards or patios and having their private baths.

As the Chimus were as much fisher folk as agriculturists the city had its own little harbor with piers and moorings, and was connected with the sea by a canal that was provided with locks or gates—a real necessity in a land where the rise and fall of the tide is so great.

Here, lying to moorings or drawn upon the banks, were canoes and craft of all sizes and of many forms. There were crude rafts formed from the inflated hides of two sea lions connected by a flimsy platform, and there were balsas or canoes made of bundles of reeds. Some of these were real sea-going vessels, forty feet in length and provided with great matting sails. And there were also catamaran-like affairs of cork-like balsa wood. These were the craft of the pearl fishers, for the Chimus loved pearls, not for their intrinsic worth but for their beauty, and possessed vast quantities of them. The mother-of-pearl shells were also prized, while the flesh of the oysters was an important part of their food and was eaten either fresh or dried.

Fortunately the Chimus kept accurate accounts of all their arts, industries and occupations in the form of superbly modeled or painted pottery and among those that have been found are many depicting the pearl divers at work. Shown resting upon the surface of the sea are the catamarans and beneath on the ocean's floor are the divers gathering the pearl shells and filling the baskets which are being hauled up. In addition, divers are represented both going down with a stone attached to their feet and coming up after having discarded the weight.

In one section of the city was the public market, always a busy spot, and on certain days swarming with buyers and sellers, men and women from far and near, and fairly ablaze with the colors of their costumes. Among the hundreds of country women, dressed in their simple skirts and bright-hued shoulder-capes, and their men in loose knee-length breeches and gaudy cotton ponchos, there would be the town folk. In place of the mother-of-pearl, sea shell and agate jewelry and the silver or bronze pins of the country women, these well-to-do residents of the city were laden with ornaments and jewelry of gold and with emeralds, opals, and lustrous pearls and were dressed in the finest most beautifully woven textiles. Among them, also, there might be a few young women attired in the very latest fashions. They were dressed in skirts of beautiful lace with blouses of lace of a contrasting color. Their black hair was bobbed, their eyebrows carefully plucked, their

Fig. 23. Gold plaque from Chan Chan showing Chimu
fishing fleet

cheeks were rouged and their lips painted. Mascara darkened their lashes and brows and their finger and toe nails were stained and polished.*

Although the throng was orderly yet there were always soldiers or police on hand, recognizable by their high bronze helmet-like headdresses, their bronze or silver breastplates and their short bronze-headed spears or hardwood clubs. Also, passing from temple to palace or *vice versa,* there were various high officials and priests. Splendidly attired and ablaze with gold, silver and gems, each wore the costume and insignia of his rank and station. Some wore tunics covered with jingling plates of embossed silver or gold and with plumed miter-like headdresses of precious metal set with gems. Others were fully as resplendent in costumes adorned with flashing rainbow-tinted plaques of pearl shell and wore headdresses representing the fish-god. And there were the high-ranking officers of the army clad in tunics of yellow, scarlet or blue feathers woven into the cotton cloth and with magnificent designs worked in feathers of every color, while upon their heads were tightly fitting caps topped by pompoms of long feather plumes.

Among all this lavish display of rich attire and brilliant color there were the cripples. Although under the beneficent law no one was poor, no member of the community no matter how lowly, ever went hungry or in rags or was forced to beg, yet one-legged or one-armed men were common as were men whose heads bore metal plates covering trepanned apertures in their skulls.

Beyond the walls of the city proper were the immense burial mounds rising for nearly one hundred feet above the plain and each composed of hundreds of tiny adobe brick cubicles, each containing a mummy accompanied by all its earthly possessions as well as food for its long journey into the hereafter.

The Chimus and the Moujiks possessed incredible numbers of objects of gold and silver in the forms of ornaments, utensils, images and decorations as well as precious and semiprecious stones, and as these were invariably buried with their dead owners, the quantity

---

* Near Lambayeque the author disinterred the mummy of a young lady attired and "made up" as described, although she had lived and died many centuries before the arrival of Pizarro. Other more recent mummies with the same "beauty aids" but less perfectly preserved, have been found in late Chimu graves near Chan Chan. (See Chapter 17, *Mining for Mummies*)

of precious metals, gems and pearls that had accumulated in the burial mounds over a period of many centuries was beyond all calculation.

Some authorities have declared that the tales of the treasures of the Chimus have been grossly exaggerated, that comparatively few gold or otherwise intrinsically valuable objects ever have been recovered from the *huacas* or burial mounds at Chan Chan. However, official figures do not lie nor exaggerate. During the time that Peru was under Spanish domain a law required that a *Quinta* or one-fifth of all treasures found was to be paid to the crown. In the old records of the treasurer of the city of Trujillo it is stated that during the year 1576, Garcia Gutierrez de Toledo paid as his *Quinta* 58,527 *castellanos* in gold taken from one mound near Chan Chan. And during the year 1592 he paid *Quintas* of 2702 *castellanos* in gold taken from the same mound which is now known as the Huaca de Toledo. It is of course highly probable, in fact almost certain, that Señor Gutierrez did *not* report more than a small part of the vast treasure he obtained, for in those days, as at present, it was seldom considered a crime to cheat the government when it came to a matter of taxes.

As the old Spanish castellano was approximately the equivalent of the British pound, or roughly four dollars, Don Garcia must have found at least $1,170,540 worth of treasures during 1576 and treasures amounting to $540,400 during 1592.

The Royal Account Books also record that in the year 1550, the Cazique Maniche, Don Antonio Chayhuac, a Christianized descendant of the Chimu king, Chummuncauchu, told the authorities of a mound or *huaca* near the ruined palace of Regulo, with the understanding that he was to receive a share of any treasures that were recovered. The total value of the treasure amounted to 42,037 gold pesos or about $75,000 of which the Cazique received 25,000 pesos, all of which was expended in local improvements and the betterment of the Indians of the vicinity.

When we consider that the above are the records of only three separate years out of centuries, and that almost continuously treasure seekers have been at work about Chan Chan, and that only a very small proportion of the graves have been excavated, we can obtain some idea of the vast treasures the Chimus had buried with their dead. And although the Spaniards robbed the city of gold, silver, pearls and gems amounting to a value of over twenty million dollars, yet the greater part of Chan Chan's treasures had been already hidden. Moreover, only a century or two before the arrival of Pizarro the Chimus had been mulcted of their most precious possessions by the Inca Yupanqui who had conquered them.

The doom of Chan Chan was sealed long before Pizarro set forth on his conquest, and years before then the Chimus had ceased to exist as a distinct civilization.

When the Inca Yupanqui ascended the throne at Cuzco, one of his first undertakings was to lead an army against the Chimus. But they were not an easy foe to conquer. Under their Chimu-Kapak they fought long and valiantly. Here and there the outlying communities surrendered but the key to the heart of the kingdom and its capital, Chan Chan, was the fortress at Paramonga.

Situated upon the levelled summit of a precipitous mountain and reached only by a narrow zig-zag road and built in the form of a square with three parallel lines of thick adobe walls seven hundred feet in length, and with salients jutting outward for ninety feet, the fort, that is still in a good state of preservation, was practically impregnable. Again and again the Inca hurled his armies at the stronghold, and again and again they were repulsed with terrific losses. Then strategy won where force failed. Back in the foot hills the Incan engineers erected a dam across the river that supplied the Chimus with water. Their crops withered and died, their reservoirs were exhausted, yet the Chimus refused to surrender. Then from the Inca came a message declaring that unless they capitulated he would shut off the sun as well as the water. To the Chimus such a feat seemed quite possible for a "son of the sun" so they promptly surrendered.

Following the invariable Incan custom, many of the Chimu leaders and nobles were transported to distant Incan provinces, while others who swore allegiance to the Inca were retained as governors and other officials.

Standing today amid the silent ruins of the once great capital of an ancient forgotten race, one cannot fail to be impressed. Here, so long ago that one can scarcely conceive of the ages that have passed, men and women lived and toiled, hated and loved, were born and died, worshiped their gods and attained to heights of art, culture and civilization that they doubtless believed never could be equaled or excelled. Here, between the Andes and the sea, they had built their great city, reared their temples and palaces, irrigated the desert, raised their crops, made discoveries, developed their arts and crafts, invented new processes and had their joys, their sorrows and their problems. No doubt among them were those who shook their heads and prophesied the downfall of a community which had attained such heights. But the majority doubtless scoffed and continued to carry on and felt there was no limit to their progress.

Then, almost in a day, they had been wiped out. All they had accomplished through hundreds of years of ceaseless effort was demolished at one blow by men of whose existence they had been in ignorance. Their arts, their civilization, their ideals were destroyed, thrown aside and forgotten. Their history, their origin, their race are all unsolved mysteries and their greatest works are crumbling ruins.

Where they once tilled their fields with implements of stone and bronze, snorting motor tractors drag gangs of steel plows. Along the roads they trod with sandal-shod feet automobiles rush with blaring horns. Across the valley they knew and loved steel rails glisten in the sun and locomotives haul their burdens of freight-laden cars. And from the cloud-flecked sky an airplane swoops roaring down and comes to rest in the great plaza where once the Grand Chimu, arrayed in all his glory, reviewed his plume-decked troops.

Standing there in the shadows of walls that were ancient at the time of Alexander, with the screech of a locomotive whistle echoing through the valley, with an automobile parked in an angle of the ruined temple walls and with the Chimus' plaza transformed into a landing field for mail-carrying airplanes, we ponder on the future of our own civilization.

Who can foresee, who dares to say what fate may be in store for us, what changes will have taken place in our own great cities five thousand or even a thousand years hence?

CHAPTER 15

Where Atahualpa Died

Beside the great Incan Road, Cajamarca dominated the lush, green fertile valley enclosed by mountain ranges and with the snow-clad peaks of the Andes looming for fifteen thousand feet against the eastern sky. Smaller than Chan Chan, the city covered an area of perhaps a thousand acres, and was totally unlike the capital of the Chimus, for Cajamarca was a city of the Chavins and many archaeologists believe the Chavin civilization was the most ancient in all Peru.

At all events the city itself was immeasurably old, for it dated back for thousands of years and had been a good-sized town in the days when Abraham was a youth.

No great walls, such as those at Chan Chan, enclosed the city which was built in circular form with narrow, paved streets radiating from the central plaza like spokes in a wheel. And instead of being built of a mixture of clay and pebbles, the buildings were of stone and were constructed in a most unusual and remarkable way. Huge blocks of pink granite, cut in irregular shapes, were loosely fitted together so as to leave crevices and openings that were filled with small stones of various colors. As the surfaces of the large blocks were highly polished while the smaller stones were left with their natural surfaces, the sunlight shining on the buildings gave the effect of innumerable great mirrors set in an intricate multi-colored mosaic. At each corner of the structures there was an immense stone column beautifully sculptured in human or animal form. Here and there the larger stones forming the walls were carved in the forms of jaguars, birds, and mythological creatures. No windows or doors pierced the outer walls of the buildings but on the sides facing the streets there were narrow windows, their frames composed of stone, carved in intricate designs, and doors with outjutting stone lintels and sculptured and painted stone frames.

Within, the houses were floored with ornamental pottery tiles and bright colored matting, while the walls were hung with beautifully woven textiles. Low stone and wooden stools, carved wooden tables and low wooden couches of carved wood covered with heavy woolen blankets were the only furnishings.

The roofs were of wood covered with many layers of interwoven palm leaves to form a thick waterproof thatch with a carved comb of wood rising above the ridgepole. Each building faced on a street connecting the radiating avenues so that the city was formed of countless more or less wedge-shaped blocks. As a result, each building was somewhat narrower at the front than at the back. To compensate for the width of the structures becoming smaller and smaller as the plaza was approached they were made longer and longer, until the inner blocks consisted of buildings several times as long as they were wide. Beyond these and encircling the great plaza, nearly three acres in extent, were the government buildings and the temple with its adjoining houses of the priests and the nuns.

These larger structures about the plaza were two or more stories in height elaborately decorated with carved and sculptured stone work and brilliantly colored frescoes and with ornate doorways.

The plaza itself was paved with carefully cut and fitted stone tiles arranged in geometrical patterns. In the center was a huge stone image of the Chavins' Tiger (jaguar) god surrounded by a circle of smaller images of the lesser deities.* Between these and the central statue was a rectangular basin filled with running water brought by an underground conduit from a mountain stream. There were no city walls, for the windowless rear walls of the buildings joined and formed a continuous stone surface with the only means

* The great plaza with its central statue of the Tiger god and the circle of smaller statues, together with the radiating streets, undoubtedly served as a gigantic sun dial with the huge Tiger god monolith forming the gnomon. It was in many respects strikingly similar to the temple site at Coclé (Chapter 11) and the Temple of the Sun at Cuzco and would have been fully as accurate for astronomical purposes as the Caracol or observatory of the Mayas at Chichen Itzá.

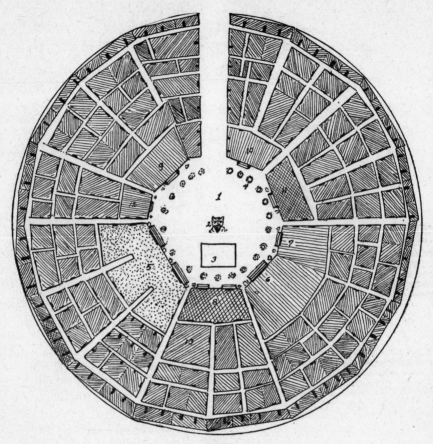

Fig. 24. Ground plan of Cajamarca
(Restoration)

of entrance through a gateway and an avenue leading to the plaza. It was in fact a unique city, in effect a gigantic circular stone fortress almost impregnable yet presenting a dignified, artistic and impressive appearance, and totally unlike any other city in Peru.*

* The ground plan may not be absolutely correct owing to the condition of the ruins which made an accurate survey impossible. However, it was approved by the late Dr. Julio Tello who was with me at the time. It is of interest to note that the fortress-city of Sinjerli in Syria (destroyed about 700 B.C.) was almost identical with Cajamarca in its ground plan. (See Fig. 25) There was the plaza

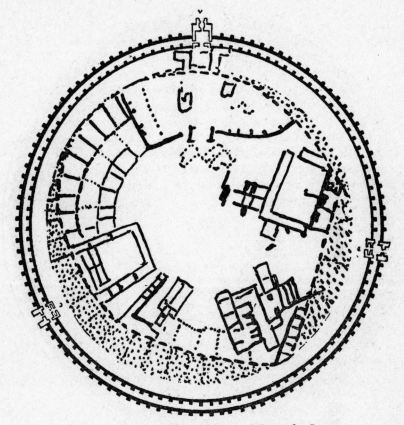

Fig. 25. *Ground plan of City of Sinjerli, Syria*
(After Garstang)

Even the Temple of the Sun was unique, for here the gods of the
Chavins, or rather the even more ancient deities of the Huallas,
were worshiped under the same roof as Inti the Sun god of the
Incas. On one side of the great room was the golden disk of Inti

with its temples, reached by a single gateway, and surrounded by the encircling
wedge-shaped houses. Unlike Cajamarca, Sinjerli was in the center of an immense circular area surrounded by a double wall of stone. Sculptures at this site
show warriors with dumbbell-shaped shields identical in form with those used
by the ancient Peruvians in the Cajamarca area (See *The Hittite Empire*, by John
Garstang).

with its rays tipped with gleaming gems, while opposite was the
fierce-faced jaguar god adorned with gold and precious stones and
with blazing yellow topaz eyes. And in the carved and painted
frieze that encircled the interior of the temple, allegorical figures
of Inti, of Wira Kocha and the jaguar were intermingled, together
with the figure of a richly attired man grasping a great feline in
either hand—the hero god Mishi or "Keeper of the Cats."

Scattered about outside the city, amid the fields of corn and
quinoa, squashes, tomatoes and potatoes, peanuts and sweet potatoes, tobacco and peppers, were the humble homes of the husbandmen and herders, all built of stone and set in the shade of groves
and orchards of cacao, avocado and fruit trees.

Beyond all, where the sides of the valley rose to meet the foothills,
great flocks of llamas and alpacas grazed, their herders ceaselessly
playing upon their *quenas* or flutes.

There were no great burial mounds or *huacas* such as rose above
the plain about Chan Chan, but a few hundred yards beyond the
city was the great cemetery of *Abencay* with its deep stone vaults
or tombs. Here the dead were interred in square coffins or chests
beautifully hollowed out from solid stone and closed with tightly
fitting stone lids often covered with carved figures and designs in
bas-relief. Covering the tombs were immense stone slabs and upon
these were the stone images of the persons whose remains were
within, surrounded by their weapons, their most valued possessions
and food.

With the tragic murder of Atahualpa by the treacherous Spaniards, Cajamarca became a place of sorrow, a city of mourning.
With the departure of Cortez and his men on their way to Cuzo,
the people gradually deserted their city, partly because of the trag-
edy that had taken place and partly because they feared the Spaniards might return to kill, rob, and enslave. Scattering here and
there, finding new homes among other tribes, the inhabitants of
Cajamarca left their city to time and the elements.

Today little remains of the once magnificent city. Mounds of
sand cover the abutments of walls and buildings. Most of the countless stones used in the construction of the city have been taken
away to be used in the building of the modern city of Cajamarca,
or for stone walls to pastures and gardens, and the great reservoir
in the plaza has long ago vanished. But here and there portions of

walls of buildings still remain with the carved stone heads of jaguars
or other beasts jutting from the surfaces and with the polished stone
slabs still mirroring the sunlight as in the days of long ago. The
cemetery is a jumbled mass of mounds of earth, broken stone slabs,
fragments of textiles and mummy wrappings and human skulls and
bones, for treasure seekers have played havoc with the tombs, wan-
tonly breaking the carved stone lids and casting aside the contents
that had no intrinsic value.

Despite the destruction of the ancient city one may still trace its
outlines, its streets and avenues, even the sites of its temples and
its palaces, and from the descriptions by the Spaniards, by means
of the many stone carvings that have been found and by the fragments of walls still standing it is possible to reconstruct the buildings of the city where Atahualpa died.

In some respects even stranger and more remarkable than Cajamarca, is Chavin de Huantar beyond the snow-covered cordillera
in a deep ravine where two rivers meet. Here, hidden beneath
mounds of earth are the ruins of a subterranean city with long
corridors, innumerable rooms, large halls and conduits of stone
buried several yards beneath the surface of the earth and with other
structures superimposed over them. The subterranean passages and
chambers are walled with carefully fitted stones, with huge stone
lintels over the doorways and with immense slabs of stone forming
the roofs. Exactly what purpose these served no one knows, for
Chavin had been abandoned and forgotten long before the coming
of the Spaniards. But as numbers of ceramic vessels, as well as some
human remains, have been found within the rooms it may be that
they were burial vaults for exalted personages or places of worship.
Also, within one of these underground corridors, the late Dr. Julio
Tello discovered a remarkable and unique beautifully sculptured
stone idol or monument that was actually suspended from the ceiling (Fig. 27). It was at Chavin that Dr. Raimondi in 1874 obtained
the famous "Raimondi stone" now in the Museum at Lima with
its ornate and complex carving of the Fish god combined with the
Jaguar god (Fig. 26). Here, too, there are underground conduits or
canals connecting with the rivers and so arranged that the entire
subterranean city or temple could be flooded while a deep wide
moat surrounds the entire place. Here at Chavin practically all of
the stone carvings as well as the pottery, which is invariably of

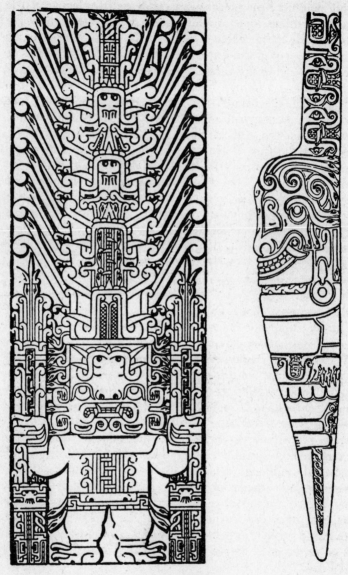

Figs. 26 and 27

highly polished heavy black ware, represent the Jaguar god in in-numerable forms, some of which are so highly conventionalized as to be scarcely recognizable. There are also many representations of Ishi the "Keeper of the Cats" in many forms. But regardless of the stylizing or conventionalization all have certain details that never vary. All show a human figure flanked on either side by felines, and although the details vary somewhat all have certain features in common. Although they are most numerous in the Chavin area of northern Peru, yet carvings or other representations of the "Keeper of the Cats" have been found among the other artifacts throughout the Central Andean region of Peru and Bolivia.

And it is a most noteworthy fact, that does much to support the theory of the Sumerian origin of the ancient Peruvian civilizations, that the "Keeper of the Cats" was an important deity of the ancient Sumerians to whom he was known as Mishi, Tas, Tashia and Ishi, and that representations of the deity found in Phrygia, Sardinia, Egypt, Persia, and elsewhere are very similar to those from South America and, in some examples, are identical in their details. (See Plate XVII.)

Also scattered about throughout the Chavin area and especially at Junin, Aija and Ancash are innumerable stone figures of a peculiar type showing symbols that were used by the Mayas and Mexicans (See Chapters 4, 5, 7 and 8).

Most of us are familiar with the old nursery rhyme of the owl and the pussy-cat, who, in a "pea green boat" set out provided with "honey and plenty of money" on a voyage of a "year and a day," finally arriving at the "land where the gum tree grows" and, finding there a "pig with a ring in his nose," they acquired the ring for the proverbial shilling and were then married by the "turkey who lives on the hill." Although it sounds like nonsensical verse yet in reality it seems a most interesting allegory and only a garbled and some-what altered version of a very ancient tradition of a Sumerian voyage of discovery to the New World. Moreover, the owl (or perhaps an eagle), and the "pussy-cat," that was a lion, actually did go to sea on a voyage that might well have lasted for a year and a day.

A few years ago, during excavations in London, a gold boat con-taining a bird of prey and a feline was unearthed, and among the other artifacts found in the Spiro Mound in Oklahoma there was a crystal boat with a conventionalized "owl" at one end and a feline at the other end (Plate XVI, 3). Both of these specimens are conclusive proof of the antiquity of the "Owl and Pussy-cat" story. However, the two did not set forth on the epochal voyage in person but only symbolically.

Fig. 28

About the year 3000 B.C. the port-city of Lagash on the Persian Gulf was the capital of the Sumer-Phoenicians and was the largest, most important port in the world of that time. The patron saint of Lagash was the god Ningursu (deified Nimirrud) whose family clan symbol was a bird of prey (Owl) above two lions. (Fig. 28 and Plate XVI, 4.) This became the official coat-of-arms of Lagash and was displayed on every ship that hailed from the famous port. So whenever a Phoenician vessel set sail from Lagash the "owl" and the "cats" were, allegorically and symbolically, on board. In all probability many of the old Phoenician vessels were "beautiful pea green," undoubtedly they carried honey which was an important export from Lagash, and they unquestionably were provided with "plenty of money" even if not wrapped in "five pound notes," and many of their voyages that are recorded on the ancient Sumerian tablets lasted well over "a year and a day." At that time, also, copal gum was a most sought for and highly valued commodity and among the Indians of South and Central America copal was and still is a very important article of trade. Hence the "Land where the gum tree grows" might well have been tropical America where the Indians (pigs) wore gold nose rings that they gladly bartered for the strange goods of the Phoenician traders; and in the persons of the feather-bedecked priests who dwelt on the great temple-mounds we have the "Turkey who lived on the hill."

In other words the familiar, seemingly nonsensical, jingle is in reality a very valuable record—despite its garbled form—and points to Sumerian-Phoenician voyagers having reached America about 3000 B.C. thus adding another link to the chain of evidence that the Sumerians had visited the Americas centuries before Sargon of Agade and his son, King Menes, established their colonies in what now is Peru.*

* Of course it may be possible that there is no connection between the nursery rhyme and the voyages of the Phoenicians and the Coat of Arms of Lagash. But in that case it is a most amazing coincidence.

CHAPTER 16

The Sacred City

About ten miles from Lima, Peru, on a bare desert over-looking the Pacific, are the ruins of the once great city of Pacha-camak. One of the most ancient cities in America, Pachacamak was for untold centuries the Mecca of the civilizations of South America. It was also one of the largest cities of all the ancient civilized races of America for it covered an area of several thousand acres and had a population of several hundred thousand people not count-ing the thousands of pilgrims who journeyed from far and near—from as far north as Colombia and as far south as Chile—to worship at the holy temples, to seek miraculous cures or to be buried in the hallowed ground of the sacred city.

Just why it should have been regarded as the holy of holies no one really knows, but as Pachacamak was not only the name of the greatest of the gods of the pre-Incan people and their descendants but also means Holy Earth of the Great Soul (or being; any exalted personage) it is quite probable that the supreme man-god was buried there and that his mummy, surrounded with all his earthly possessions and untold riches, still lies beneath the great temple erected to his memory and devoted to his worship.

Before the Spaniards came, Pachacamak was a magnificent city with its great temples and their lofty mounds covered with multi-colored frescoes and ablaze with gold, with its thousands of houses, stores, markets and lesser shrines, and set in the midst of green fields of growing crops, with the sparkling river and the Andean foothills in the distance. Today little remains of the city's past glories. The once cultivated land has become a desert of shifting sand and only the ruins of buildings, temples and palaces remain.

Dominating the city and its vast burying grounds, are the remains of the great twin temples of the Incan and the pre-Incan gods, for here in the sacred city devotees of either deity were free to worship the god of their religion.

There has been a great deal of confusion in regard to these temples for it has long been customary to refer to them as the Temple of the Sun and the Temple of Pachacamak which is incorrect. Inti, the sun god of the Incans, was believed to be the visual manifestation of Pachacamak the supreme god, hence the "Temple of the Sun" and "Temple of Pachacamak" would be one and the same. In reality the other temple, which was ancient when the Sun god temple was built, was dedicated to Wira Kocha, the bearded man-god of the pre-Incans. This was pointed out by the late Dr. Julio Tello who was not only a leading archaeologist but a full-blooded Peruvian Indian and undoubtedly the most outstanding authority on all matters relating to Peruvian archaeology.

Both temples were built upon the summits of immense pyramids fully two hundred feet in height and composed of rubble with their entire surfaces faced with cut stone slabs covered with polychrome frescoes. Stone stairways led to the summits, zig-zagging back and forth to make the gradient easier, and with great stone monoliths at each turn.*

Facing the broad level areas at the tops of the pyramids were the temples, chapels and altars of their respective deities. Although in all of these respects the two were very similar yet in the details of the temples and their idols they differed greatly.

At the Temple of the Sun or Pachacamak the top of the great mound was encircled by a series of deep niches in each of which was a sculptured figure covered with gold and silver. Its inner

* As an example of the "belittlin'" attitude of certain archaeologists, a member of the staff of the American Museum of Natural History stated, in his criticism of my work: "Pachacamak covers an area of about 40 acres. The large pyramid I would estimate as about 30 feet high." Uhle, who made a careful survey and an accurate map of the city, stated in his report that it covers an area about 2½ miles in length by 1⅓ miles in width or, roughly, an area of about 2200 acres. Referring to the large pyramid Uhle states: "It stands about 250 feet above the plain." When, in 1928, Dr. Tello and myself measured the pyramid by triangulation, we made it approximately 175 feet in height. If, at the time of my critic's visit, the pyramid had shrunk to 30 feet, by now it should be a depression rather than a mound!

temple contained a great sun disk in the form of a human face flanked by jaguar heads and with its rays tipped with huge topazes, while opposite this was a large silver disk of Mama Quilla, the moon goddess, with its rays tipped with immense pearls. On gold and silver trays resting on sculptured tables, were the sacred gold *pachas* or drinking vessels, gold incense burners and concave silver mirrors mounted in gold gem-encrusted frames, that were used in lighting the sacred fires at the time of the solstice and the beginning of the Incan New Year. Covering the walls of the wooden building were magnificent tapestries embroidered with gold thread and set with pearls and precious stones, while the door was plated with gold sheets elaborately embossed with mythological figures with emeralds and other gems forming their eyes.

The Temple of Wira Kocha was also of wood fastened together with gold nails and with the interior walls covered with murals depicting scenes in the history of the people. The outer surfaces were also painted while the heavy timber doors were completely covered with mosaic work of turquoise, mother-of-pearl, jasper, agate, lapis-lazuli, coral, scarlet sea shell, bitumen and crystal set in gold and studded with emeralds, zircons, topazes, sapphires, opals and other gems.

Seated upon a red jasper throne within the temple was a heroic sized black stone figure of Wira Kocha. Decked in the finest of textiles, loaded with golden ornaments and jewels, the benign bearded face of the most ancient and most revered of Peruvian gods gazed serenely toward the east. About him in the little chapel were life-sized images of the other deities of the pre-Incans: Ishti with his outstretched hands grasping two great felines; Saycunin and Urcon; the complex Fish god; Kuti-Kundar the Condor god; and others.

Today only the great rubble pyramids remain. Only traces of the frescoes are visible. Most of the stone facing has been carried away to be crushed for paving the road that passes through the ruins or to be used in building the church and other structures in the nearby village of Lurin. And treasure seekers and archaeologists have dug deep into the mounds themselves. But the stone stairways still remain, there are traces of the chapels and other buildings on the summits and the niched wall encircling the sun pyramid still is in fairly good condition.

Surrounding the bases of the pyramids were the vast cemeteries containing tens of thousands of cotton-wrapped mummies of those who had died, and near at hand was the so-called Temple of the Virgins of the Sun. But the ruins of this building would seem to preclude the possibility of the vestal virgins having dwelt there. The doorways are so low and so small that a normal human being is forced to bend double to enter and within, the cell-like cubicles, with no windows and no means of ventilation, have such low ceilings that a person cannot stand upright and are so small that no ordinary mortal could lie at full length, even diagonally.

In a way the structure is similar to the Temple of the Dwarfs at Uxmal, Yucatán, and it is not at all improbable that it was built to house dwarfs who, as I have explained in a preceding chapter, were kept by the Totonacs of Mexico, perhaps to be sacrificed or perhaps because they were regarded as more or less supernatural beings.

The coming of the Spaniards spelled the doom of the sacred city. Pizarro's brother, Hernando, had been sent on a scouting trip and with his followers reached the city of Pachacamak. Rumors of its vast treasures had reached Pizarro but nothing very definite was known as to its exact location.

But if the Spaniards had little reliable information in regard to the city, the people of Pachacamak had complete knowledge of the white men and their ruthlessness, and long before the scouting force arrived the greater portion of all objects of precious metal and the precious stones had been stripped from the temples and cleverly hidden in the nearby Valley of Lurin.* However, the people had not expected the Spaniards to arrive so soon and much of great value still remained in the city. The idols were still within the temples although the gold and the magnificent mosaic work that covered the doors had been hastily removed and the Spaniards found only a few bits of gold and a few emeralds that had been dropped by the priests and overlooked. But the Dons did not return empty handed to Cajamarca. Having torn down and destroyed

* This vast treasure never has been found. But I have no doubt that there are Indians still living who know the secret of its hiding place. To them, however, it is sacred and nothing would induce them to reveal the caches, for despite their veneer of Christianity many of the Indians still believe in and secretly worship the deities of their ancestors.

every image, idol and statue they could find, they finally discovered that the woodwork of the temples at Pachacamak was fastened with golden nails. When this had been burned and the precious spikes were raked from the ashes they were found to weigh nearly a ton, worth over half a million dollars at the present valuation, and far more in those days.

Despite tortures of the most fiendish sorts, the priests and officials refused to disclose the hiding places of the city's greatest treasures, although one priest, unable to withstand the agonies inflicted by the Spaniards, told them of a horde of silver in a storehouse and of caches of precious metals buried near the Temple of the Sun. So great was the quantity of silver that the Spaniards shod their horses with the metal. Then, convinced there was nothing more of value left in the city, they rode away.

The city never recovered. Deprived of their deities' images, with their temples destroyed, the people deserted the city. No longer did pilgrims travel from far and near to worship or to be interred at their Mecca. Soon Pachacamak became a dead and deserted city, a memory of the past, a place tenanted only by the burrowing owls, the soaring vultures and the desert rats. The thatched roofs of the buildings decayed and vanished, the adobe walls, uncared for, crumbled and fell apart. The stone walls and cut stones of the mounds were broken up for use on the roads or were used to build houses and corrals of the farmers at Lurin, and where once were gardens and green fields the desert sand drifted and filled in the unused irrigation ditches and covered the untrodden streets. Alone with its dead the forsaken city lies silent in the shadows of the once magnificent temples. Even the dead have not been left in peace. Where the bodies of the faithful had lain at rest for centuries men have dug, seeking the gold and silver objects buried with the bodies. Ruthlessly the cotton-wrapped mummy-bundles have been dragged from their graves, the robes, garments and textiles have been ripped from the dessicated bodies that, torn limb from limb, lie scattered about, tossed aside to be trod underfoot. Treasure seekers, curio hunters, tourists and archaeologists all have played their parts in the desecration until there is scarcely a square yard of the sand in and about Pachacamak that is not pock-marked with opened graves. Everywhere are the miniature craters and the pits where graves have been excavated, and everywhere are the skulls and bones, the

human hair, the fragments of textiles, the worthless sandals and
slings and the broken pottery that have been disinterred and thrown
away. In many places the bleaching skulls form veritable windrows
and one can scarcely move anywhere without treading upon human
remains. Everywhere also are great piles, often six feet or more in
height, composed of garments, sandals, bones, mummified birds and
dogs, work baskets and wooden ware, cotton spindles and innumerable other objects that the *huagueros* consider of too little value to
salvage.

Bad as this was the worst was yet to come. Until 1929 the great
Temple of the Sun upon its artificial hill had remained almost intact. Most of the frescoes and much of the stucco work had disappeared and little of the stone facing remained. But the walls still
stood, solid massive and impressive. The ramp-like stairway could
still be followed and one could still trace the outlines and details
of the shrines upon the summit. Then within two years, man
wrought more havoc than the elements of centuries. Some one
claimed to have an ancient document telling of vast treasures buried
beneath the temple. A syndicate was formed and steam shovels were
put to work tearing down the mound, destroying the stone facings
and burrowing into the pyramid itself. Luckily the syndicate's funds
gave out before the destruction was complete and protests of archaeologists resulted in the government forbidding further excavations.

To the archaeologist, Pachacamak has proved a real treasure
trove. Incalculable quantities of pottery, textiles, weapons, utensils,
wooden ware and other specimens have found their way from the
graves to the museums of the world and there is scarcely a collection
of Peruvian antiquities that does not contain some object from
Pachacamak. Yet despite the almost continual digging that has been
carried on for four hundred years and more, there probably are as
many undisturbed graves as have been opened. It is almost impossible to dig anywhere in any spot, in the open desert, in the courtyards or within the ruined houses, without coming upon an un-
opened grave, for when Pachacamak was in its heyday many of
those who died in the city lacked certain ceremonies entitling them
to burial in the cemetery. Moreover, even where the mummies have
been disinterred one may dig deeper and find more bodies. During
the untold centuries of Pachacamak's existence layers or strata of
graves have been formed, one superimposed upon another, to a

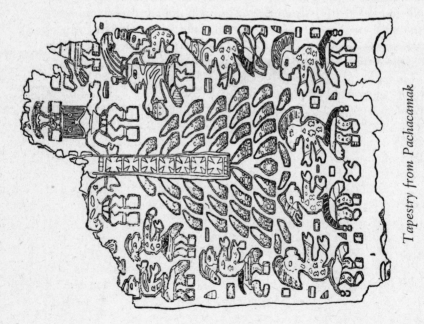

Tapestry from Pachacamak

Comparison of Hittite symbols with those on the tapestry

Fig. 29

depth of twenty or thirty feet or more. Each layer represents a distinct culture, an era in the civilization of ancient Peru. The most ancient Chavin and Hualla, the Tiahuanaco, the Parakas, the Nasca, the pre-Incan and the Incan eras, all are represented. And at the bottom of the deepest excavations are the tops of carved wooden stakes indicating still other graves below.

What race built Pachacamak, what people first interred their dead in its holy ground no one can say, for no archaeologist, no treasure hunter has yet reached the very bottom layer of burials. Perhaps the first people of Pachacamak were ancestors of the Chavins, perchance they were from the immeasurably ancient city of Tiahuanaco in Bolivia who, it has been estimated, built their amazing cyclopean stone cities fully ten thousand years ago. Perhaps those whose bodies lie deepest beneath the surface of Pachacamak's sands were members of that most mysterious puzzling race whose perfectly preserved mummies, wrapped in innumerable magnificent robes and laden with gold have been found in the burial caverns of Parakas in southern Peru. Perchance they are "Sumerians" who, many now believe, came overseas about 3000 B.C. and founded the civilization, the religion and the cultures of the ancient Peruvians. Some day, perhaps, scientists will reach the very bottom layer of burials and the mysteries and puzzles of the origin of Peru's civilization may be solved.

CHAPTER 17

Mining for Mummies

One might think that the people of Lurin, who dwell at the very edge of the ruins of Pachacamak, might be afraid of ghosts, for as a rule the Latin-Americans, and more especially the humbler folk, are exceedingly superstitious. And surely, if spirits ever walk, then Pachacamak should be most thoroughly haunted. But apparently the people who dwell in the shadows of the ruins have not the slightest dread of ghosts or spirits. Perhaps, to their way of thinking, only Christians have ghosts, or it may be that they feel that the ghosts of Pachacamak have enough and to spare to attend to within the confines of the ruined city and will not wander far afield. Whatever the reason, the close proximity of the city with its thousands of dead, and which at night is a most uncanny and spectral spot, does not seem to trouble the living in the least. Indeed, those who dwell upon the borders of the ruins have had no small part in the desecration of the Pachacamak graves, and human bones and grinning skulls lie scattered about their dooryards.

Even those who have business abroad do not hesitate to ride at dead of night through the ruins, passing the cemeteries with their countless graves as casually as though the bleached bones were so many rocks, and trampling many a skull under their horses' feet.

But in these respects the inhabitants of Lurin differ not at all from all the other inhabitants of Peru—both natives and foreigners. In fact were the dwellers in and about Lima at all nervous for fear of ghosts or did they respect the dead, there would be no Lima, or for that matter any other cities or towns in most parts of Peru, for the country is one vast cemetery.

From Ecuador to Chile and from the coast to the Andes there is scarcely a square mile without its cemeteries, its mounds or its ruins filled with dead. No one would dare estimate the number of bodies that were interred or that yet remain even in a small area of the country.

Many cemeteries cover hundreds of acres; many burial-mounds are stupendous, and in many ruined cities every available bit of ground is filled with mummies. The Huaca Juliana just outside of Lima—nearly half a mile in length, nearly a quarter of a mile wide, and over one hundred feet in height—is composed of countless brick cubicles containing mummies, and this is but one of dozens of almost equally large burial-mounds in the vicinity of Lima alone.

The Avenida Progreso that connects Lima with Callao, is cut through another immense mound and for months after the highway was completed the roadsides were littered with human skulls— many with the dried skin and hair still attached—human bones, mummy wrappings, broken pottery, wooden implements, and other artifacts ruthlessly torn from the tombs and dumped aside by the steam-shovels. Even today, bones, wrappings, and skulls may be seen protruding from the sides of the mound where it was cut through to form the road. Many of the hazards on the Lima Country Club Golf Course are ancient graves and mounds, and in the new urbanization developments about Lima the homes of the suburbanites are erected over ancient graveyards. It is not at all unusual to see a modern residence with scattered skulls, scalps, mummy wrappings and bones within a few feet of the front door, and in cultivating their flower gardens the residents are as likely to turn up skulls as stones.

I doubt if there is another country on earth where the inhabitants dwell happily and contentedly in the midst of countless dead; but as I said before, no one gives the matter a thought and the people do not appear to regard bodies and bones of men a thousand or more years old in the same way as they regard cadavers of persons who have died and been buried recently.

Ever since the days of the Spanish conquest, mining for mummies has been a more or less lucrative industry in Peru. Not that the mummies were desirable or valuable, but because the Incans and pre-Incans interred ornaments, weapons, utensils, and implements with their dead, and some of these were of silver or gold. How many tens of thousands of mummies have thus been disin-

terred and destroyed no one can guess. And in addition to the countless numbers thus dug up by the professional mummy miners, or
huaqueros as they are called, thousands more have been disinterred
by archaeologists, curio seekers and others, while many thousands
more have been destroyed in the course of constructing railways
and roads, digging irrigation ditches, cultivating land and carrying
on various public and private works.

One would suppose that, years ago, the supply of mummies
would have been exhausted. But so vast was the number of dead
buried in Peru that despite all that have been disinterred practically
no impression has been made, and what is more, scientists are constantly finding mummies and remains of hitherto unknown races
and cultures.

Strictly speaking, the mummies are not mummies. That is, aside
from those in one or two districts, the bodies were not embalmed
nor purposely preserved. They merely were buried in the dry desert
sand, in adobe brick tombs, or in cylindrical rock-lined graves
where, owing to the dry climate and a certain amount of nitrates
in the earth, they become dessicated and are indefinitely preserved.
And the same conditions also preserve the innumerable articles interred with the bodies. The finest textiles, the most delicate laces,
the most gorgeous of feather robes and headdresses are as fresh, as
bright and as perfect as on the day they were made, and from these
various objects it is possible to reconstruct and revisualize much of
the life, the customs and the habits of these Peruvians who lived
from one to perhaps five thousand years ago.

Obviously the majority of bodies are those of poor and humble
peasants, of farmers, fishermen, and their ilk whose mummy-
bundles contain very little of interest or of scientific or intrinsic
value. Stone shell or clay ornaments, an occasional stone implement, gourds filled with maize, peanuts, or other food; baskets containing needles, thread and weaving implements, pouches filled
with cotton seeds; llama-hair slings and cotton spindles are the usual
objects found, together with pieces of pottery and various kinds of
woolen and cotton cloth. But one never knows beforehand what
may be found when mining for mummies in Peru. There is no
means of distinguishing the burial place of a peasant from that of a
prince, a priest, a chief, or a medicine-man, and oftentimes a wonderful collection of archaeological treasures may be revealed.

From one grave I obtained a magnificent bronze battle-axe with handle complete, a most beautiful and effective weapon still capable of slicing a man's head from his shoulders or cleaving his skull. From another grave—in a small, insignificant mound on the outskirts of Lima, a mound so small and unpromising I had never bothered digging into it, I disinterred the mummy of an old medicine man. Upon his head was a crown of black feathers, he was dressed in elaborate robes, and tucked into the folds of these were numbers of small woven pouches containing his stock of medicines, his "herbs and simples," and his instruments. About his neck was a silver collar and a string of lapis lazuli beads from which was suspended a carved wooden llama and a silver pin in the form of a heron's head. Evidently he belonged to the heron clan, for the pottery found with him bore designs embodying herons while a carved wooden spoon—possibly used in dispensing his medicines— also bore the figure of the heron.

There were also several stoppered bottles made from gourds, each containing remains of dried-up medicinal preparations, a curved bronze surgical knife, a number of bronze pincers—used for extracting hairs—a feather wand, a bundle of knotted *quipos* or message strings and a peculiar wooden knife-like implement. Altogether the old doctor's mummy-bundles contained over one hundred different specimens—a veritable miniature museum in itself. In another grave I found the mummy of a woman who judging from her garments, must have been high in the social whirl of her day; a woman of wealth and station and a leader of fashion. No doubt when she walked Peruvian soil and queened it over her less fortunate sisters, she was regarded as the best dressed woman of Peru, as she deserved to be. Her gown, which might well have been the model from which present day evening gowns are copied, was of the finest lace, the upper portion of rich brown, the lower portion of old ivory, while over this was a drapery of pale gray-blue lace, the whole so perfectly preserved that it might be worn by any woman today. About her head was a fillet of chased silver; she wore a necklace of polished carnelian and turquoise beads as large as pigeons' eggs; about her wrists were bracelets of silver, pearl shell, and semi-precious stones, and her long hair was confined in a net of loosely woven human hair and was fastened at the back by means of a fibre band decorated with delightfully carved figures cut from mother-of-pearl.

And instead of being wrapped in coarse textiles, this Peruvian lady of over two thousand years ago was wrapped in a shroud of thirty-five yards of the most beautiful white lace! Talk about old lace! Here was really old lace, moreover, lace made of wool as well as cotton, and as perfect as on that far distant day when sorrowing friends and bereaved relatives wrapped the dead woman's body in the filmy material she loved so well in life.

But even more interesting were the other objects buried with this Moujik woman. There was a hand loom with a strip of cloth half finished upon it, and there was a work basket filled with needles, woolen and cotton thread, yarn and a leather thimble, showing quite clearly that even if she were a leader of fashion she was no drone, no idle rich, but an industrious young lady. Still she must have been as vain as any woman of today and as careful of her personal appearance, for two beautifully woven and decorated pouches or "vanity bags" contained her toilet accessories and her cosmetics—practically exact counterparts of those carried by every girl and woman today. There was a mirror of polished marcasite set in a carved and painted wooden frame, a comb made from palm wood, a powder box formed from a gourd and a powder puff of soft feathers; there were bronze pincers for removing superfluous hair, a bronze knife for paring her finger nails, a little gourd phial containing cinnabar paste with a silver spatula for applying it to the lips, several pins, a cuticle stick much like the modern ones of orange wood; a dainty spoon—perhaps the owner was squeamish and preferred an individual spoon when taking her maté tea. There were also various other articles that may be found in almost any woman's purse, ancient or modern.

The discovery of such interesting and scientifically valuable mummies is, however, a matter of luck and nothing more. To be sure, certain localities contain a larger proportion of richly clad, richly decorated mummies than others, yet as a whole I should say that not one in five hundred mummy-bundles contains gold, silver or other valuables, and that not one in fifty contains anything other than the commonest textiles, the most ordinary utensils and the plainest pottery. Luck may have no standing in the realm of science, it may be impossible to prove—either by logic or by any known scientific formula—that such a thing or condition exists, yet it enters very largely into all or nearly all scientific discoveries and achievements.

Especially is this the case with such branches of science as archaeology and ethnology. I have known competent, trained archaeologists to delve and dig for months without notable results, and then along comes some amateur at the game and, at the first spadeful of earth, he turns up priceless archaeological treasures. In the many years I have devoted to ethnology and archaeology in South and Central America, luck has ever been my strongest ally and it proved faithful to me in Peru.

For nearly six years I had delved in prehistoric ruins that were teeming cities a thousand or more years before Christ was born. I had resurrected pottery, weapons, tools, and textiles from tombs that had been sealed in the days when Ur was at its zenith. I had mined mummies in the desert sands, had burrowed into immense burial-mounds, and had dug into strange, bottle-shaped graves on rock-strewn *punos*.

Scores of mummies had been brought to light. I had been very lucky. I had secured feather robes and ornate headdresses from the shrivelled, desiccated bodies of long-dead Moujik chieftains; marvellous ceramics from the immense mummy-bundles of the mysterious Nascans; beautiful pottery from the cell-like niches wherein the Chimus placed their dead; copper, bronze, and silver ornaments with here and there a bit of gold. I had obtained carved woodwork and objects rich with mosaics; beads of lapis, of turquoise, of semi-precious stones; I had found the mummy of an ancient medicine-man, the lace-wrapped mummy of a prehistoric debutante—in fact nearly every object known to or used by the Incan and pre-Incan races.

But never had I discovered the mummy of an Inca. By that I do not mean the mummy of one of the Incan people. On the contrary, having been the most recent of Peruvian aboriginal cultures—barely six hundred years of age—that of the Incans left the most abundant of all remains. And as the Incan people as a whole were woefully lacking in worldly goods, as they were a most efficiently utilitarian race who rather neglected the arts for art's sake only, and who considered neither gold, silver, nor precious stones intrinsically valuable, and as practically every museum in the world possesses large collections of Incan culture artifacts, I had, as a rule passed by their mounds and burials and had confined my work to more promising and less known graves and tombs of the Incans' predecessors. So when I say I had never found the mummy of an Inca I mean the mummy of a person of royal blood—a reigning Inca, a noble, a prince, a governor of a province; and for that matter I never dreamed of finding one.

Mining for mummies is an expensive business—or pastime—and I had found by experience that mining Incan mummies was a waste of time and money.

Neither is mining for mummies pleasant work. It is a hot, tiresome, and exceedingly dirty occupation. The light dust of ages; the mingled sand, disintegrated animal matter, decayed outer textiles of the mummy-bundles, and portions of bodies which have failed to dry up, surrounds one in a cloud, and one literally breathes mummies. It is bad enough digging under such conditions where the chances are even if not in favor of finding something scientifically worth while. But it is heartbreaking labor thrown away when the chances are all on the side of finding little or nothing.

Still, somewhere, buried in some tomb, or grave, or mound, there must be mummies of Incan nobility—even the bodies of the supreme reigning Incas themselves. And as the Incan nobility—which included the priests, the law-makers, the provincial rulers, the generals, and practically all Incan officials, were gloriously arrayed and adorned with the finest products of Incan looms, with ceremonial paraphernalia, with insignia, and with ornaments of precious metals, their mummies must, I knew, be veritable archaeological treasure-troves.

No one, as far as known, had ever found one of them, however, and hence there was little real first-hand knowledge of just how the Incas and their nobles were attired, for the reports of the old Spanish conquerors do not agree on these matters. Why no one had ever found a royal mummy was something of a mystery. Perhaps, I thought, they were most carefully secreted to insure that they would never be disturbed. Perhaps the old Dons tortured those who knew of their burial-places until the unfortunates revealed where the royal mummies might be found and stripped of their valuables by the conquerors. Or again there was the rather remote possibility that the Incas were not interred with their riches but were buried in ordinary clothes and wrappings like those of their subjects.

At all events it would have been a hopeless task to have dug all or even a small portion of Incan graves in the faint hopes of finding the body of an Inca. And I did not trust sufficiently to my proverbial good luck to cause me to feel that I might dig at random in any one spot and be rewarded by coming upon the mummy of one of those "golden ears" as the Spaniards called the Incan nobles, because of the gold shells or ear-coverings worn by them.

This custom, by the way, according to tradition, had a most curious and interesting origin. One of the sons of the Inca, Pacha-Kutik, lost an ear in battle, and to hide the mutilation he wore oval golden coverings over his ears. Then, in order that he might not be conspicuous—as well as to commemorate his bravery—the Incan princes all followed his example and wore the *huancos* which in time became the recognized insignia of royalty.

But that I should ever find a mummy with the golden ears never entered my head. And then "Lady Luck" stepped in and played her little joke.

I had long intended to try digging in a very small, very inconspicuous mound which, somehow, seemed different from the others in the vicinity. I had taken my medicine man with his hundred odd implements and articles from another small mound, and I had begun to have a "hunch" that small mounds might prove richer fields for excavations than the larger ones. At any rate they were easier to dig and could be excavated more thoroughly. Moreover, this particular mound contained very little adobe brickwork but was mainly composed of loose gravel and earth. So at last, selecting a spot that appeared to be promising, I started work. Dust flew in clouds, under the blazing sun perspiration ran in streams, but presently a human skull was unearthed. There was no sign of a mummy or even a wrapping; evidently the cranium had fallen from some body that had been buried near the surface and had weathered out in the course of centuries. Then a bed of sticks and leaves was disclosed—sure indications of a burial beneath. Carefully this was removed, revealing a few fragments of animals' skeletons, some bits of textiles, and two or three pottery jars. Then two more skulls— one a woman's, the other an infant's—and a few bones. I was, as the children say in Hunt the Thimble, "getting warm." Somewhere below that thick layer of tightly packed leaves and trash was a mummy; but whether that of some humble farmer or a man or a woman of high station was impossible to guess.

To go farther with the pick and shovel would have been to court disaster, so on hands and knees I commenced digging carefully with a trowel. Presently I came upon a small, tightly wrapped bundle of basketry containing the mummified body of a little Incan dog. The next moment my trowel struck wood, and most carefully scraping away the sand and dust I discovered four upright stakes. They were lashed together with fibre ropes to form a quadrangle and the intervening space was packed with fine dry fibres.

My interest and excitement now ran high. Never had I found a burial of this sort, and with the utmost care I lifted the fibre. A cry of amazement and delight came from my lips. Brilliant yellow and scarlet feathers were revealed, and very gently I lifted a gorgeous crown from the mass of brownish hair that covered the skull beneath. It was a regal affair and in a perfect state of preservation. But more surprises were in store. Beside one of the upright posts was a wooden shield; beside another a bronze-headed spear with palm-wood staff, and a magnificent bronze axe was beside the third stake. Little by little I withdrew the masses of fibre that filled 'the grave, until at last the mummy could be seen, a shapeless bundle wrapped in heavy striped cloth. But it scarcely could be called a mummy. Little of the body remained except the bones. Scarcely a trace of skin adhered to the skeleton, and though every care was used the bones dropped apart when the bundle was lifted from the grave. But the wrappings were intact and as I commenced unwrapping the bundle I scarcely could believe my own eyes. Never had I seen such a mummy. There were textiles of the rarest and finest weaves and patterns; ornate pouches, bundles of *quipos*, woven sashes and belts. And as each strip of cloth or each garment was removed more and finer objects were disclosed. There were implements of bronze and wood, charms or amulets, a carved wooden sceptre or staff tipped and ornamented with gold. About the bony wrists were golden bands with raised figures of birds and the Sun-god. Below the knees were golden bands from which hung little metal ornaments tipped with scarlet feathers. Upon the skeleton's chest were three golden disks each embossed with the tiger-head image of Inti. And at the front of the headdress, above the exquisite *llautu* or head-band about the painted wooden false face, was the golden symbol of the rainbow—the royal Incan standard— topped by a pompom of scarlet and black feathers with a little gold sun hanging over the forehead. All or any of these alone would have proved the mummy that of a royal personage, for only Incan nobility was permitted to wear the rainbow symbol and the golden Sun-gods. But best of all, there were the golden *huancos* that in life had covered the ears of the deceased. Their presence left no doubt of my tremendous luck. I had unearthed the mummy of an Inca!

Sometimes the mummy miner has very different experiences. Sometimes inexplicable things are found, sometimes one draws a blank, sometimes—well, almost anything may happen. One surprising and far from pleasant discovery was made while excavating graves at the immense ruined city of Cajamarquilla near Lima. Digging into one grave I came upon some wonderfully preserved textiles. As I drew them forth I became almost as astonished as when I had found my priceless Inca. Upon the "wrappings" were buttons! Yes, actually buttons, and incredible as it seemed—a metal buckle. Then a strange but unmistakable and nauseating odor issued from the grave, and among the folds of the amazing wrappings I caught a glimpse of a human hand, a horrible swollen, discolored, putrid thing. Very hurriedly I shoveled the sand back into the grave, for obviously the body had not been interred more than a few days previously. Yet here it was occupying a grave amid hundreds of pre-Incan and Incan graves, miles from the nearest village or house. Not until days later did I learn that the aborigines of the neighboring hills, the descendants of those who once dwelt in the great city of Cajamarquilla, still brought their dead to the ancient burial-ground of their people and interred them amid the bodies of their ancestors.

To one mining for mummies in Peru the Nasca area is like the mother lode. Unlike most of the ancient Peruvians, the Nascans buried their dead in square subterranean tombs with posts at the corners and roofed with wood. As the tops of the posts usually project above the surface of the ground the tombs are readily located and excavating is a simple matter. Very often the tombs contain several mummies and they invariably contain numbers of pieces of pottery. In many ways the Nascan pottery is superior to that of any other prehistoric American race, and is so characteristic and so unique that anyone may recognize it at a glance. Largely it is in soft reds, white, buff, brown, and black beautifully modeled and with a satiny semi-glossy slip-glaze. It is in the thin delicate nature of this ceramic ware, the perfect firing and the truly artistic and beautiful polychrome decorations that the Nasca pottery excels all other Peruvian types. In addition to the conventional plates, bowls, cups, jars, and pots there are horns and trumpets, Panpipes, bells, whistles, and flutes, as well as many vessels in the forms of fruits, vegetables, animal and human figures, all highly decorated with artistic designs in which birds, flowers, fruits, and human figures predominate.

To the mummy miner the pottery alone would be ample reward but the real treasures are the mummies. Nowhere else in all Peru are there mummies like those of the Nascans. Not only are the bodies most perfectly preserved, but the wrappings and coverings are rich, elaborate and gorgeous. Ordinarily the Peruvian mummy is doubled up with the chin resting on the knees, is covered with a poncho or blanket and together with a few personal belongings, ornaments, weapons and food is wrapped in coarse sacking and quilted cotton and finally encased in a coarsely netted container of rope.

Very often there is a mask of wood, copper, silver or even gold covering the face and sometimes there will be a feather crown or other form of headdress still in place. But the Nasca mummies are of a very different type. Not only are they interred with the finest pottery, the richest garments and the most prized weapons and ornaments, but in addition they are wrapped, bundled, decorated and disguised until they bear no outward resemblance to human bodies. The entire mummy, head and all, is then wrapped and roped into a bulky bundle on top of which there is an artificial head with hair sewn in place and with a mask of silver, gold or wood, painted, carved or chased to represent the face of the deceased. Topping all is a gorgeous crown of feathers usually with a fillet of silver or gold. The bundle is robed in the finest textiles and feather work and is draped with necklaces and covered with ornaments, cloth, doll-like images, scores of woven pouches and bags, ornamental pins and gew-gaws.

Unwrapping one of these mummies is a most fascinating job.

One never knows what magnificent and amazing contents may be revealed. Always there are the wonderful textiles, for the Nascans were most expert weavers and there are many examples finer than any made by machinery today, but all woven on crude hand looms. Much of the cloth is plain weaving but the greater portion is tapestry in which the most elaborate and intricate designs in many colors are brought out by a sort of embroidery upon a woven base.

Very often, too, one may come upon robes of the amazing feather cloth made by sewing thousands upon thousands of small, bright colored feathers on a woven background to form intricate designs in contrasting colors and used for belts, headbands, garments and even large ponchos and blankets. And not infrequently the mummy bundles contain beautifully wrought ornaments and utensils of silver and gold. Taken all in all when the mummy miner opens a Nasca tomb he really strikes pay dirt.

Unfortunately the native *huagueros* have found opening and robbing Nascan graves so lucrative that thousands have been looted and today it is not at all an easy matter to locate a Nasca tomb that is still intact.

To the archaeologist the Nasca culture is of intense interest for we know little regarding the Nascans. About all we do know is that they occupied a vast area of country near Pisco and Ica in central Peru, an area that is now barren desert but in their days was irrigated and intensely cultivated and was probably fertile and covered with tropical verdure, that they dwelt in adobe houses, that they seldom worked stone and never erected stone idols or images, that they were highly cultured, with a knowledge of engineering and astronomy and that they were among the most expert and skilled weavers and potters of all American races. Some day, someone mining for mummies in the Nascan area may find the key that will solve the puzzle of these ancient people.

CHAPTER 18

Forgotten Cities

Throughout Peru, and over the border in Bolivia; hidden in trans-Andean jungles, perched on mountain sides, on plains and deserts and in fertile valleys, are the countless ruins of villages, cities, forts, palaces, and temples of long-forgotten ancient Peruvian civilizations.

Many never have been explored or examined by archaeologists, others have been investigated and partially excavated and have yielded an enormous number of artifacts of inestimable scientific value, yet have failed to solve the mystery of their origins. When these ancient cities were built, who built them, why they were abandoned and deserted, no one knows, perhaps no one ever will know.

The amazing citadel of Machu Picchu has been publicized as one of these cities of mystery ever since it was first made known to the outside world by Hiram Bingham in 1912. But in reality there is no mystery about Machu Picchu. The Spanish conquerors knew of it, but it was so remote, so difficult of access that, as far as known, they never visited it. The Incans also knew it and at the end of the Manco revolt the defeated Inca and his followers took refuge in Machu Picchu and occupied the ancient city for a number of years.

Long before then, however, Machu Picchu had been abandoned, partly because of the frequent and disastrous raids by the savage head-hunting tribes of the surrounding jungles and partly because of the scarcity of arable land capable of producing sufficient food to supply the inhabitants.

In many respects Machu Picchu is probably the most remark-

able city in all America. A city unique in its situation, it was built
upon a narrow spur or shelf in the depths of the Andes, with a
sheer peak rising for thousands of feet on the one side and a precipice dropping for a thousand feet or more on the other side and
accessible only by a narrow path along the top of a ridge. In many
places the walls and structures actually overhang the cliff and appear as if about to fall into the abyss below. Everywhere, crowded
upon the little plateau, are walls, houses, palaces, temples, granaries and other structures, seemingly placed hit or miss without
order or plan and with narrow streets, often carried by stone steps
up the slope. Everywhere also, are combinations of Incan and pre-
Incan stone work. Walls of polygonal pre-Incan type stones may be
topped by the equally typical Incan stone work. Incan type walls
with Incan type doors and niches join walls of pre-Incan type,
and there are many structures that are neither the one nor the
other, that are unlike any others in Peru. Although a deal of excavatory work has been carried on first and last, no human remains
and few artifacts of unknown or undetermined cultures have been
found. Largely they are Incan, a great many being late Incan,
probably buried at the time Manco occupied the city, while some
are of the more ancient pre-Incan type.

How long the strange mountain city has been in existence no
one knows. It unquestionably antedates the Inca regime. In all
probability the Incans found it abandoned, took possession, repaired
and added to it, and erected the majority of the structures that are
ruins today. Undoubtedly it was used more as an outlying border
fortress than as a residential city, as a protection against savage
raiders, but there is no record, no knowledge of when it was deserted and left to the elements and the jungle growth that effec-
tually concealed it for centuries.

Today the Peruvian government has cleared away the trees,
creepers and brush and it may be visited in comparative ease by
motor cars operating on a railway line, but it is a hard stiff climb
up the steep slope to the ruins on the narrow shelf midway between
the valley and the clouds.

Unquestionably there are other ancient cities still hidden in
the jungle-covered mountains bounding the valley of the Urubamba
River. In fact during the past few years some of these have been
found, the vegetation has been cleared away and the ruins exposed

to view, but none so far discovered can compare with Ollantay as far as remarkable monolithic stone work and architectural beauty and engineering feats are concerned. As I already have mentioned, the gigantic stones of which much of the fortress is composed were transported for many miles across country and over two large rivers. Even with an army of ant-like men hauling and straining, with huge rollers beneath the stones, it would have required a very long time and an amazing knowledge of engineering to have brought even one of the immense blocks of granite to the fortress-city, and there are hundreds of them. Also it must have been a herculean undertaking to have lifted the monoliths to the summit of the terraced hill and to the tops of the high walls. Many years, many lifetimes, even centuries must have been devoted to building the city which, like Macchu Pichu and other great Andean cities, was abandoned centuries before the coming of Manko-Kapak the first Inca.

At Vira Kocha, also, there are remarkable ruins, prominent among them the great stone viaduct that carried water from the mountain reservoirs to Cuzco and other towns. More remarkable yet and one of the unsolved mysteries of ancient Peru are the great sunken, circular auditoria or stadia not far from Cuzco. Here in the valley, are several enormous circular arenas, strikingly like our modern football and baseball stadia. They are paved with stone and provided with tiers of stone benches capable of seating several thousand people.

No one knows their purpose or use. They may have been true stadia where games, dramas, athletic events or performances of some sort were held or they may have been pre-historic senate chambers or forums. It is all guess work and one guess is as good as another.

Another puzzle still unsolved are the chulpas. These are stone towers about thirty feet high by ten or more feet in width, usually cylindrical but sometimes square, standing far from towns or other buildings and usually on hilltops or near water although sometimes in valleys. They are two stories in height, usually with two rooms, one above the other, but with no stairways or connections between them. The lower chamber is provided with a low narrow doorway but there are no windows. As in some of these chulpas human remains have been found it has been suggested that they are tombs, but the fact that human skeletons are buried in only a few rather does away with this theory. Another guess is that they were storehouses or granaries but in that case how could the grain or other substances have been placed in or taken from the upper chamber? If, as some surmise, they were signal towers or watch towers, how did the men on watch reach the summits of the structures when there are no openings in the stone-covered tops?

Recently an entirely new theory has been advanced by Mrs. Verrill, who has made a very deep and exhaustive study of ancient Asiatic civilizations. In certain parts of the Old World, in the Indus River Valley, in Algeria and in Tibet, there are stone or mud brick towers almost identical with the chulpas that are known in India as *stupas* and in Algeria as *chouchas*. These were, (and still are, in Tibet) the abodes of religious hermits who have passed years or at times their lives within them.

It would seem highly probable that the Peruvian chulpas may have been used in the same way. This also would explain why human remains are sometimes found within them, for being in remote spots and seldom visited by outsiders, the hermit occupant of a tower might die and leave his bones within the cell. At all events it is the most reasonable theory yet advanced to explain the chulpas and fits all the conditions. It is also significant that *chouchas,* one of the names for the Old World towers is strikingly like *chulpas,* the Incan name of the towers in Peru.

To enumerate all the forgotten cities and ruins in Peru of whose history we know nothing, would require far more space than a single chapter or several chapters. But of them all none is as puzzling, as intriguing or as remarkable as Tiahuanaco just over the border in Bolivia, a few miles from the shores of Lake Titicaca, and nearly fifteen thousand feet above the sea. Here on the very roof of the continent, in a barren, bleak and dreary land, are the remains of the most mysterious and probably the oldest known city in the New World; a once magnificent city of a highly civilized people whose origin, history and fall are unsolved mysteries, whose engineering feats seem almost superhuman, whose stonework has no counterpart in the New World and who had vanished from the face of the earth centuries before the coming of the first Inca. It is as though the entire civilization, the entire prehistoric race, had been restricted to the area about Tiahuanaco; as if the people and their civilization had descended upon the spot from another world and, as mysteriously as they had arrived, had returned to whence they came.*

Although we have absolutely no certain knowledge regarding them, yet the influence of their arts and their religion extended throughout Peru, Bolivia and from the Andean region to the shores of the Pacific.

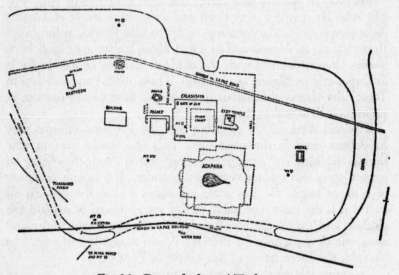

Fig 30. Ground plan of Tiahuanaco

Despite the fact that Tiahuanaco has been exposed to the elements for countless centuries; although the Incan people, the wild Collas, the Spaniards, the Bolivians, the tourists, the treasure seekers, the scientists and the railway builders have done everything within their power to destroy, desecrate and obliterate the work of the Tiahuanacans; and although the most remarkable and priceless antiquities have been carried away or broken to bits; yet much of the city's immense temples, its stupendous buildings and its amazing monoliths still remain. Fortunately those portions of Tiahuanaco which have defied time and man are the portions that

* *Tiahuanaco* in the Incan language means "The Place of the Dead" or "The Place of Those Who Were."

speak most eloquently of the high civilization and the seemingly impossible feats of the vanished race who dwelt and worshiped there.*

The ruins are scattered over an area of several square miles and are bisected by the Guayqui-La Paz Railway. In fact the greatest destruction of the ruins was done by the railway. Hundreds of tons of the finest and best preserved stonework and immense idols having been broken up and used for ballast. But long before the advent of the railway Tiahuanaco had suffered at the hands of innumerable vandals. The ancient Spanish church in the nearby village of Tiahuanaco is built entirely of stones from the ruins of the city, and in front of the church are two huge stone idols broken in half to reduce them to movable size.

The greater portion of the Indians' homes in the village have door frames, lintels, steps and other portions made from beautifully sculptured stones taken from the ruins, and wherever the streets are paved the pavements are made from cut stones of the ancient city. Outside the village, everywhere, the farmers have utilized every bit of stonework they could carry to build the walls enclosing their fields. Even those portions of the ruins that have been left in place have been scarred, chipped, and defaced by rifle bullets when they served as targets of the Bolivian soldiers.**

The ruins are now twelve miles from Lake Titicaca but there is no question that in the days when the city was built it stood on or very near the shores of the lake, for traces of a dock or mole are to be seen just north of the principal ruins. Moreover, the city was once completely encircled by a wide moat filled with water from the lake.

Although the city originally covered a vast area and was probably continuous over that area, the ruins are now more or less separated and may roughly be divided into three sections known as the *Akapana* or "Hill of the Sacrifices," the *Kalasasaya* or "Temple of the Sun," and the *Tunca-Puncu* or "Place of Ten Doors," in addition

* The Incans had no knowledge of who the Tiahaunacans were. According to Aimara traditions the city was built by strangers who came from across the lake and called themselves the Stone People.

** Some years ago the Bolivian Government passed laws protecting the ruins. Great numbers of the best and most important objects, including several gigantic stone idols, have been removed to the open air Museo de Tiahuanaco at La Paz.

to several smaller groups, isolated buildings and numerous monuments and idols.

Most conspicuous of all is the Akapana, an immense truncated pyramidal hill one hundred and seventy feet in height and measuring four hundred and ninety-six by six hundred and fifty feet at the base and with each side almost mathematically in line with the respective cardinal points of the compass. Originally the entire surface was faced with huge rectangular stone blocks and smaller stones, but the greater part of these has been carried away by the railway workers and the natives.

An immense stone stairway once led to the summit but only a few of the steps of enormous stones now remain. The greater part of the top of the man-made hill is occupied by a huge artificial lake provided with beautifully cut and fitted and most scientifically designed overflow conduits. Although the original purpose of the Akapana is not definitely known, yet there seems little doubt that it served the combined purposes of a place of worship and a gigantic baptismal font very similar in its design to such fonts on artificial hills in the Near East and known to the Sumerians as *Apasus* or *E-Abzus*.

One thousand feet from the northern base of the Akapana is the *Kalasasaya* or "Temple of the Sun." Here the earth has been formed into an immense rectangular terrace about ten feet above the surrounding plain and measuring about five hundred by four hundred feet square. Leading from the plain to the terrace that originally was paved with stone tiles, is a stairway flanked by enormous stone columns. Each of the steps consists of an immense stone slab ten feet in width and twenty feet in length and weighing forty or fifty tons.

Along the four sides of the area are great stone columns fifteen to twenty feet in height and spaced sixteen to twenty feet apart. At the time when the city was occupied these columns were topped by stone lintels to form an enclosing colonnade, for notches and cut mortises in which these were set are still visible on many of the columns that, through the ages, have been badly eroded by the elements and the desert sand blown by the frequent gales prevalent in this area.

Originally the great column-enclosed terrace contained innumerable idols, images and other objects, for their scattered remnants are everywhere as are stone tables or altars and fragments of highly decorated pottery. Despite the wanton destruction and vandalism that has taken place the most interesting and imposing, as well as most remarkable, feature of the temple still remains almost intact.

This is the so-called Gateway of the Sun at the western end of the terrace, the largest known example of single stone cutting in the world. It is hewn from a single block of fine grained exceedingly hard andesite thirteen feet and five inches in length, seven feet and two inches in height and nearly two feet in thickness and is pierced by a doorway four feet and six inches by two feet and nine inches cut through the center.

The western surface of the upper portion is decorated with low bas-relief designs of severe geometrical form and with four rectangular niches perhaps designed to hold small images or objects of gold or silver, two in the upper portion and two in the lower, on each side of the opening. On the opposite side the surface is covered with beautifully sculptured symbolic figures in low relief and has two deep niches, one on each side of the doorway. The sculptured figures are arranged in a series of equal sized squares surrounding a much larger central figure representing a deity supposedly the sun god and in either hand he holds a scepter or ceremonial staff. The rays about the head of this figure terminate in miniature jaguars' heads. Flanking this deity are the forty-eight squares, twenty-four on each side, arranged in three rows of eight figures each. All face the god as if running toward him, and each carries a small scepter or staff. The upper and lower rows are semi-human figures with wings and crowns and are identical in every respect, while the figures in the central row are repetitions of the others aside from the fact that they have the heads of condors. Below all these is a line of sixteen carvings consisting of twelve human heads in flat relief flanked by two condor heads. No one hitherto has been able satisfactorily to explain or interpret this remarkable sculpture which unquestionably was of great ceremonial or symbolical significance. According to ancient Peruvian mythology, a giant Condor god carried the sun across the heavens each day, and he frequently is represented battling with a jaguar, the god of night or darkness, thus symbolizing the eternal conflict between night and day. Perhaps the sculptures upon the Gateway of the Sun represent the various lesser deities paying homage to the supreme deity. But the most plausible interpretation of the figure is that advanced by Professor Arthur Posnansky who devoted nearly 50 years to the study of the Tiahuanaco ruins and published a monumental volume on the subject.

He points out that the Kalasasaya, in addition to being a temple, was a portion of a truly amazing astronomical arrangement for determining the solstices and months and that the figures on the Gate of the Sun are calendrical, the various months being represented as running toward the sun god.

At a considerable distance from the other ruins is the *Tuncu-Puncu* or "Place of Ten Doors," the largest, most remarkable and in many respects the most interesting of all. At first sight these ruins appear to cover the summit of an artificial mound about fifty feet in height and two hundred feet square. But in reality the "mound" consists of ruined masonry, foundation stones and stone walls of the enormous magnificent building which has fallen in and been partly covered with debris and drifting sand. Formerly the Tuncu-Puncu was known as the "Palace of the Incas" but it antedates the Incans by many hundreds of years, although at one time the abandoned city was occupied by the Incans for a short period.

The true purpose of the vast structure is not definitely known. It may have been a regal palace or perhaps a sort of forum or a tribunal of justice, or just as probably a temple, or it may have served all of these purposes. Today it is such a complete ruin that it is practically impossible to determine its original form. Its most outstanding features are its stupendous slabs of cut stone, its innumerable magnificently sculptured cornices, columns, blocks and lintels and its titanic stone steps. Only those portions far too heavy and massive for transportation remain, for nearly everything of reasonable size has been carried off to be used in building the Spanish church and the Indians' houses.

Many of the huge stone slabs are of almost incredible size, the largest measuring thirty-six by seven feet and weighing from one hundred and seventy-five to two hundred tons, while slabs weighing one hundred tons, fifty tons and less are everywhere. Bordering the edges of some of these largest slabs are immense platforms hewn from the rock and cut into square, seat-like forms. Possibly these served as thrones or perhaps thrones were placed upon them, but it is far more probable that they were designed to hold statues or idols. Also, on the edges of nearly every block and slab there are deeply cut grooves in "T" shape with holes drilled into the stone at the ends of the deep grooves. In many places where the stones lie side by side these mortised recesses are in line and it is at once obvious that they were designed to hold metal keys or staples for binding the blocks together. In fact numbers of the bronze staples have been found in the debris while some have been found still in place. All however were not bronze for several have been found which are of solid silver. From their shape and the hammer marks upon them it is evident that the staples were cast or forged in oval or squarish section and after being inserted in the grooves were hammered in until the metal spread and became immovably locked in the slots. There is no question that the removal of these fastenings caused the collapse of many of the walls.

Bronze or rather copper is scarce in the area and the natives found a potential copper mine in the abandoned city. Then when the Spaniards found Tiahuanaco and discovered the silver staples they unquestionably wrenched and tore away all that were in sight; but the Tuncu-Puncu was already partially in ruins before the Spanish conquest and countless numbers of the metal fastenings undoubtedly are still buried beneath the massive stones.

Originally the Place of the Ten Doors must have been a most impressive, ornate, and beautiful structure, for innumerable fragments of sculptured stone are scattered everywhere. In every case the designs are formed of straight lines, squares, angles and severe but graceful geometrical designs. On some the carving is incised, on others it is in relief, while in many instances the pattern is cut deeply into the rock; but in every case there is not the slightest flaw in the true, sharply cut mathematical accuracy of the stone carving. Every angular edge is as sharp, smooth and true as if done with a plane or some similar instrument.

Occasionally a stone bears the swastika design and crosses of various forms are common. Very numerous also, are square or cross-shaped, deeply cut niches with the interior cut in a number of steps, each a trifle smaller than the other, until at the very bottom of the niche the design may be only two or three inches in diameter whereas the pattern on the surface of the rock may measure two feet or more across.

There are also countless square or rectangular holes evidently designed to support the ends of great stone beams or lintels, for many of these have one or both ends cut to fit exactly into the recesses. So extremely accurately cut are these various designs that careful measurements with micrometer gauges and other modern instruments showed that nowhere was there a variation of more than one fiftieth of an inch from true while the straight edges of the carvings showed no unevenness when a steel rule was placed upon them. That the Tiahuanacan builders were expert engineers as well as architects is obvious; moreover, they did not work by guesswork or rule of thumb, for plumb-bobs, levels, and various measuring devices have been found amid the ruins. Yet no one has ever as far as is known discovered a single tool or implement of any description which could have been employed in cutting the mathematically true sharp lines and angles, the deep stepped-in recesses, the mortises and tenons in the hard rock.

Almost as puzzling and incomprehensible is how the ancient people of Tiahuanaco transported the stones that were used in their buildings. The nearest quarries are miles away and many are on islands in the lake or on its farther shores. We know that the rock used at the ruins came from these for there are numerous great slabs and blocks at the quarries that are partially cut away with a few that are roughly squared out and ready to be carried to the city. What an enormous amount of man power, what immense rafts must have been required to have carried two hundred or even one hundred ton blocks of stone over miles of water and across even more miles of land! Rollers or similar means must have been used and as rollers would sink into the sand and be useless they must have had tracks of some sort. But the discovery of huge stone wheels amid the ruins may be the answer. One such wheel was found by Dr. Bennett, as I have previously mentioned, and on my first visit to Tiahuanaco I discovered two more. One was almost completely buried under the masses of tumbled-down stone at the Tuncu-Puncu while the other was hidden under small rock fragments and sand just outside the ruins. These wheels are seven feet in diameter, about sixteen inches in thickness, and have square holes in the center. They are cut from the same stone as that of the ruined buildings and the surfaces show the same type of tool marks and workmanship.

If a rotating axle were fitted to these great wheels, slabs or blocks of stone could be trundled across the plain, for the sixteen inch tread of the wheels would prevent them from sinking into the earth or sand. With the extreme scarcity of timber in the vicinity and with no wood of sufficient size for constructing large wheels, stone would have been the only available material, and apparently the Tiahuanacans worked stone as easily as ordinary human beings work wood. In the case of stone wheels, however, a stationary wooden axle with the wheels rotating upon it would have been out of the question, for the wood would have been worn away in a very brief time and the amount of friction would have been tremendous. But by using greased ropes or even withes of twisted vines or bark as slings and with a rotating axle with squared ends immovably fixed in the wheels, all problems would have been overcome.

Such a method of transporting heavy objects is feasible and has been used repeatedly in recent times. In fact in my youth I saw numbers of large stone blocks to be used in building a church transported through the city streets by chain slings looped over rotating steel axles.

Astonishing as is the Tiahuanaco stone work and the herculean feats that were performed by the people, even more amazing is the fact that in many ways they were quite up-to-date and were far ahead of European races centuries later, for throughout the ancient city there is a complete subterranean sewerage and drainage system of stone conduits and pipes very carefully and accurately graded to insure the water being carried off. Also there were sluice gates to control the water in the encircling moat or canal. And finally an immense, rather complicated but very accurate astronomical arrangement by which they determined the solstices, the months of their years and other calendrical matters.

Tiahuanaco, however, had three distinct eras. The earliest was archaic with rough, crude images and idols and only fairly well sculptured stonework but with many huge monoliths and buildings constructed of massive stones. The second period was a vast improvement over the first in the sculptures, stonework, and all other respects, while the third and last period reached the amazing perfection of stone cutting that we find in the ruins of the Tuncu-Puncu, the Gateway of the Sun, the gigantic stone images, and the intricate systems of underground sewers. Although the three eras are more or less easily distinguished, yet, on the other hand, they often merge one into another as though the work of one period had been interrupted only to be resumed at a much later period. But the work done in the third or last period never was finished. For some unknown reason the city was abandoned before the greatest buildings had been completed. Everything was halted, all work stopped and Tiahuanaco was deserted.

What great catastrophe, what threat, what cataclysm caused this no one knows. It has been suggested that the area was shaken by terrific earthquakes, that neighboring volcanoes suddenly erupted, that climatic changes caused by the melting of the glaciers or otherwise forced the people to desert their wonderful city. But none of these theories seems to fit the conditions as far as can be judged. There are no signs of destructive earthquakes having taken place, none of the ruins are covered by volcanic ashes or eruptive material and although there unquestionably have been great alterations in the earth's surface, the land either rising or Lake Titicaca sinking, such changes are so gradual as to be unnoticeable. And climatic changes that would have followed would scarcely have induced a teeming population to abandon the ancient city, their homes and their fields. Even if they were accustomed to a climate far warmer and rainier than that of the area today, such changes would have been gradual, the people would have adapted themselves and their lives to conditions and as the Indians of the vicinity raise their crops and graze their llamas there today, the people of Tiahuanaco could have done as much, if not far more. Personally I believe that Tiahuanaco became untenable because of frequent raids by the semi-savage warlike Aimara and Colla Indians who swept down upon the city, destroyed farms and crops, slew the inhabitants and raided very much in the manner of some of our own tribes in the early days of our winning the west. Macchu Pichu and other fortress cities were abandoned because of the raids of savage warriors and they were far better equipped and designed to withstand the raiders than was Tiahuanaco whose only safeguard was a moat. Moreover, the Incans had well trained, well armed soldiers, but as far as we can judge by the remains so far found the Tiahuanacans were not a militant people and had neither forts nor even serviceable weapons.

Whatever the truth may be the people vanished from the city they had labored so long to build; they must have scattered far and wide, mingling with other people, joining other communities, and being gradually absorbed. We know that such must have been the case for their influence, the typical Tiahuanacan figures, designs and patterns, the deities and mythological characters of their race, are found almost everywhere among the remains of nearly all the ancient Peruvian races from Chile to Colombia and from the lower foothills of the Andes to the coastal plains of the Pacific slopes. As the remains showing this Tiahuanacan influence are invariably far beneath the remains of other races and often are in the very lowest strata we may be sure that the Tiahuanaco civilization was very ancient, probably the most ancient in America. How ancient it was is still somewhat of a question but scientific investigations during recent years have thrown considerable light upon its antiquity.

In 1926, 1930, and 1940 various astronomers, mathematicians and civil engineers have worked at the problem using the ancient astronomical device of the Tiahuanacans as their basis and determining the amount that the earth's axis has altered since the monoliths and gnomons and other devices were erected. Among those who have tackled this fascinating problem were Dr. Arnold Kohlshotter, Frederick Becker, Dr. Hans Ludendorf, Prof. Arthur Posnansky and Dr. Rudolph Muller.

Using the formula of the International Ephemeris Conference adopted at Paris in 1911, Professor Posnansky determined that the second era dated back for the incredible period of 13,000 years. Later Doctor Rudolph Muller carried on very extended and careful observations and calculations, using two different formulas, and stated that his calculations showed by one method an age of 9300 years and an age of 14,600 years by the use of the other equation, and that somewhere between the two extremes was the actual time element, so that Professor Posnansky's computation was very nearly correct. As a result of his statements Professor Posnansky was ridiculed, scoffed at and his entire work discredited by other scientists and archaeologists. It would seem almost impossible, really beyond belief, that over 13,000 years have elapsed since Tiahuanaco was built. If it is that old then it is the most ancient city in the entire world, and older than any other remains of cultured man with the exception of certain ruins in Asia.*

It may seem strange that trained and famous scientists should work on the same problems with the same formulas and produce a time element varying nearly 5000 years. Under the conditions they faced, such an error, even a far greater error, might very easily be made. The accuracy of the calculations depended upon the exact positions of the monoliths, the marking stones and the position of the Gateway of the Sun. Undoubtedly all of these had been accurately placed when first erected, but time, the elements, earthquakes, the gradual elevation or subsidence of the land might well have shifted the positions of the stones and a very slight alteration in their positions would, in the completed equation, cause a difference of thousands of years. Even if we accept the lowest of these scientists' figures (9300 years) it would make Tiahuanaco the oldest city in the world.

Some archaeologists now claim that the Chavin culture of the northern coast area of Peru antedates that of Tiahuanaco, although artifacts showing Tiahuanacan influence have been found *beneath* the remains of the Chavin people.

Also, there are valid and historical evidences, as will be explained in another chapter, indicating that the greater portion of Tiahuanaco was built about 3000 B.C. which would still make it the most ancient city in the Western Hemisphere.

* The extremely great age of the ruins is proved by the discovery of human skulls that have been completely fossilized. They are now in the museum at La Paz.

CHAPTER 19

The Incas Take Control

Merely as a lake, Titicaca is something to brag about. Not only is it one of the really big lakes of the world but added to this is the fact that it is over two miles above the sea. Moreover, it is unique in many respects. Its waters contain but one species of fish, a smelt-like fish found nowhere else in the world; the only known fresh water sea horse, and a pearl-bearing shell found only in these waters. Its shores are unlike those of any other lake, and no other lake on earth can boast of a view of an unbroken range of snow-capped mountains nearly one hundred miles in length and nowhere less than twenty thousand feet in height. Its waters have been navigated by civilized human beings for a longer period than those of any other lake in the Americas and beneath its surface lies a treasure so vast no one dares guess at its value. Upon its shores was built the oldest city in all America if not in the entire world, while finally it is the legendary or rather mythological birthplace of Manko-Kapak, the first Inca, and his sister-wife Mama-Ocllo, the founders of the vast Incan Empire of Tiahuantisuyo.

According to tradition, Manko-Kapak and Mama-Ocllo appeared one morning upon the sacred lake and announced to the wondering people that they were divine "Children of the Sun" and had been sent by their father the Sun God to lead and civilize the people. Perhaps the legend is best told in the words of the ancient Quechua saga:

Over the lake the mist lay softly white.
Silence hung over all, no creature stirred—
When from afar the splash of paddles came,
And as the rising sun broke through the mist—
A balsa floated on the lake's calm breast.

Straight from the flaming sun it glided onward,
Until it grated on the rocky shore,
When from it stepped a man and woman—
Beings like gods, in gorgeous robes arrayed.
Thus from the sacred Lake of Titicaca—
Born of the Sun God came the holy pair,
Mako, first Inca of Tihuantisuyo
With Mama-Ocllo, sister-wife so fair.

It is a very beautiful, a very poetical and a very romantic legend, but in all probability only an allegory and nothing more. However, it is not at all improbable that it was founded on actual fact, for there is every reason to believe that the first Inca and his consort came from across the lake from the east, and if so it is logical that they should have declared they came "from the sunrise," a statement that would easily and quite naturally and consistently be interpreted by the aborigines as being "born of the sun."

There is no question that the oldest traces of Incan occupancy are those about the shores of Lake Titicaca, especially on the Island of the Sun and Island of the Moon, which would seem to bear out the legend of the place of arrival of Manko-Kapak. Whatever the truth may be, it is certain that Manko-Kapak was the first of the Inca rulers, but there is a tremendous gap to be filled in the history of the Incas before him and in the Inca genealogy.

All researches seem to indicate that Manko and his wife came from the district of Sapalla or Kosala about fifty miles from Cuzco and that they were of the Panaka family or clan.

Just what took place after the arrival of Manko Kapak is uncertain, for traditions vary greatly. The most common is that Manko, his wife and a small army of followers journeyed to where Cuzco now stands and drove his golden staff into the earth and so founded the city. Another legend has it that he found Cuzco inhabited and to impress and win over the people the Inca covered himself with gold and stood in a shaft of sunlight so that he appeared to glow like the sun itself.

Probably there is as little truth in the one as in the other. Beyond any doubt this first Inca found Cuzco an inhabited city with many of the huge walls and splendid buildings that are still standing today, for despite the claims of some archaeologists, there is abundant and incontrovertible evidence to prove that for many centuries before the arrival of Manko-Kapak the Andean region had been occupied by a highly civilized race.

We know that this must have been the case, not only from the ruins and remains of their work, but because it manifestly would have been impossible to have accomplished such feats of construction and engineering in the short space of time that elapsed between the arrival of Manko-Kapak and the Spanish conquest. There had been only twelve Incas between the time of Manko's appearance on the scene and the death of Atahualpa, or actually eleven, for Inca Yupanqui and Pachak-Cutik were twins and ruled together, and assuming that each Inca reigned for fifty years—which is highly improbable and incredible—the dynasty could not have existed for even 600 years prior to the arrival of the Spaniards. There is no question about this for the genealogy of the Incas, subsequent to the arrival of Manko-Kapak, is well known and definitely established as follows:

INCA'S TITLE	ACTUAL NAME	NAME OF EMPRESS
1. Manko-Kapak Inca	Panaka-Chima	Mama-Ocllo
2. Sinchi-Roca Inca	Panaka-Raurac	Mama-Kora
3. Lloque-Yupanqui Inca	Panaka-Hahuak	Mama-Chahua
4. Mayta-Kapak Inca	Panaka-Uska-Mayta	Mama-Cuka
5. Kapak-Yupanqui Inca	Panaka-Apuk-Mayta	Mama-Kori-Illpay
6. Inca Roka Inca	Panaka-Willka-Quirau	Mama-Mikay
7. Yahuar-Huakak Inca	Panaka-Aucak	Mama-Chikya
8. Wira-Kocha Inca	Panaka-Soksok	Mama-Runtu-Kayan
9. Pacha-Kutik Inca	Panaka-Hatun Inaka	Mama-Ipa-Huarku
10. Tupak-Yupanqui Inca	Panaka-Kapak-Tupa	Mama-Anak-Huarku
11. Huayna-Kapak Inca	Panaka-Huaykak	Mama-Chimpu-Ocllo
12. Cusi-Huascar Inca	Panaka-Huayak	Mama-Pahua-Ocllo
13. Atahualpa Inca	Panaka-Karyashwa	Mama-Chuqui-Llantu

Undoubtedly the first Inca found the country in a more or less chaotic condition. The ancient civilization had deteriorated and was in a state of decadence. There was no unity, no coordination among the people of the many cities and communities and although all were of the same race there were various clans and tribes and these were in a state of constant friction and warfare. Neither were there definite laws; human sacrifices were held, vast areas of land were neglected and every community had its own ruler.

Starting at Cuzco as their headquarters, the first Incas developed the nucleus of a new form of civilization. They promulgated laws, instructed the people in new arts and industries, introduced a new religion and invented a new language for universal use. They united many diverse tribes and when peaceful methods failed they conquered and subjugated tribes and communities until finally the entire country was united to form one great empire.

The fact that the people firmly believed that the Incas were divine, the "sons of the sun," that they had appeared from nowhere and were therefore regarded as sacred, made the Incas' undertaking far easier than it would have been otherwise. Also, there is no question that they were of a different and in some ways more intelligent race. According to all Spanish accounts and to tradition, they were fair-skinned, tall, with finely cut features and large strongly aquiline noses and had red or brown hair. Whether or not this red hair was natural or artificial is not known, but the people believed that it was because they were Children of the Sun and their red hair was a mark to set them apart from all others.

We must accept the theory of their alien race or else believe they were inspired and actually possessed some of the divine attributes accredited them in the legendary lore of the people, for there are no signs indicating a slow and gradual development or evolution of a new culture following the Incans' arrival on the scene. Rather it was marked by an abrupt and revolutionary order of things, exactly as if the laws, customs, arts, religion, sciences, industries, and social organization of the new regime had been brought, ready made and fully developed, from another land—as was doubtless the case.

Very rapidly the empire was extended. Cuzco became a great populous city. Preeminently agriculturists, the Incas brought millions of acres of arid land under cultivation by constructing vast irrigation systems. They developed new and better varieties of the native vegetables; they encouraged arts and industries that were being neglected, they repaired the pre-Incan roads, the buildings, walls, and temples, and erected new ones. To use a modern slang expression they were "live wires" in every sense of the word. But they were first, last, and all the time devotees of efficiency and prone to sacrifice art for the sake of utility. Where the pre-Incans had hewn, carved, and fitted gigantic stones with which to build, the Incans used smaller, easily handled, more or less roughly squared blocks and often employed cement or mortar to bind them together.

Their pottery was inferior in its beauty and art to that of their predecessors but they introduced very superior weapons, and their textiles and metal work were of a very superior quality. Unquestionably these and other industries and arts were not truly Incan but were carried out by the descendants of the pre-Incans whose handiworks were fostered, encouraged and preserved by the Incas. Even today each community has its own arts and industries and anyone familiar with them can at once recognize and identify the source of a textile, piece of pottery or carving or almost anything made by the Indians.

Although the Incans availed themselves of the arts, industries, and products of the pre-Incans, yet there was practically nothing in common with the civilization of these earlier people and that of the Incas, any more than our own civilization has any direct connection with that of the Chinese or the Mayas even if we do borrow and use Mayan and Chinese motifs and arts for many purposes.

Also, the several Incas, like anyone else, varied greatly in characters, interests, temperaments and other matters. Some were patrons of the arts and industries, others were peacefully inclined, some were organizers, others philosophers while some were born conquerors and soldiers. Among these was Yupanqui-Inca who conquered and subdued the Chimus and brought all the central plains communities from Chan Chan to Nasca under control of the Empire, but it was not until the accession of Huayna-Kapak that the Incans reached their zenith of power and their country attained its greatest extent and wealth. Huayna-Kapak was an ambitious, indomitable empire-builder, a soldier, a statesman, and a conqueror who may well be likened to Julius Caesar or Napoleon. He dreamed of extending Incan dominion to include all of his known world and under his reign the boundaries of the empire were pushed forward for thousands of miles in every direction. Southward the irresistible triumphant armies of the Inca swept on to Central Chile. Eastward they penetrated the tropical Montaña jungles beyond the Andes, and they swept northward through what is now Ecuador, subjugating every race and tribe they met until the powerful kingdom of Quito was conquered and the daughter of the dethroned monarch was espoused by the victorious Inca.

Huayna-Kapak, however, was not a ruthless destroyer. He did not lay waste the areas he conquered, he did not wipe out peaceful communities or burn and ravage. His one dominating idea was to weld the many tribes and communities into an Incan entity. Moreover, in addition to his offensive campaigns and his conquests, he conceived and carried out immense public works and improvements, and accumulated a food reserve sufficient to support the entire population for over two years in case of war or famine. The great Incan road was put in perfect condition, bridges were renewed and side roads constructed, yet by the irony of Fate his lifetime efforts to bring unity, peace, and prosperity to the people resulted in the disruption and destruction of the empire when hostilities broke out between Atahualpa and Huascar and Atahualpa met his death at the hands of Pizarro.

As mentioned in a preceding chapter, the Incas very wisely did not attempt to regulate or control the religions of their subjects. Sunworshipers themselves and regarding Inti the sun as the visual manifestation of a Supreme Being known as Pachu-Kamak, yet they permitted other races to worship their own gods in their own way in their own temples.

The great majority of these people worshiped a Supreme Condor God or *Kuntur Tiksi* whose representative was a divine human being called *Wira Kocha*. Although they were doubtless ignorant of the fact the two religions were merely variations of a much more ancient faith.

The pre-Incan supreme deity or Creator is almost invariably represented as a puma or jaguar more or less humanized and usually surrounded by various symbols of divine power such as jaguars,

condors, fishes and snakes, the first three being symbolic of the
god's dominion over air, earth and the sea while the serpents are
symbolic of the sun's rays and indicate the deity's dominion over
heaven. In a great many cases, also, the face of Kuntur Tiksi is
within a circle of rays representing the sun. Wira Kocha on the
other hand is represented as a benign bearded human being believed to have been endowed with supernatural or divine power as
a representative of the supreme deity. To symbolize this union
Kuntur Tiksi is usually represented with a beard.

The Incans' Sun god *Inti,* was believed to be a being who suffered and died at each solar eclipse but was reborn each time and
was subject to a supreme divinity, the Creator of the Universe or
Pacha-Kamak whose abode was *Hanak-Pachak* or heaven, while an
evil deity known as *Supay* was believed to reside in *Haek-Pachak*
or hell. Although the names of the deities differed in the two
religions, yet their attributes were very much the same and the
Inca's sun-god *Inti,* is usually represented either as a sun-disk with
a jaguar's head or as a human-faced sun-disk with jaguar heads
at each side, and very often with a beard.

Thus it is obvious that the two religious factions were mere offshoots of a much older faith just as our Baptists, Methodists, Epis-
copalians, Congregationalists, etc., are all offshoots of the original
Christian religion. In fact the similarity between the Incan and the
Christian faiths is truly remarkable. Just as we believe in a supreme
God and in Christ, His son, who suffered and died and reappeared,
so the Incas believed in a Creator and a divine humanized son.
And just as we worship both God and Christ, so the Incans worshiped their *Pacha-Kamak* and their sun-god *Inti* who died and
was resurrected. They even had confession with the priests hearing
the men's confessions and the priestesses hearing those of the
women.

The title of *Inca* meant "of the sun" and when they declared
themselves "sons of the sun" they were doing no more than do
modern kings and emperors who claim "divine right" to reign or
are referred to as "heaven born."

So similar to the Christian faith was the religion of the Incas
that one worthy friar, who was much broader minded and more
intelligent than his fellows, wrote a book on the subject and in it
argued that as the two religions were so much alike the Indians

should not be considered as infidels. However, the sole result of his book was to bring him before the Inquisition where he was convicted of heresy and burned at the stake, while all known copies of his work were destroyed. However, during one of the revolutions in Peru I had the rare good fortune to find among the loot taken by the mob, a well preserved copy of the volume.

Like ourselves the Incans had religious or Church holidays and secular or legal holidays. The most important of the former was the *Kapak Raymi* or Birth of the Sun, the Incan New Years.

This was the greatest and most sacred of all Incan festivals and celebrated the summer solstice or beginning of the Incans' New Year as well as the Birth of the Sun and the birthday of the Inca, for regardless of the actual day of his birth he was regarded as a "son of the sun" and his birthday anniversary was coincident with that of the sun itself.

Prince Checko gave a very detailed and graphic description of this festival. No doubt his description was accurate, for in his youth he had witnessed the ceremonies. His story was set down in quaint old Spanish script by the secretary to the Viceroy Toledo and may be translated as follows:

"From his palace the Inca was carried in his golden litter or *juantu,* that was covered with diamonds, turquoise, amethysts, rubies and emeralds, and was lined with the finest robes and pillows of feathers and down, by his bearers and was surrounded by thirty-two guards of the race of the *Lucanas* who claimed the privilege of this honor. He was clothed in rich robes of fine cloth with a wide border of fine embroidery in silver and gold. In his hand he carried the *champi* of gold, which was an elegant mace and was his scepter. His hair was cut short around his neck but for two fingers (plaits) falling by his ears, and was confined by a band called *llauto,* a diadem of bright colors that bore above it two red plumes of the bird *pillco-pichiu* rising above two other plumes of white from the eagle, in two bunches above the forehead. On the left side of the diadem came another royal symbol called *huasca-payalla* that was in the form of a plate of gold set with gems.

"Covering his ears were oval shells of gold. About his neck was a collar formed of fifty-two emeralds each the size of a pigeon's egg and from this collar were hung topazes of great size that were carved to represent the sun and the moon and the fifty-two phases of the moon. Beside the Inca was his woman and sisters and cousins. With them went the Virgins of the Sun, the chief of the holy men (high priest) the chief of the court of princes, the wise men (council) and governors and lords and officers of the warriors, together with all the nobles, the governors of the provinces, the centurions and the chiefs of the cities and provinces. The sentries to the number of two thousand *Canarias* and two thousand *Chachapoyas*, with their painted wooden shields and garbed in bright-colored ponchos and with great lances, occupied niches, like windows without openings, round about the city, the walls, the Inca's house and the plazas. The great orchestra consisted of three hundred and seventy-five *taquica—mayocs* with *pincullus* and *quenas, antaras, pututus, charancos, quepas, huancaras* and *tinyas*. (These instruments were in the nature of flutes, pipes, little organs, guitars, cornets, trumpets and drums.) The music they gave was plaintive and sad. As the sun rose above the mountains of Sallac and Piquicho, where is the castle of Sacsayhuman, it was watched by fifty thousand and more as it moved toward the temple. At sight of its rays, cries and hurrahs of joy arose. At this solemn moment the Inca rose from his litter, and facing the sun, raised his first finger to the height of his mouth. At once a great silence came, and the Inca pronounced the words: *Capak-inti-illariymin*, and the multitude in chorus replied *Punchao-paca-riyrcum*, which was the chant of the great arrival of the sun of the morning on the day of *Capak-Raymi* when the sun-lord reached nearest to the land and thus told the people of the coming of a new year. Ending the chant, the escort and holy men sang victoriously with the people in chorus, passing the chant from place to place until it resounded from the mountains in its echoes. At the close of the chant, from various parts of the city where they had already been allotted, maidens famed as singers accompanied by other virgins sang together five chants to the sun, the moon, the stars, the rainbow and the Inca, the last verses of each song being given by one thousand five hundred acolytes arranged for this solemn day about the temple of *Kori-Cancha*.

"The chants ended, the Inca drank with the chief holy man a great drink of *chicha* from a sacred golden cup called a *pacha* formed to represent the sun and other figures, and from which the *chicha* ran through a path or gutter to a spout whereof the Inca and the chief holy man of the temple sipped. Then all went within the temple and the Inca made obeisance (or *mucha*) to the gods and to his ancestors, until the rays of the lord of the day struck upon his gold image, whereupon the sacred fire was lighted by the Inca who held in his hand a mirror and reflected the rays upon charred cotton.

"Then from this fire the Virgins of the Sun struck other fires and kindled the sacred fires throughout the temple, and with great shouts the people hurried to light their fires, for since the coming of the night before, no light or fire had been left burning in the land. Great rejoicings were made through the day, and in place of water *chicha* ran from the fountains, and at the plazas and on the streets were great jars of *chicha* from which all who desired might drink their fill, for this day was the birthday of the Inca and the birth of the sun, the great Inti, and the New Year of the people of the land.

"Having thus offered prayers and having given thanks to Inti, their god, and the priests having pronounced their augeries,* the Inca in his golden litter borne upon the shoulders of the princes, together with his household and the populace went to the great pampa not far distant from Cuzco where games and tests of skill at arms and mock battles and diverse other feats were carried out with favors to those who were champions bestowed upon them by the Inca."

The only "great pampa" not far distant from Cuzco is the plain with the strange stadium-like structures previously described. It would seem highly probable, therefore, that the sham battles and contests of skill and strength, as well as the choosing of the royal *Cechollo* or poet-laureate took place at these ancient auditoriums. (See Chapter 18).

The birth of the sun ceremonies marked the end of a national holiday of five days' duration. These were the nameless or "lost" days of the Incan calendrical system. As the Incan year was 360 days the surplus five days at the close of each year were nameless and were devoted to universal entertainment and merry making. No work was done during these holidays for they were regarded as a

---

* At this time sacred white llamas were sacrificed and the augeries were based on an examination of their internal organs.

.dispensation granted by Inti to enable the hard working people to enjoy themselves before entering upon the new year.

Then at the Birth of the Sun and the New Year ceremonies, the holidays came to an end.

In addition to worshiping the sun-god Inti, the Incans adored the moon or *Mama Quilla,* regarding the planet as the sun-god's wife, and believed that an eclipse indicated she was hiding her face while she gave birth to a star. At such times prayers were offered and chants sung to her and there was a great rejoicing when she again shone forth. At the "dark of the moon" Mama Quilla was thought to be merged with the sun-god and there are many carvings and decorations of pottery and metal objects showing the moon being swallowed by the symbolic jaguar representing Inti.

CHAPTER 20

The Amazing Empire

The so-called Incan civilization, utterly destroyed by the Spaniards in their conquest of Peru, was in many respects the most advanced, the most extensive and the most remarkable of all American ancient civilizations. In their government and social organizations, their amazing engineering feats, their highly advanced knowledge of mathematics, their architecture, their ceramic and textile arts, their communication systems, their sea-going vessels, their armies, weapons, utensils and many other matters they were immeasurably ahead of the civilizations of Mexico and Middle America. In addition, they were the greatest agriculturists of the world. By means of vast irrigation systems they had transformed deserts into fertile lands and had developed, perfected and cultivated over eighty per cent of the food plants in use today, in addition to innumerable medicinal plants, many of them among our most important and valued drugs.

Although referred to as the "Incas" yet there never was a race or nation of that name. Inca was the title of the ruler or emperor and it would be just as erroneous to call the British "Kings" or our people "Presidents" as to call natives of Peru "Incas." The title Inca, or as pronounced in Quechua, INGA, means "of the Sun," the rulers of the ancient Peruvians having claimed direct lineage from Inti the Sun-god. However, for the sake of clarity it *is* permissible to refer to the ancient Peruvians as Incans, for the many diverse races inhabiting what is now Peru, Bolivia, Ecuador and parts of Brazil and Chile, were all under the Incan domain. But the high and advanced civilization of the area was only partially of Incan origin. Largely it far antedated the Incan regime, which was probably only a few centuries old at the time of the Conquest, and the greatest accomplishments, the most noteworthy engineering feats, the most amazing architecture, the advanced agriculture, much of the religion, and the various deities and other features of the ancient Peruvian civilizations were of pre-Incan origin. Yet no one definitely knows who the pre-Incans were, whether they were of the same race as the later Incans or another people, whence they came or why or how they vanished leaving only their stupendous stonework, their arts and crafts, their great cities and their feats of engineering, their deities and their mummified bodies as evidences of their existence and their accomplishments.

The fact that they completely destroyed an advanced civilization older than the civilizations of Europe did not bother the Spaniards in the least. They had reared the Cross, they had tortured and put to death countless infidels who refused to become Christians, they had come into possession of thousands of slaves and, most important of all, they had secured the greatest treasure in precious metals and gems that the world had ever known.

Some historians and archaeologists have claimed that the stories of gold and jewels taken by the Spaniards are greatly exaggerated, that the fabulous riches of Cuzco and other Incan cities were largely figments of the Spaniards' imagination and that their statements regarding the loot were unreliable. Figures, however, do not lie and as Pizarro and his followers were compelled by Royal edict to render a strict accounting of all treasures obtained, and as the Crown of Spain received a "quinta" or fifth of all treasures, there are available records in the Spanish Archives. According to these documents Pizarro and his ruffians obtained loot amounting to a total of over two hundred million dollars in our money. And we may be quite sure that it was more rather than less, for human nature has not changed and unquestionably Pizarro and the priests, who were the scribes, auditors and accountants, juggled their figures and reports and gypped the King of a goodly portion of his *quinta* and pocketed the difference. In fact upon his return to Spain Pizarro was haled before the Court charged with embezzlement and falsification of his accounts. But it was impossible to prove the charges, more especially as the Church was involved, and, to protect themselves, the padres stood by Pizarro.

Moreover, the statements made to the Spanish Viceroys by surviving Incan noblemen, who embraced Christianity, bear out the tales of fabulous riches of the temples, the Incas and the priesthood. Also it must be remembered that the Incans placed no intrinsic value upon gold or silver and gems; gold was prized only because of its ductility, its color, symbolical of the sun, and its enduring qualities. Moreover, it had been accumulating for countless centuries for it never left the country and only the comparatively small amount interred with the dead was lost.

Although the Incans had no monetary system and gold had no intrinsic value in ancient Peru, yet by an odd quirk of Fate it was the precious metal stolen from the Incans that instituted the gold standard by placing Spain in possession of over one half of all the gold in Europe.

In its form of government the Incan Empire or Empire of Tihuantasuyo (literally, the Four Corners of the World) was the most marvelous social organization the world has ever known.

Never, before or since, has there been anything like it for the government was a combination of communism, a monarchy and a republic.

Moreover, it had been eminently successful and had endured for centuries. But the only reason it had endured was because the people knew of no other form of government. For them the entire world lay within the boundaries of their empire.

A vast empire it was, extending north and south from Quito, Ecuador to Chile, and from the shores of the Pacific to the head waters of the Amazon deep in the trans-Andean jungles, an area larger than Europe without Russia and Germany, and with a population estimated at ten million inhabitants. Neither were the people all of one race. The Empire was made up of countless communities each with its own tribal tongue; hence to avoid the Babel that would result, a common language was devised, a sort of Esperanto, combining the simplest and best features of various dialects. This language, known as the Quechua, is perhaps the simplest, most expressive and perfect in the entire world. It is still spoken by more than half of the Peruvian people and is the universal language of the interior of the country. Although everyone was compelled to learn and use the Quechua, yet the people were free to use their own dialects among themselves. In the same manner, although the people were permitted to worship their own deities in their own temples, yet side by side with these were the Incan Temples of the Sun, dedicated to Inti or the Sun God who was regarded as the visual manifestation of the Supreme Being.

That such a diversity of races, many of whom were traditional enemies and the majority of whom had been subjugated by conquest, could have been welded into a union of industrious, law abiding, contented and intensely patriotic people is one of the most astonishing features of the amazing empire and speaks volumes for the organizing ability, the intelligence, and the power of the Incas.

The Incas or emperors were by no means supreme. In many respects the governmental system was republican and the Inca himself was really little more than a president possessing no more real power than does the Queen of England today. Somewhat corresponding to our president's cabinet were the four wise men or Aputus, presided over by the Apu-Tucuy-Ricac. These men were appointed by the Inca just as our president appoints his cabinet, and every law or decree issued by the Inca had to be passed unanimously by them. Once the Aputus had made their decision it could only be revoked or altered by the Tribunal of Princes or Apu-Auquis which correspond to our Supreme Court. In addition to the Federal government each district had its own governor or Curaca, and each town and village had its prefect or mayor known as a *Suyuyoc*, as well as a town council or board of aldermen composed of officials called *Auquis* who served as a court, jury and governing body combined. The provincial governors were appointed by the Inca but the mayors, and other local officials were elected by the people.

Next in importance to the Inca was the High Priest, yet unlike the Aztecs and Mayas the priesthood did not control the government. Church and State were entirely separate and priests were compelled to obey the laws like any other members of the community. Moreover, the budgets of the Church and State were also separate.

Although the Incas maintained a most luxurious and expensive court, yet they appear to have been paternally benign and rarely indeed took any advantages of their position or their immunity to oppress their subjects.

They were intensely religious and were hedged in by innumerable conventions and restrictions. Both the Inca and his queen were compelled to bathe and change costumes four times daily and never could wear the same garment twice, and in time of war the Inca was compelled to take personal command of his armies and to risk his life in the front ranks like any common soldier. Moreover, once every two years he was required to make a complete tour of his domain and to listen personally to all complaints or pleas of his people. Whatever the Incas faults may have been, slothfulness, lack of initiative, and incompetence were not among them. As executives they equalled if they did not excel any rulers the world has ever known, and the fact that for more than five hundred years they succeeded in maintaining their amazing government without any revolutions or other serious troubles or interruptions proves this.

Of course the universal belief that the Incas were semi-divine had a great deal to do with their success. Men might grumble or even revolt under the rule of a mere mortal, but it was a very different matter to protest against the rule of one who was the Son of the Sun and a human manifestation of the Sun god or supreme divinity. Just how much faith the Incas themselves had in their alleged descent from Inti the Sun god it is impossible to say. Very probably they actually believed themselves possessed with divine rights, just as some modern kings have claimed to be God-inspired. But regardless of the beliefs of the royal family as to their origin there is no question that the people as a whole regarded the Incas as offspring of the deity and revered them as much. So, in addition to the customary belief that a king can do no wrong, the people of the Empire of Tiahuantisuyo knew that a divinity could do no wrong and therefore considered themselves under divine rule, for even the Incas' subjects whose supreme deity was the immeasurably ancient Wira Kocha, regarded Inti the Sun god as a divinity.

In addition to its imperialistic and republican features, the Empire in many respects was thoroughly communistic. Practically all individuality and freedom of thought were completely subservient to the community as a whole. From birth until death the lives, actions, tasks, social status, marriages, dwelling places, divorces, and even the destinies of the offspring were planned, regulated, ordered and carried out by inexorable laws, rules, and decrees. Every man, woman and child of the millions were tagged, tabulated, and filed as efficiently as cards in a cabinet.

The locality a person lived in was indicated by the designs and colors of his or her garments, and even today each village has its distinctive type of wearing apparel. At birth a child's place in the scheme of things was ordained. Every child automatically became a ward of the government when it reached the age of five years, and was reared, trained and educated for the occupation, position or industry to which its life was to be devoted.

From five to ten years of age the boys' duties were educational; from ten to twenty they hunted, helped their elders and were generally useful. From twenty to twenty-five they were employed in public works, such as building roads and bridges, agricultural terraces and irrigation canals. Also at this period in their lives many became soldiers and were carefully and thoroughly trained at the government's military college, while those selected to become officials or teachers took a three years' course in the government's schools. Not until they were over thirty did the men work in the fields. From fifty to sixty, if still able-bodied, they cultivated the smaller vegetable gardens and those who lived to be over sixty became councillors or advisors to the local officials. Some, too, were trained as *Checollos* or bards, whose duty was to wander from place to place, singing the ages-old Incan songs, reciting poetry or repeating the innumerable proverbs.

So carefully and systematically was the economic status of the population watched and regulated that never was there a shortage or a surplus of labor, of skilled artizans, of husbandmen or soldiers in any portion of the immense empire with its population of millions.

Every community was planned in advance. Every village was restricted to a definite number of this, that or the other profession so as to maintain a perfect balance between supply and demand. If spinners were needed more girls were trained to spin and weave. If soldiers were required more boys were sent to the military schools. If a community needed additional agriculturalists the numbers required were taken from some area where there was an excess of farmers.

Every man was compelled to marry by the time he was twenty-four and every woman, aside from those destined to become nuns, was forced to find a husband by the time she was eighteen and at any time, if the officials decided it was for the good of the community or the state, or if the married parties did not have children or did not behave as they should, they could divorce them irrespective of the wishes of the interested parties.

On the other hand, men and women were permitted to carry on their own love-making, for even the Incas knew better than to attempt to regulate that matter or to make matches by law or rule, and neither did they go so far as to experiment with eugenic marriages. As long as a man had taken a wife by the time he was twenty-four, and as long as there were no old maids over eighteen years of age, the officials were satisfied that matters were as they should be.

When there happened to be men and women past the marriageable age the village prefect or *Cammachicue* lined up the youths and girls in the plaza and each male was forced then and there to choose a mate. In case a man desired some particular girl and another chap came first in line he had to accept the next best. Any surplus of single men or women were then sent to some community where there was a shortage of one sex or the other and the proceeding was repeated until all were mated.

Despite the facts that marriage was compulsory and divorce simple, there were most severe penalties provided for infidelity and other offenses. Adultery was punishable by death or torture or both, and brutality, immorality, etc., were severely dealt with and were grounds for divorce.

Regardless of whether a couple was married by compulsion or by choice the groom paid for her with presents and *chicha* and asked her parents' consent to the marriage. Following this was a period of eight days of "proof," a sort of trial marriage, within which time the groom could reject his bride if she failed to come up to expectations physically or in her ability to sew, weave, cook or perform the essential duties of an Incan housewife. As a result of this most excellent custom, girls who were ugly, ill tempered or deficient in wifely arts and industries were soon rejected, and as there was a penalty for remaining single they were forced to mend their ways and to acquire a knowledge of what they lacked, or take the consequences.

Widows were always in great demand and were much preferred to virgins because of their greater skill and experience. They were known as *Chukisonkos* or hearts of gold, and never remained widows for long, although the law did not compel them to marry a second time. However, widows never married widowers, though whether it was because the widows preferred men who had never been married or the widowers preferred unsophisticated maidens, or whether custom or law forbade the mating of widows and widowers, is not known.

Socially there were no distinctions among the people with the exception of the nobility and priesthood. Aside from these all were equal socially and economically. No one could be rich, no one poor in a land where money was unknown, where gold and precious stones had no intrinsic value and where every man, woman and child had precisely the same amount of property and all shared equally, all contributed equally to the support of the commonwealth, the Army, State and Church.

All habitable land was divided into three equal parts, one for the Sun or Church, another for the Government or Inca, and the other third for the people. The lands assigned to the Church provided the revenue to support the many temples and the multitudinous priests. The Inca's share supported the Court and Army and paid for all public works and the surplus provided the reserve supply which was carefully put aside for use in time of famine and to feed the Army in time of war.

The People's portion was divided among the inhabitants of the area but it was not owned by the individuals who were merely lessees and whose titles expired each year when new allotments were given, these being increased or decreased in size according to the economic need of the inhabitants. All lands were cultivated by the people, those allotted to the Church being attended to first, then came the lands of the aged, the sick, the soldiers in active service and the widows and orphans. Not until these had been cultivated were the people permitted to work their own lands, and finally all joined and with elaborate ceremonies cultivated the lands of the Inca.

Very often the area alloted to the Inca was the poorest land, for the ruler argued that he could best afford to reap small returns as he had land everywhere and all members of the commonwealth cultivated them.

Everything actually belonged to the Inca, and the mines were worked solely for his benefit. Also, at the time of shearing, the llama and alpaca wool was all placed together in government storehouses and by officials chosen for the purpose, was apportioned to the women of each family. Cotton was divided in a similar manner, although in some areas where cotton was the principal crop, the farmers were permitted to keep and use the cotton they raised. In addition to all this each community was required to pay the government a certain amount of the commodities it produced, the quantity being regulated in proportion to the amount grown or manufactured, but no other taxes were imposed.

For bravery in battle and for extraordinary services the Inca sometimes awarded areas of land. But severe penalties were provided for any official taking advantage of this and there are records of governors of provinces having been put to death for having taken land that rightfully belonged to the people and bestowing it upon higher officials in order to gain favor. Under such conditions political graft did not flourish in ancient Peru.

In addition to the shares of everything produced by the people within the true boundaries of the Empire, there were enormous tributes demanded and collected annually from conquered tribes and races who acknowledged Incan dominion yet did not form integral parts of the commonwealth. All of this tribute, which consisted almost entirely of gold, silver, and precious stones, went to the State and the Church. Adding to all this enormous amount of riches there were innumerable mines which were worked, aside from the gold taken from streams by individuals. As none of the gems or precious metals were exported, as they were imperishable and as only a minute fraction of the whole was buried with the dead, they accumulated through countless centuries until at the time of the Conquest there was more gold in Peru than in all the rest of the known world.

Although Mancio Sierra, writing from Cuzco on September 15, 1589, stated that at the time of the conquest the Spaniards never found a liar, a thief, or a sluggard in the entire Empire, yet there were many laws and heavy penalties for the prevention of any sort of crime, offence or misdemeanor, and even laziness or failure to work was punishable. Judged by our present days standards the penalties for breaking the laws seem far out of proportion to the seriousness of the offences, but by comparison with the laws of Europe in force at that time those of the Incas were just and the punishments mild. The most serious of all crimes was blasphemy directed at the Sun, the priests, or the Inca. Death after the most terrible tortures was the penalty which, fortunately for the people, was practically unknown. On the other hand and to prove there was no discrimination, even more severe penalties were provided as punishments for religious persons who misbehaved. A Virgin of the Sun or any nun who violated her vows was to be buried alive and her home town completely destroyed together with all of her relatives. Any priest who failed in his duties, who was guilty of extortion or who took advantage of his position to impose upon the people was to be put to death by torture and his body burned. This to the Incans was the most terrible of all penalties for they believed in a resurrection and that destruction of the body destroyed the soul also.

Death was the penalty for murder or adultery and for incorrigibles or habitual offenders, as well as for cowardice on the part of soldiers, officials and members of the nobility, all of whom were supposed to be above fear of anything. Theft or any form of dishonesty resulted in the offender being branded for life. Liars and scandal-mongers were flogged for the first offence, beaten with a club for the second and for the third offence had their tongues nailed to a board. Although most petty crimes were punishable by flogging, in some cases the culprit was forced to carry a heavy stone wherever he went during the time imposed by the law.

To enforce all these laws a well trained and efficient police force was maintained but the members of the force must have led a very easy life, for, as reported by Mancio Sierra, offences of any kind were practically unknown anywhere.

Next to the Inca and his Court the priests and their satellites were the most exalted and important members of the nation. Above all others was the High Priest or *Villca humu* who was in charge of the Temple of the Sun in Cuzco and presided over a supreme council of nine priests or *Hatun villca*. Each of these was in charge of some designated area and of the numbers of lower priests or *Yana villca* who served the various temples of the area. The members of the priesthood were of both noble and common birth and most of the members were elected to their positions, the electoral college consisting of priests and representatives of the Inca. Although the Inca could not appoint the high priest he usually managed to have a close relative—often a brother—elected to the position. Finally there was the soothsayer or prophet, usually a very old man who had served as high priest. Below the group of priests I have mentioned were the *Huatacs* or confessors and below them the *Humu* or *Nacac* who were lay brothers and did the menial work.

There were also orders of monks and nuns, the latter being divided into four classes or groups. First, the *Yurac aclla* who were dedicated to Inti the Sun God. These could never marry and were celibates. Next the *Vayru aclla* who could not marry but were concubines or spiritual brides of the Inca. The third group was the *Paco aclla* who could be bestowed by the Inca as wives to the *Curacas* or governors and other officials.

Finally there were the *Yana accla* who could be given as brides to the commoners as rewards for special services. The girls of the first three groups were daughters of the nobility while those of the *Yana accla* were of humble origin. In addition to their religious duties all of these nuns were engaged in weaving the finest textiles to be worn by the Inca and his Queen and in making and decorating the royal garments. There were also girls who were daughters of royal families who were reared and trained in convents but took no vows and could leave and marry at any time.

Aside from the priests and Virgins of the Sun stationed at Cuzco every temple of any importance throughout the entire empire had its local high priest, its lesser priests and lay brothers, and its nuns, and in each of these temples every detail of the worship, each ceremonial, and every chant and prayer was carried out exactly as in the great temple of the Sun at Cuzco.

One might think that in a land where there was no currency, where precious metals had no intrinsic value and where supply and demand were always balanced by law, that there could be no business, no buying and selling, no commerce. But the Incas had foreseen this condition and had duly provided for it. Aside from the agricultural products, the industries of each village were established by law and no other trades or occupations could legally be carried on. One village might be devoted to carding and dying wool, another to weaving. One hamlet might produce *ponchos,* another textiles for garments, and so on. As a result, every community was forced to trade with others in order to obtain all the articles required for maintenance and existence. Obviously, it would be most inconvenient for a man or woman to travel the rounds of half a hundred villages, situated miles apart, in order to secure what he or she required in exchange for the articles their own village produced. So the Incan government arranged for central markets in various areas, where at intervals the people for miles in every direction could meet and barter and trade and intermingle and converse. The result was an enormous national commerce and a commingling of the various tribes and communities, in addition to a holiday or *fiesta* for the people. So satisfactory was this custom or rule that it still prevails today even though the present day Indians know and use money. However, fully ninety per cent of the business carried on at these markets is by barter. So fixed and ingrained has the ancient rule become that it is not at all unusual to find the people of two or more villages a few miles apart journeying fifty miles or more to a market-town and bartering their goods with one another, to return, often side by side, to their homes, but never dreaming of strolling from one village to another to exchange their wares.

Of all these ancient central markets that at Huancayo is the most important and largest. Nowhere else in all Peru can the Indians be seen so easily and in such numbers as at Huancayo on market day. There is nothing like it elsewhere in the world and it is the great weekly event in the dull lives of the inhabitants, for as in Incan days the Sunday market is as much a grand *fiesta* as a matter of business, and from many miles about, often from villages fifty miles distant, they flock to Huancayo.

At dawn on Sunday they begin to arrive, dressed in their best, their *ponchos, mantas* and the women's skirts and blouses ablaze with color. Bending under huge bundles on their backs the women trudge along; tiny children carry loads heavier than themselves; shouting and laughing the men urge on their laden llamas and burros and all are happy and keep up a babel of conversation in the Quechua tongue.

No matter how great a load a woman may carry there is always space for a wide-eyed baby. In fact without a load upon her back a Quechua woman feels uncomfortable and at a loss. Often if there is no burden and no infant to be carried, a woman will pick up a stone or a billet of wood, and slinging this on her back will glide off with a satisfied expression, feeling far more at ease and more properly equipped than without the superfluous load. And they never cease spinning. No matter what she may be doing, unless her hands are otherwise engaged, whether walking or seated or standing and gossiping, every woman will ceaselessly twirl her spindle as her deft fingers feed the carded wool or cotton to form thread that often is as fine as the finest silk thread made by machinery.

By eight o'clock the market place and all the surrounding streets will be packed with the Indians. They are there by thousands, natives of scores of villages, people of dozens of tribes, and the members of each still retaining the distinctive costumes decreed under the ancient Incan laws. No words can describe, no painting could do justice to the kaleidoscopic, ever changing, dazzling yet harmonious color of the scene. And everywhere, spread upon blankets and *ponchos,* in great baskets or in piles, are the myriad products of the people. Every art and industry is represented. There are *ponchos* and blankets, rugs and garments, hats and caps, beautifully woven textiles and ornately decorated arm coverings, sandals and silver ware, wooden ware and leather goods, pottery of every size, form and color, skins of jaguar, llama, alpaca, vicuña, puma and bear; great masses of fluffy carded and dyed wool of sheep, llama and alpaca; baskets and wonderfully carved and colored *tortumas* or calabashes; whips and dance masks, charms and amulets, and an endless assortment of fruits, vegetables, grain and dried meat —a cross section of the native products and industries of central Peru, the whole forming a scene as filled with life, gaiety and color as in those far off days when the Inca sat on his golden throne in Cuzco.

CHAPTER 21

Round and About the Incan Capital

Nowhere in all the world was there another city like Cuzco, the Incan capital. The architecture of its impressive, severely beautiful palaces and public buildings was unique and it was the richest city on earth at the time of the Spanish Conquest, a city where gold had no value, where the precious metal was even used as cornices and sheathing on the temple and adorned the portals of palaces.

The city was laid out in the symbolic form of a condor, the fortress of Sacsayhuaman forming the head, the Rodadero and Andenes representing the neck, while the body was the city proper with the Kori-Pata for the tail and the surrounding hills simulating the spread wings. Enclosing the city was an enormous wall of pre-Incan work constructed of huge beautifully cut and fitted stones, some weighing as much as thirty tons each. On every hand were magnificent residences, palaces, temples, and government buildings with numerous *pampas* or plazas shaded with trees and with beds of flowers. The streets, although narrow, were at nearly right angles dividing the city into more or less regular rectangular blocks. To insure a never-failing water supply a mountain stream flowed through a masonry canal with stone-flagged bridges spanning it at each street. Between the larger buildings and away from the great central plaza or Kusi Pampa, were thousands of the humble homes of the two hundred thousand inhabitants of the city.

On the Street of Ahuacpita was a great factory wherein hundreds of expert women wove every type of cloth, rugs, *ponchos,* blankets and garments for the use of the officials of the Incan army. Near here was the finest of all the magnificent palaces, the Aclla-Huassi

with its facade adorned with golden plates and with a golden lintel
to its doorway flanked by ornate columns of solid gold. Almost as
splendid was the palace of the Inca Roca with its elaborate frescoes,
its numerous windows and its doorway at one of the angles of the
walls and with gracefully fluted columns of polished jasper at either
side of the heavy door of embossed silver inlaid with semiprecious
stones.

Largest of all was the huge palace of the first Inca, Manko-Kapak,
surrounded by its wall built of marvelously fitted stone blocks,
while close to it was the palace of the Inca Sinchi-Roka rising above
its retaining wall of enormous stones. At the end of the broad
avenue of Kora-Kora were the royal baths of Tiksi-Kocha and on
the same smoothly paved avenue was the strange house of twelve
corners built by the Inca Pachak-Kutik, with the vast palace of the
Yupanki-Inca a few blocks away.

For centuries each of the Incas had erected his own palace, and
surpassing all others in its massive, imposing, severe architecture
and simplicity of design, was the palace of the Inca Wira-Kocha.
Finally, in the great central plaza, was the Collque-Macha-Huay, a
beautifully sculptured female figure from whose breasts flowed
streams of sparkling water which, on festival days, was replaced by
streams of *chicha* which the people could drink to their hearts' content. But the true wonder of the Incas' capital was the Temple of
the Sun or Korikancha.

Architecturally the Temple of the Sun is one of the most remarkable structures in the entire world. It is built of immense blocks of
amazingly fitted stone, no two exactly alike in size or shape, but so
accurately designed and cut that the circular interior with its radial
flooring is geometrically and mathematically perfect. No modern
engineer equipped with the latest, most delicate instruments and
the most up-to-date appliances and mathematical tables, could excel
the work of the long-vanished, long-forgotten designers and artisans
who constructed this ancient temple.

In the temple garden were trees, plants and shrubs of silver and
gold. Among the leaves and branches of precious metals there were
birds, animals and insects of gold with jewelled eyes and wings.
Even the fountains, the tools and implements of the gardeners' trade
were of the same metals and at the verge of the golden basins of
the fountains were lifelike crocodiles of gold.

The interior of the temple would have made Aladdin's cave look tawdry by comparison. The Fray Alonzo Martinez, who was a priest sent by Pizarro to verify Atahualpa's statements, wrote the following vivid if somewhat quaint account of the interior of the temple as it was before the arrival of Pizarro:

"Above the great altar was an image of Inti in the form of an enormous disk of gold with a human face cut upon it. About the edges projected rays of the same metal, each tipped with silver stars in which were splendid jewels. To the right of this image of the sun was that of his woman, the sacred moon or Mama-Quilla, figured with the face of a woman cut upon a plate of heavy silver and whose crown ended in a series of stars of gold. In a side nave, close to the image of the moon, were seen great idols cut from blocks of stone and crowned with plates of copper gilded and tinted in many colors to represent the Huaya-Cauri or rainbow that these pagans hold sacred. In small places like ovens were sacred vessels, some of clay and others of silver and gold, showing upon them the conquests, the laws, the pagan religion, the mythology and the history of these people. To one side and the other of the principal portal of the temple, where they faced the image of the sun, were twelve Chuquihuancos of gold, which were life-sized statues of the Incas who had gone before, and at the feet of each of these and beside it was the respective mummy of every emperor who had died.

"Facing the place of the statue of Manko-Kapak was the twelfth door of the temple that gave entrance to the sacred garden of Will-camuya. The walls of the temple were overlaid with sheets of gold within and without and the ceiling was studded with stars of gold and gems.

"The cornices of the twelve doors and of the windows were of gold, and on the outer part of the temple was a band of gold a yard in width that embraced all the temple. The cornices of the doors of Venus and the moon were of silver and those of the ten other doors were of gold, and the mummies of the dead Incas were seated upon stone thrones or chairs called Tiyanas that were encrusted with gold plates."

At the time Pizarro and his men reached Cuzco much of the great treasures described by Fray Martinez had been stripped from the temple. The twelve golden statues of the Incas, together with many of the gold, silver and jewelled vessels and ornaments, as well as most of the objects from the marvelous temple garden were included in the treasures hidden in the mountains when, on their way to Cajamarca the carriers had word of Atahualpa's fate and concealed their precious burdens. Also, the great golden sun disk and some other objects had been removed and hidden, although many years later the golden disk was found buried in the Wilca Pampa and was sent to Spain by the Viceroy, only to be forever lost when the galleon carrying it went to the bottom of the sea at Silver Shoals north of Hispaniola.

Of all the great Incan cities destroyed by Pizarro and his men, Cuzco alone still exists as an inhabited city, with many of its buildings, its walls and streets much as they were when Pizarro first saw it.

Partly this is due to the fact that the Spaniards found it next to impossible to raze the palaces and temples or to destroy the walls of cyclopean stonework. But largely the city was preserved because the Spaniards planned to occupy and use it as their own capital. As a result, the remnants of Cuzco's former glory dwarf and make insignificant the conquerors' edifices about them. Even the Temple of the Sun still remains although greatly altered to be sure, for upon its foundations the Spanish priests built their church of Santo Domingo, yet the perfection of its masonry, its mathematically exact curves and radial lines may still be seen and in places one may yet find traces of the groove from which the massive golden belt was stripped.

Also, despite the efforts of the Spaniards to destroy, despite the great conflagration that swept the city during the Inca Manco's rebellion, a number of the great palaces and most of the massive walls still remain. It is beyond question the most historic spot in all Peru and is redolent of romance—the romance of a lost civilization, a mighty, peaceful and happy people ruthlessly betrayed, robbed, murdered, enslaved and almost annihilated solely to satisfy the fanatical priests and for the treasures they possessed and which, to them, had no intrinsic value.

Of all the spots in and about Cuzco none hold greater and more historic and romantic associations than the mighty fortress of Sacsayhuaman (Nest of the Eagle) that still frowns down upon the city from its lofty mountain top.

Upon the summit of the walls of that immeasurably ancient fort

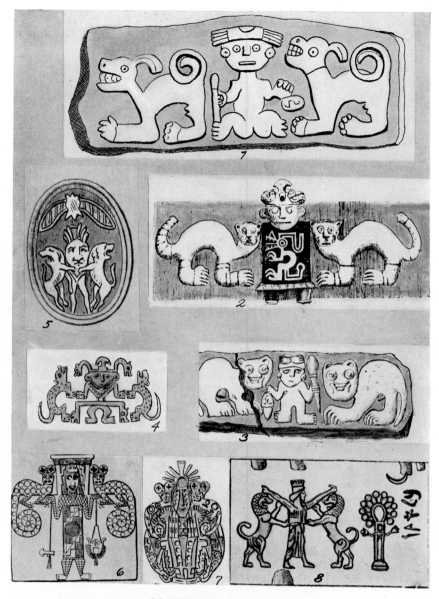

PLATE XVII (Chapter 15)

1 Incised stone lintel with "Mishi" the "Keeper of the Cats." Huaylas, Peru.
2 Pottery decoration of "Mishi" from Carhuaz, Peru.
3 Stone lintel with Mishi. Aija, Peru.
4 Decoration on pottery. Huarmay, Peru.
5 Medallion of "Ishi" from Sardinia.
6 "Keeper of the Cats" on copper plate. Northwestern Argentine.
7 The double Lion God on copper plaque. South America.
8 Stone carving of "Ishi" the double Lion God, from Syria.

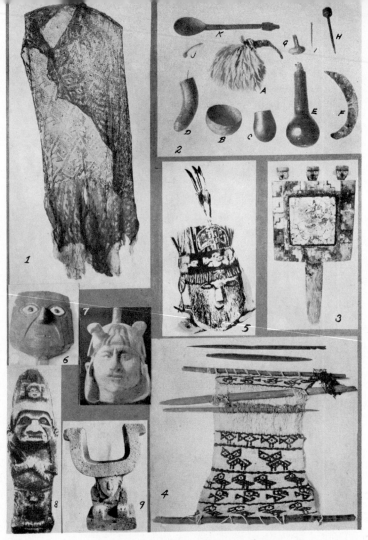

PLATE XVIII (Chapter 17)

1 Lace dress from mummy of Peruvian girl of over 2000 years ago.
  From grave at Lambayeque, Peru.
2 Contents of the girl's "vanity bag": A—Powder puff of feathers. B—
  Powder container of gourd. C—Gourd container for mascara. D—
  Gourd with lip paint. E—Container with nail polish. F—Bronze
  knife. G—Bronze tweezers. H—Hardwood nail-cuticle stick. I—Bronze
  needle. J—Bronze pin. K—Silver spoon.
3 Mirror of polished marcasite in mosaic-covered wooden frame from
  mummy-bundle of the ancient Peruvian girl's grave.
4 Unfinished textile on hand loom. From girl's grave.
5 Mummy mask of royal Incan. Gold ear-coverings, gold rainbow symbol
  on crown, gold sun symbol over the "borla" or fringe on forehead.
6 Mummy mask with mother-of-pearl and emerald eyes, Lambayeque.
7 Pottery portrait head. Lambayeque, Peru.
8 Stone carving of the Chibchas, Colombia.
9 Stone chair. Manabi culture, Ecuador.

PLATE XIX (Chapter 17)

1 Mummy-bundle from Parakas, Peru, before unwrapping.
2 Parakas mummy partly unwrapped showing rich robes, gold scepter and ornaments, etc.
3 Parakas mummy completely unwrapped seated in basket.
4 Portion of tapestry robe from a Parakas mummy.
5 Section of Nasca tomb with mummy-bundles and pottery.
6 Mummy-bundle from Nasca with outer wrappings removed.
7-8 Pottery from Nasca graves.
9 Incan "Quipo" of knotted strings.
10 Odd instrument used by Pacific islanders for navigating.
11 Gigantic astronomical device on desert near Nasca, Peru.

PLATE XX (Chapter 18)

1 Gateway of the Sun. Tiahuanaco, Bolivia.
2 Ruins of the Tunca-Puncu (Place of Ten Doors). Tiahuanaco.
3 Huge monolithic idol and portion of stone columns of Temple. Tiahuanaco.
4 Stone columns enclosing the Kalasasaya or Temple. Tiahuanaco.
5 Monolithic idol shown in Fig. 3.
6 Small stone idol from Tiahuanaco.
7 Sculptured figures on Gateway of the Sun at Tiahuanaco.
8 Gateway and stairs leading to the Kalasasaya or Temple at Tiahuanaco.

PLATE XXI (Chapter 19)

1 Hand loom with partly finished textile and weaving implements.
2 Textile belts from graves at Pachakamak, Peru.
3 Textiles from graves at Pachakamak.
4 Ancient textile from Temple of the Sun, Island of the Sun, Lake Titicaca.
(Museum of American Indian, N.Y.)
5-6 Lace from the wrappings of a girl's mummy. Lambayeque, Peru.

PLATE XXII (Chapter 22)

1 Pre-Incan wall partly covered with late Incan masonry. Cuzco, Peru.
2 Cyclopean stone work at Malta. Note similarity to pre-Incan work.
3 The "Lion Gate" at Mycene, Greece. Note resemblance to pre-Incan work.
4 Giant stones in walls of Sacsahuaman Fortress (Eagles' Nest) near Cuzco, Peru.
5 The "Citadel" at Sacsahuaman Fortress.
6 Corner of a cyclopean wall at Cuzco, Peru.
7 A portion of the principal temple at Machu Picchu.
8 Method of locking stones together at Ollantay.
9 Method of locking giant stones together by staples. Tiahuanaco, Bolivia.
10 Stones locked together by staples at Palace of Nimrod, Assyria.
11 A stone lion from Tiahuanaco.
12 Stone lion from the valley of Mexico.

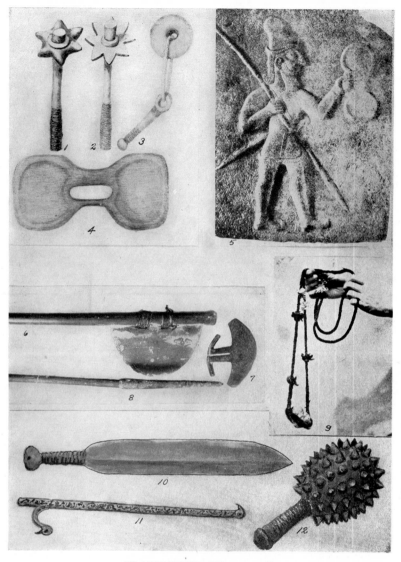

PLATE XXIII (Chapter 23)

1 Stone-headed star-shaped mace. Peru.
2 Mace with bronze head. Peru.
3 Mace with free-swinging head. Peru.
4 Wooden shield. Peru.
5 Stone bas-relief from Syria showing warrior with shield identical with those from Peruvian graves.
6 Battle axe with bronze head. Lambayeque, Peru.
7 Bronze battle axe. Pachakamak, Peru.
8 Bronze-headed spear. Lambayeque, Peru.
9 Biblical type of sling used by ancient (as well as modern) Indians of Peru.
10 Sword-like club of hard wood. Lambayeque, Peru.
11 Atlatl or spear-throwing stick. Chan-Chan, Peru.
12 War club of hard wood studded with bronze. Chancay, Peru.

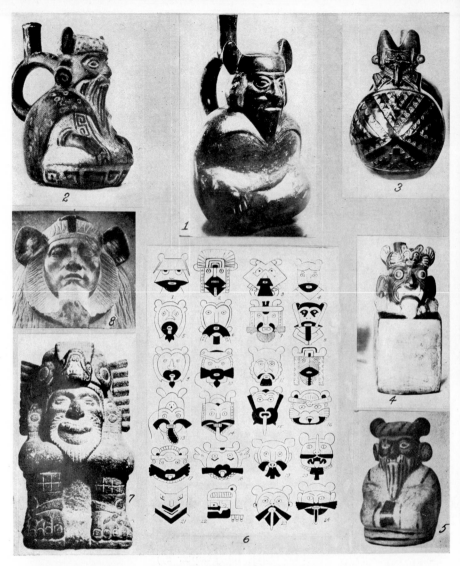

PLATE XXIV (Chapter 26)

1 Black pottery portrait jar of Wira Kocha, the bearded god. Chan-Chan, Peru.
2 Buff and red pottery portrait jar of Wira Kocha. Chan-Chan.
3 Double jar of black pottery with head of Wira Kocha. Chan-Chan.
4 Red and yellow jar with head of bearded god. Piura Valley, Peru.
5 Jar with portrait of Wira Kocha. Piura Valley.
6 Conventionalized forms of the bearded god from pottery from various areas in Peru.
7 Stone figure of Quetzalcoatl (the plumed serpent god). Mexico.
8 Stone figure of a deity from Egypt showing the lion's ears headdress, the rainbow symbol, etc., as shown on Wira-Kocha jars.

whose titanic stones were hewn, fitted and erected countless centuries before Columbus set sail from Palos, centuries before the birth of Christ, I stood late one afternoon awaiting the sunset. The spot whereon I stood was the apex of a single cut stone, a monolith of flint-hard andesite over twenty feet in height and weighing, perhaps, two hundred tons, yet but one of hundreds that, fitted together without mortar or cement, formed a sheer smooth wall with scarcely a visible crevice between the stones.

All was silent, deserted. I might well have been the only living man on earth, the last human being, standing on the prehistoric fort that crowned the lofty mountain top.

But I had only to glance down at the valley below in order to see Cuzco with its teeming human ants, its scurrying beetle-like automobiles and a toy-like locomotive laboriously puffing as it drew its train of passenger cars from the station.

What, I wondered, would the Incan warriors, who once garrisoned the fort, have thought had they looked upon the Incan capital as it is today? What, for that matter, would the conquering Spaniards have thought of the city they had laid waste could they have seen Cuzco as it appeared four centuries later?

How many times Incans, pre-Incans and Spaniards must have stood there in the waning light of dying day and gazed across the fair green valleys, the hillsides with their terraced gardens, the tumbled snow-topped Andean ranges and the capital city of the Incas.

Upon the very spot where I stood Incan warriors had battled furiously for lives and freedom, for their Inca and their homes. Perhaps upon the stone beneath my feet that gallant Incan general, last survivor of the garrison, had defied the Spaniards single-handed until at last knowing the cause hopeless, he had thrown aside his weapon and with a prayer to Inti and a shout of defiance had leaped from the parapet to find freedom and peace in death upon the rocks below the precipice. I could picture him in my mind, a heroic figure in the blue and white uniform of the imperial guards, his golden casque with scarlet plume upon his head, swinging his long-handled battle axe, slicing Spaniards' heads from their shoulders, heedless of cross-bow bolts or musket balls and arrows, until even the Dons drew back and cheered his heroism and his valor.

And I could visualize him as when, for a moment, his foes ceased their onslaught, he looked westward at the setting sun and breathing a prayer to his god, he tossed his blood-smeared axe into the abyss and leaped after it.

I glanced down and shuddered at the thought of hurtling through space to the jagged rocks hundreds of feet below. Yet his death had been easier and more merciful than those of his fellows and his Inca who were tortured, burned at the stake and garrotted merely because they fought for their homeland and freedom and refused to disavow their own benign gods and accept the faith of their inhuman conquerors.

Now, Cuzco, the City of the Sun, that once contained a greater wealth of gold and gems than all of Europe, gleamed softly golden in the rays of the sinking sun. Although it no longer was the capital of the Incas, although many great changes had taken place during the four hundred years and more that had passed since the last Inca sat upon his golden jewel-encrusted throne, yet in the glow of the fading day I still could trace many of the landmarks that had been so familiar to the warriors who once had paced the walls of the Eagle's Nest and had looked proudly and longingly down upon their capital.

There, massive and square, was the palace of the Inca Roca. I could trace the broad avenue of Ahuac-Pita leading to the circular Kori-Kancha, the Temple of the Sun, now transformed into the Santo Domingo church, near the railway station. There, also, was the bulky mass of the palace of Maita Kapak-Inca wherein Gonzalo Pizarro dwelt. There was the palace of Ipa Huako that once had housed the famous yet infamous Francisco Pizarro, and was now occupied by the Prefect of Cuzco. Half-hidden in the lengthening purple shadows cast by more modern structures, was the once magnificent residence of Manko-Kapak, the first Inca. With my eyes I followed the Calle de Triunfo, known to the Incans as Kora Kora, to that strange polygonal structure, the House of the Twelve Corners. But all were overshadowed by the giant cathedral, the Jesuit College and the Christian churches, just as the ancient faith of Cuzco's builders had been overshadowed by their conquerors' faith, and all built from the remains of razed palaces and temples. The sound of their jangling, discordant bells reached my ears even on Sacsayhuaman's heights, as they called men to bow their heads to the Angelus, to worship in temples dedicated to a God of peace and love and goodwill toward all on earth, yet founded on blood, torture, wanton cruelty, and destruction.

Swiftly the shadows spread across the city like a veil of mourning for the sins committed there, and all about me the mountains and the fortress walls gleamed like gold in the sun's last rays. No wonder the Incans worshiped and adored the fiery source of all light and heat. Standing there as he dropped lower and lower toward the Andean peaks, and as the turquoise sky turned to rose and crimson and the golden glow suffused all the visible world, I felt awed and reverent and to my mind came the words of the ancient Incan Chant to the Setting Sun:

> Now wearied with his journey through the sky
> Inti, the Sun god, glorious to see—
> Hastes to his couch beyond the ocean's rim
> And robed in gold and red sinks down to rest.
>
> Above him in the vast arch of the sky
> His banners flaunt their folds of gorgeous hues
> Waving farewell to him who rules the world.
> Then swiftly darkness wraps the tired earth
> Within the soft cool mantle of the night.
>
> Inti's eyes close, and now the Sun god sleeps,
> The mountains are but shadows—spectral things,
> The pampas, seas of blackness; night has come,
> The day has ended and the whole world rests.

As the afterglow faded from the sky I picked my way carefully across the rock-strewn mountain top to where a battered Ford awaited me. How had the mighty fallen! The Quechua chauffeur, descendant of Incans, was sprawled across the torn and patched seat, his eyes closed, his mouth open and snoring lustily. Ghosts of long-dead warriors, of Spanish adventurers; the glory of the Andean sunset, the Sun god of his forefathers meant nothing to him.

Sleepily he yawned, rubbed his eyes and reluctantly climbed from his extemporized couch and cranked his ancient ramshackle car. Then as the venerable "Model T" shook and rattled to the racing motor, and he climbed back to his seat, he turned to me with a grin.

"Does the Señor wish to visit a cabaret?" he enquired. "We of

Cuzco are up to date. We have a most excellent cabaret, with the *musica* of the jazz and the Señoritas dancing *muy desnudo*. Does the Señor wish—"

My "No!" and my look silenced him. Ye gods! To visit Cuzco, the City of the Sun, the one time capital of the Incan empire, and spend one's time in a cabaret!

With a sigh of deep disappointment, the degenerate Child of the Sun gave his attention to the gears and shook his head deprecatingly. To him the ways of the Gringos were past all understanding, for who could be crazy enough to wander about, staring at old buildings, poking amid ruins, gazing at stone walls when one might sit in a brightly lit cabaret and drink beer and listen to a jazz band and see painted, bespangled Señoritas dancing *muy desnudo*?

CHAPTER 22

Unsolved Mysteries

The most striking and remarkable features of Cuzco and other ancient Peruvian Andean cities are the stupendous, amazing walls constructed of most perfectly cut stones put together without mortar or cement, yet so accurately fitted that even today a thin one hundredth of an inch blade cannot be inserted between them. No two blocks of stone are alike, either in shape or size. Some weigh only a few pounds while others weigh more than twenty tons. Some are rectangular, others hexagonal, and some have as many as twenty-four or even thirty-two angles, and the edges of every stone are smoothly, evenly, sharply beveled or chamfered. No expert modern stone mason working with the best steel tools and the most highly perfected stone-cutting machines could produce anything more accurate. Anyone at all familiar with stone working can see that each and every block must have been mathematically planned and laid out beforehand, for it manifestly would have been impossible to lift the immense blocks in and out and gradually trim them to a fit.

Moreover, in many cases the stones are cut in such shapes that they could not have been laid in position but must have been pushed into place between the adjoining stones.

The only way in which stones could have been fitted with such incredible accuracy was by cutting each block to extremely fine measurements or by using a template, a process that would indicate that the people who built the walls had a most thorough and most advanced knowledge of engineering and the higher mathematics.

Evidently, also, the cutting of these stones and the building of the walls was neither very difficult nor slow work, for they are everywhere in and about Cuzco and throughout the surrounding territory, and very often where a roughly, hastily built wall of cobbles or rubble would have served just as well.

In nearly every case the walls are thicker at the base than at the top so that the surfaces slope slightly inward, and very rarely do they show any carvings, sculptures or ornamental work, although here and there some of the stones, usually in pairs, have small conical projections upon them. In addition to the walls, nearly all of the larger buildings and palaces of pre-Spanish days are built in the same way and so enduring and strong are the structures that they have remained intact through flood and the great fire, while the Spaniards, despite their utmost efforts to tear them down, found it such a next to impossible task that they made the best of it by erecting their own buildings within or upon the ancient walls. For this reason some of the finest examples of this Cyclopean masonry, as it is called, have been found concealed beneath cheap masonry and stucco.

Marvelous as are these structures in and about Cuzco, they pale into significance beside the Fortress of Sacsayhuaman. Upon a mountain top artificially leveled and terraced is the mighty fortification covering several hundred acres. It is built in a series of zigzag walls with passages between, with salients at the angles and a large circular inner structure, and is as well designed and laid out as any fortress built by our modern army engineers. But to see it one would feel that it must have been made by giants. Everywhere are enormous blocks of stone weighing fifty, one hundred or even two hundred tons with many that weigh more than three hundred tons, each and every one as accurately and smoothly cut and surfaced and as perfectly fitted as are the smaller blocks forming the walls and buildings in Cuzco.

How were such titanic blocks of stone brought to the top of the mountain from the quarries many miles away? How were they cut and fitted? How were they raised and put in place? No one knows, no one can even guess. There are archaeologists, scientists, who would have us believe that the dense, hard andesite rock was cut, surfaced and faced by means of stone or bronze tools. Such an explanation is so utterly preposterous that it is not even worthy of serious consideration. No one ever has found anywhere any stone tool or implement that would cut or chip the andesite, and no bronze ever made will make any impression upon it. Moreover, even were there stone hammers and picks capable of cutting the rock it would have required lifetimes, centuries, to have hewn a three hundred ton or even a fifty ton block of the stone into anything even approaching the monoliths that are there by thousands. Furthermore, every engineer, every stone mason who has examined the Cuzco stone work has declared that it would have been utterly impossible to have cut, fitted and chamfered them without using a chisel and a maul; that only by striking a chisel a sharp blow could the stones have been cut. But no one has ever found a stone chisel capable of cutting the dense hard rock. A stone chisel, even if of a material harder than the rock, would be shattered and broken when struck. Even had the ancient Peruvians possessed tools of tempered steel it would have required a vast army of expert stone masons many lifetimes to have cut and fitted the tens of thousands of the blocks that are in Cuzco, alone, not to mention the thousands upon thousands of others at Ollantay, Viracocha, and elsewhere.

As to slowly, laboriously chipping at the rocks with crude stone hammers I defy any man or men, laborers or scientists, white, black or brown, using stone or bronze tools, to visibly or measurably cut the surface of one of the blocks forming these structures. I know whereof I speak, for when excavating the ruins of the Coclé culture in Panama, I tried out the possibility of cutting rock with rock. There the many monoliths, often elaborately carved and sculptured, were of diorite, a rather soft rock compared to andesite. Selecting a section of a broken column I drew a rough scroll upon it with a piece of chalk, selected five of my Indian laborers, and giving them a peck or more of stone hammers and other implements we had found, told them to go ahead at sculpturing the design I had drawn. For ten days they labored industriously from morning until night and although they broke or wore away every implement they made no noticeable impression upon the column.

If the archaeologists who so off-handedly declare that the stone blocks of Cuzcan walls and buildings were fashioned by means of crude stone tools why don't they prove the truth of their words by showing us how?

Also some of them declare that these Cyclopean structures are all "Incan," that none are over a few centuries old, and that there were no such people as the pre-Incans whose works were immeasurably ancient before Manko-Kapak, the first Inca, reached Cuzco. Tommy rot! Even at the time of the conquest the Incan people had no slightest knowledge of when or by whom the Cyclopean structures were built.

All of the old chroniclers agreed on this, and even the Prince Checko, who was nearly eighty years of age and had become a Christian and was more familiar with his people and knew more of their history and traditions and customs more intimately and more accurately than any Spaniard, stated to the Viceroy Toledo that the Cyclopean walls had "always" been there; that his people did not even have a tradition as to who built them, and that they had always believed them to be the work of gods or made by magic.

Actually there is no evidence to support the claim that these structures and other remarkable feats of engineering were the works of the Incans and that there was no pre-Incan Andean civilization.

On the contrary, all the evidence indicates a culture or a civilization long outdating the Incan culture and far surpassing it in many respects. There are no transitional remains showing that the one merged into the other and it would seem illogical and ridiculous to think that there should have been a decadence in the arts and the engineering accomplishments of a race that, in political organization, agriculture, metallurgy and many other attainments had advanced rather than retrograded. Nowhere do we find walls or other structures built of stones that are intermediate between the titanic, accurately fitted blocks of pre-Incan origin and the stonework typical of the Incans. In many places, it is true, even in and about Cuzco, there are Cyclopean type walls and buildings composed of both the polygonal blocks of stone and the Incan type of rectangular small stones laid like bricks in regular tiers. But in every case it is obvious that the latter were placed in position long after the Cyclopean structures were built. At times they were used to fill or repair gaps or openings in the more ancient walls, in many cases they formed the upper portions of palaces or other buildings superimposed upon the pre-Incan walls or foundations, and in a great many instances they were used in adding to or extending the older walls. Some of the best examples of these combinations are to be seen at Ollantay and Vira Kocha. At Ollantay the ancient engineers accomplished feats that in some respects were greater than those performed at Cuzco. Many of the enormous, accurately fitted many-angled blocks of pink granite, measuring as much as twelve to eighteen feet by six to eight feet square, and weighing fifty to one hundred tons were not only raised to the upper tiers of the walls but were carried up a steep mountain side and were transported for many miles from the quarries and across two large rivers. But throughout the ruined fortress-city are walls, additions and patchwork of the Incan type made of local rock entirely different from the beautifully polished pink granite Cyclopean work.

Another, and perhaps best of all examples of the Incan stonework in combination with the earlier type, is the amazing stronghold and city of Machu Picchu. Here, everywhere, are innumerable combinations of the two distinct types of architecture and buildings, yet search as I might amid the ruins I failed to find a single structure or a single stone that was of an intermediate type; all were distinctly and typically either Incan or pre-Incan just as they are in Cuzco and elsewhere.

The character, forms and types of pottery and other artifacts of the pre-Incan and Incan cultures are as distinctive as the stone work. Anyone at all familiar with ancient Peruvian ceramics can tell at a glance whether an earthenware vessel is of Incan or pre-Incan origin.

Under these circumstances, with no shred of concrete evidence to substantiate their claims, why will certain supposed authorities boldly and positively declare that there was no pre-Incan Andean civilization in Peru, that all stone work remains are Incan and that none are very ancient, the oldest dating back to about 1300 A.D. or a little more than two centuries before the arrival of Pizarro and his fellows. No one with an atom of common sense can believe this. It is truly amazing that any sensible man, supposed to possess more than average intelligence, should propound such a theory. It required our own European ancestors thousands upon thousands of years to advance from a state of savagery to cultured communities with walled cities, castles and palaces, churches and cathedrals built of stone. Yet those who would have us believe that the pre-Spanish civilization of Peru began with Manko-Kapak about 1300 A.D. must credit the Indians with having possessed far greater intelligence, far more ability, vastly greater knowledge of engineering and the arts than our own ancestors in order to have attained in less than three centuries a civilization equal to if not surpassing that of the Europeans who had devoted millenniums to its development. Let us look a little further into this matter.

Many of the great cathedrals of Europe were hundreds of years in the building. Hundreds of highly skilled artisans worked steadily, equipped with excellent tempered steel tools, cutting and carving, setting stones in place; living and dying with their work unfinished and leaving their sons, their grandsons and their great grandsons to carry on until, after centuries, the building was completed.* Yet according to some of these modernizing archaeologists the Peruvian Indians, equipped with nothing better than stone and bronze implements, erected hundreds upon hundreds of palaces, forts, walls and temples and other structures far larger, more massive and entailing fully as great a knowledge of engineering, mathematics and stone cutting as any building in Europe, all in the brief space of less than three hundred years from the time they were primitive savages dwelling in thatched huts!

If, as archaeologists would have us believe, all of this amazing ancient Peruvian stone cutting was accomplished by the use of stone tools, where are these tools? It is a noteworthy and significant fact that good stone implements are conspicuous by their absence in Peru and adjacent Bolivia. Far more and much better stone tools are found in the graves and mounds of the uncivilized Indians of the United States than among the remains of the Incan and pre-Incan people. Stone weapons—mace-heads, axes, spear and arrow points, yes; but never a stone implement capable of cutting the hard arsenite and andasite rock of which the mighty walls and buildings were composed. For that matter I do not know of any rock or mineral in Peru and Bolivia (aside from meteoric iron) that is harder than arsenite. If the stone work was done by means of stone tools there should be countless thousands of the implements scattered about, and here let me call attention to a most interesting and a most significant fact. The better, more advanced and elaborate the stone cutting and carving of an ancient American race, the fewer the stone tools. Really good stone implements are very few in Mexico and are mainly of the extremely ancient archaic culture. Very few, and those poor, were found in Coclé. They are

* Notre Dame was 551 years in its building, Rheims 200 years, Tours 380 years, Nantes 406 years, Canterbury 400 years, Worms 100 years, and St. Stephen 200 years.

almost unknown from Tiahuanaco in Bolivia and Peru where the most remarkable and by far the greatest feats of stone cutting were accomplished, and they are by no means abundant in Yucatán where the Mayas had only soft limestone and sandstone to be cut. Yet in North America, even in New England, in the Guianas and elsewhere where there were no civilizations, no stone monuments or other stone work worth mentioning, excellent stone tools are exceedingly abundant. Let the stone-implement fans explain this if they can.

It must be admitted, however, that some of these belittlers of the antiquity of Peruvian civilizations have only to be "shown" in order to change their minds.

When in 1925 I unearthed mummies in Lamabyeque, including that of the prehistoric woman described in Chapter XVII, and claimed they were two thousand years old, I was laughed at, derided and criticized. But when in 1946 Dr. Junius Bird of the American Museum of Natural History, with associates, carried on excavations in the Viru Valley and disinterred some very ancient mummies, he announced that they probably dated back for at least two thousand years and that there were even more ancient burials beneath them.*

The strongest, most convincing, and irrefutable proofs of the great antiquity of the ancient Peruvian civilizations are found in their known agricultural achievements. Everywhere, in all tombs or depicted upon pottery, sculptures and textiles, other than those of the pre-pottery people of the northern coast, are maize, cotton, cacao, peanuts, squashes, beans, potatoes, peppers, sweet potatoes, tomatoes and other cultivated plants, as well as Guinea pigs, llamas, alpacas, and dogs. Moreover, the vegetables and fruits were highly developed, cultivated varieties. In fact the ancient Peruvians, long before the advent of the Spaniards grew every main variety of maize and beans and most of the varieties of squash, pumpkins, potatoes and other vegetables known to us today.

They had black corn, sweet corn, field corn, popping corn and several varieties we do not have such as the giant mote corn, yet the original ancestor of maize is unknown as is also the case with the original wild ancestors of the squashes, sweet potato, peppers,

* Wm. D. Strong; National Geographic Magazine, Page 453.

beans, Guinea pigs, llamas, alpacas, and the so-called Inca dog.

To have cultivated and hybridized and developed food and other plants from the original wild forms to their highest perfected state would have required countless centuries, and to have domesticated and bred unknown wild animals to the status of llamas, Guinea pigs and dogs would have required fully as great a period of time. Yet the most ancient Peruvian people (aside from the pre-pottery coast race) possessed all of these, proving beyond all controversy that the various cultured people who we consider the most ancient, were, in reality, the descendants of people who had devoted ages to the cultivation and perfection of plants and animals. No race, no matter how well equipped, no matter how industrious and intelligent, could by any remote possibility have accomplished such results in a few hundred years. Our most expert agriculturists, our best animal breeders, during the four hundred years and more that have passed since the Europeans reached America, have never yet produced a single new distinctive form of maize, a single new type of llama, a single entirely new bean, potato or other cultivated plant or domestic animal known to the most ancient Peruvians. New varieties, new hybrids, yes; but nothing absolutely and entirely different from those known to the ancient Peruvian people. In fact they raised a number of food plants which our horticulturists have never been able to duplicate, such as frost-proof tomatoes, mote corn, purple insect-proof potatoes and certain kinds of squash.

Also, our archaeologists have always and consistently claimed that no pre-Columbian American race knew of the wheel, despite the fact that numerous wheeled toys had been found among ancient remains in two places in Mexico and that Dr. Bennett, in his first report of his excavations at Tiahuanaco in Bolivia, stated that: "In pit number 7 in a small temple said to be the oldest in Tiahuanaco, associated with ancient stone images and other objects," he found a large stone "wheel or ceremonial grindstone." Apparently this admission must have been a slip of the pen, for in his subsequent printed report no mention was made of the wheel. However, you can't fool all of the public all of the time, as Barnum discovered, and a few months ago, after they had been reminded of the wheeled toys by my wife, the archaeologists, in the official organ of the American Museum, announced that the ancient Americans *did* know the wheel, although they never made any practical use of it.*

Why a certain number of scientists should be so "belittlin'" of the early American civilizations is a mystery fully as great as any of the mysteries of the ancient people. It may be because they are jealous and hate to admit that any race other than the Anglo Saxons ever accomplished anything worthwhile, or that the civilizations of American aborigines could by any possibility have equalled or excelled those of the white men, or again perhaps, it is a feeling of superiority, a tendency to look down upon the Indian as an inferior being. Be that as it may, they constantly are announcing that many things relating to the early American cultures have been highly and flagrantly exaggerated; that the aborigines never performed any great engineering feats, never had more than a superficial knowledge of astronomy and mathematics, never did this, never accomplished that.

Utterly disregarding the documentary evidence of letters and reports by the Spanish padres and conquerors, even of later Viceroys and the testimony of Inca nobles, these modernists either deny or fail to mention that Cuzco was very rich in gold at the time of the conquest, that there were golden shrubs, birds and other creatures in the garden of the Temple of the Sun, and claim there is no evidence that there was a gold band about the temple, that the great gold chain of the Inca Huayna-Kapac was a myth and that the amount of booty taken by the Spaniards was exaggerated, despite the official files and accountings still preserved in the Archives of Spain. We are told that the royal palaces of Montezuma were rather ordinary mud dwellings and that the Incan road was little more than a foot path and that the longest tunnels were "cut through the hills for short distances." ** I scarcely would consider one of these tunnels that was cut through a mountain for 900 feet, and is still in use, as being "short."

Still more remarkable and inexplicable is the ever increasing tendency of a number of archaeologists to modernize the ancient civilizations, to cut down the long established, long accepted ages to a few centuries. To be sure, they do not agree as to dates by any means. Their estimates varying to the extent of several hundred or even a thousand years or more. And if the adherent to recent

* Goodwin F. Ekholm. Natural History Magazine, October 1950.
** W. C. Bennett; *Handbook of South American Indians*, Vol. 5, Page 55.

date propaganda comes upon a glyph recording a date earlier than his he calmly states "that, in reality, they are anachronistic, carved sometime later than the apparently very early dates inscribed on them."

If this modernization keeps on it won't be so very long until we are told that the first Inca did not appear until after Columbus, that the Aztecs had been only partly cultured when Cortez put an end to their advancement and that Cuzco was not only "built in a day," but in the early sixteenth century!

One of the most fascinating unsolved mysteries of the ancient Peruvian races is that of the Parakas culture, first discovered by Dr. Julio Tello about twenty-five years ago, on a narrow desert cape in Central Peru, not far from the area of the Nasca culture, itself an unsolved archaeological puzzle. Dr. Tello found the remains of two cities built of beautifully cut pink porphyry rock.* And here, interred in huge artificial caves or great tombs he came upon numbers of mummy bundles totally unlike any others known. They were huge affairs of conical tent-like form often seven or eight feet in height by five or six feet in diameter at the base and when opened were found to contain mummified bodies wrapped in layers upon layers, yards upon yards, of the most exquisite textiles ever found.

In addition the bundles contained quantities of pottery of unique types, ornaments, implements and utensils of gold and silver, feather headdresses and fans, dried fruits and vegetables and innumerable other objects entirely new to archaeology and completely different from anything previously known in Peru.

Subsequent excavations proved that there were three eras or strata of culture of the Parakas area. The first or oldest was immeasurably ancient. Many of the textiles and pottery vessels, as well as the painted frescoes, showed llamas with five toes on the front feet instead of two as in the llamas of the present time. Moreover, skeletons of five-toed llamas were found which would seem to prove that these prehistoric people lived in the dim and distant past when llamas still possessed five toes—a period so remote that we cannot even hazard a guess at it. But many scientists are of the opinion that the five-toed llamas of these people were merely freaks

* Although Dr. Tello at first thought these were remains of abandoned cities, he subsequently found that they were merely walls enclosing the great cemetery.

and were perhaps regarded as sacred because of their five toes. Whatever the truth may be—and the chances are we will never know—the fact remains that they antedated nearly all other ancient cultured races of Peru.

Quite aside from the question of its age the Parakas civilization presents most intriguing unsolved mysteries. Why were all the mummies so far found obviously of the highest, most noble class? Why should a numerous and highly cultured race have been restricted to a comparatively small and isolated cape? Why should they have erected stone walls when their nearest neighbors, the Nascans, used adobe?

Not because stone was the most convenient material at hand. On the contrary the stone was quarried and cut many miles from the site and was carried across wide desert wastes. Whence did they come, whither did they go? Did they come from overseas, were they survivors of the Tiahuanacans? There are numberless theoretical answers to the Parakas puzzle but up to the present not one can be proved correct. We can merely shrug our shoulders and, like the Spaniards, say "Quién sabe?"

CHAPTER 23

Outstanding Achievements

As so many of the most noteworthy achievements of the ancient Peruvians were pre-Incan and as it is often impossible to say whether each of these did or did not antedate the Incas' regime, it obviates a great deal of confusion and serves every purpose to refer to them all as ancient Peruvians.

ENGINEERING

In some ways the greatest engineering feat of these people was the so-called Incan Road. Over four thousand miles in length, it stretched from Quito in Ecuador to Tucuman in Central Chile and traversed some of the roughest, most mountainous country in the world. There were ranges fourteen to fifteen thousand feet in height to be scaled, vast canyons thousands of feet in depth to be crossed, roaring torrents to be bridged, deserts to be traversed and morasses and swamps to be passed. But the pre-Incan engineers who constructed the road treated such matters as though they were nonexistent. The highway, twenty-five feet in width, was carried up the loftiest ranges by easy gradients and zig-zags; where precipices barred the way the living rock was hewn away or retaining walls were built up for hundreds of feet to support the roadway.

Ravines and chasms were filled with solid masonry to form causeways; canyons and torrents were crossed by suspension bridges supported by immense cables of wool or fiber anchored to holes cut through solid rock or fastened to massive abutments of wonderfully constructed masonry; peaks and cliffs were pierced by tunnels sometimes several hundred feet in length. For hundreds of miles smooth pavements of stone were laid across burning deserts; dykes were constructed across swamps and shallow lakes and for part of its length the amazing highway was surfaced with asphalt.

At frequent intervals branch roads led east and west, to the sea on one hand and to the trans-Andean *youngas* or jungles on the other. The roadways to the west connected with a second longitudinal highway twenty feet in width that followed the coastline for two thousand miles.

Throughout the entire length of the road, at distances of not over twenty miles apart, were *tambos* or rest houses, while at every forty miles was an Imperial Inn. The *tambos* served as stopping places for travelers and stations for government runners or *chasquis*, while the Imperial Inns were storehouses for food, supplies and equipment for the army, in case of war, or for the relief of villages in time of famine. They also served as eating places for the army when on the march and as stopping places for the Inca and other officials when traveling. There was also a system of sentry stations, watch towers and forts, as well as a system of signals, using mirrors during the day or flares at night, by which the men who constantly were on watch could transmit messages from one end of the road to the other in less than four hours.

For rapid transportation relays of runners or *chasquis* were stationed at each *tambo* and as no one runner had to cover over twenty miles from his station to the next, and in mountain sections only ten miles, messages or cargo could be carried with truly remarkable speed from one place to another. Fresh fish caught in the Pacific were delivered in Cuzco, over three hundred miles distant and beyond mountains fifteen thousand feet in height, within twenty-four hours from the time they were taken from the water, which is ten hours sooner than is possible by the way of the railway today. Fish from Lake Urubamba, caught in the morning, were served at Cuzco dinners the same evening while fruits and vegetables from the coastal plains were delivered in Cuzco within fifteen hours.

Also, throughout the entire length of the road, posts or stone pillars accurately placed showed the exact distance to the next rest house or *tambo*. So easy were the gradients on this amazing highway, and so evenly paved the surface, that it would have served admirably as an automobile road, yet it was used solely by pedestrians and llama trains. So well and enduringly built was the road, so perfectly drained and supported, that even at the present time, after a lapse of over five centuries, many portions of the highway and several of the ancient bridges are in daily use by motor cars and trucks, while some of the tunnels now serve for the Andean railways.

No ancient people, not even the Romans, ever constructed such a highway, yet in some respects the Incan irrigation systems called for even greater knowledge of engineering than the highways. There were great artificial rivers or canals bringing the water for hundreds of miles across mountains and deserts. Many of these were carried over ravines and canyons on stone viaducts and were so well built and well designed that they are still in use. Even more remarkable were the careful and well planned systems of canals and ditches that led the water to the fields and farms and formed an intricate, complex but perfect network covering thousands of square miles.

In many ways fully as remarkable or for that matter even more remarkable as engineering feats, were the walls and buildings constructed of the amazing polygonal or Cyclopean type of stonework which I have already described. To quarry and cut a block of stone weighing several hundred tons and transport it across many miles of rough country, ferry it over wide rivers, and lift it to a mountain top would be a titanic undertaking even today. Railways would have to be built, immense steam cranes used and steel cables and pulleys employed. To be sure it is no great feat for a modern steamship to lift a hundred ton locomotive and swing it aboard ship, but that is simply a lifting job and adequate power and derrick booms are all that are needed. But it is quite another job to carry such a weight overland and across rivers and to the summit of a thousand foot mountain. How such feats were accomplished by the ancient Peruvian engineers no one can satisfactorily explain. If man power alone were used it would have required so many men hauling and tugging that they would have been in one another's way. And how could they have fastened the necessary thousands of ropes to a stone monolith? Of course rollers or wheels of some sort must have been used and in that case a strong hard roadbed or tracks must have been laid. And to cross rivers either exceedingly strong bridges or huge rafts would of necessity have to have been built. Regardless of how many men were employed, how many rollers used, how many bridges, tracks and barges constructed, it would have taken a tremendous length of time to move one such block from the quarry to the building site, yet hundreds upon hundreds of them were transported. One very competent American engineer, who visited Cuzco and other ancient Peruvian cities, declared that with all modern equipment it would require months, probably a year to accomplish the feat if starting from scratch with no tram lines or other preparations made. When we stop to consider how long it takes to move a house or other building a few blocks over paved city streets and from one site to another on the same level, we may more fully appreciate the task the pre-Incans faced. Their problems did not end even when the gigantic blocks of stone were eventually upon the mountain top. They had to be cut to size, tooled and fitted and raised into position, yet at Ollantay, Sacsayhuaman and elsewhere there are countless blocks of stone weighing from one hundred to three hundred tons, cut and faced with such precision and placed without mortar or cement, that the thinnest knife blade cannot be inserted between them. Moreover, to transport and cut these stupendous rocks must have been a fairly simple and easy matter to the ancient Peruvian engineers, for numerous smaller stones would have served every purpose just as well.

Few persons realize what an advanced knowledge of engineering the Incans possessed. The entire country from Ecuador to Chile and from the trans-Andean borders to the shore of the Pacific were surveyed, measured, divided into definite sized areas and mapped. They even had relief maps made to scale and modelled in pottery or carved from stone.

The entire irrigation system of the Incan Empire was planned and mapped as were all the roads, villages, public buildings, etc. Moreover, buildings were designed and planned by highly skilled architects and scale models were made, often in both horizontal and vertical sections, showing every detail of construction so that the builders were working from blueprints in clay.

MEASUREMENTS

Naturally, in order to accomplish such feats, measuring devices were essential and these had been worked out and standardized.

Although the Incan numerical system was decimal all measurements were based on the primitive digital five, or fingers of a hand. Measures of length were of two kinds, those used for everyday purposes and those employed in making surveys or measuring great distances.

LONG MEASURE

		Inches
yuku (or one hand)		5
1½ *yuku* made 1 *kaipa*		7½
2 *kaipa* made 1 *rhokok*		15
2 *rhokok* made 1 *sikia*		30

2½ sikia made 1 *rikira*   75

1000 *rikira* made 1 *tupo* 75,000 inches = 6250 feet

Nautical mile	6080.20 feet
Difference	169.80 "

The entire length of the Incan road was marked with TUPU stones showing the distance from one *tambo* to another. The standard of these measurements, a *rikira*, was always kept in Cuzco just as our own standards of measurement are kept in Washington.

SURVEY MEASURE

thatkaiy—5 feet (60 inches) equal of two *sikias*

5000 *thatkaiy* made 1 *turo*—25000 feet or about 4½ miles (4 *tupu* miles)

30 *tupos* made 1 *yuamani*—about 135 miles (or 120 *tupu* miles)

As two *sikias* of the ordinary long measure equalled one *thatkaiy* of the survey measure and as one and one-half *thatkaiy* of the survey measure equalled one *rikira* of the ordinary measures the standard *rikira* stick at Cuzco served to check any of the various measurements.

There was only one measurement of area, the Square *topo*, which was approximately four-fifths of our acre. This measurement is still in use but today it varies in different localities from twenty-two by forty-four *thatkaiys* about Cuzco to twice as much in the vicinity of Arequipa. In the same way the old Incan *tupu* of linear measurement varies in different sections of Peru and to the great majority of Indians it is an indefinite distance, the term being used to denote "far" while the term *tuamani* means merely a great distance or "very far."

The fact that the Incan mile or *tupu* came within 169.80 feet of our own geographical mile of one minute of a degree of the earth's surface would seem to prove that the Incans had evolved their linear measurements from a degree and must have known that there are three hundred and sixty degrees in a circle.

The standardization of their linear measurements made possible the Incans' accurate surveys which doubtless were accomplished by simple triangulation and a knowledge of the cardinal points of the compass. It is really surprising what accurate maps may be made in this manner, but after all, when a surveyor uses a transit he is accomplishing the same thing, merely substituting his instrument for a couple of measured sticks.

As far as known the Incans had no exact form of liquid measure but they did have measurements of weight and both beam scales or steelyards and balance-scales were used. Some of the latter that have been found are very ornate and beautiful with highly carved and decorated beams of ivory, bone or even silver and with chased or engraved bronze or silver bowls. As a rule, however, they are quite plain. Although customarily used in trading, one commodity being balanced against the other, yet small pieces of copper of various sizes were also used as weights, especially when measuring powders, dyes, and other small articles weighing not over a pound. The largest of the balance scales I have seen would weigh several pounds in the tray.

These ancient balances are still in use and when at Aitchi Kaitchi on the eastern side of Lake Titicaca I found the Colla Indian women in the market weighing commodities on balance scales they had obtained from ancient graves. For weighing large or bulky objects the Incans used beam scales or steelyards made of wood and often elaborately carved. These are still in use but have no regular standard weights.

Mathematics and Astronomy

As I have already stated, the Incans had a decimal numerical system but it was based on the "hand" or digital count of five which is almost universal among American Indian tribes. So firmly fixed was this basic count of five that it entered into all of the Incan mathematics and their astronomy. Thus the Incan year was of three hundred and sixty days which is a multiple of five so that they had seventy-two weeks of five days each and twelve months of six weeks, or eighty days each. The odd five days were the nameless or "lost" days immediately preceding the New Year and Birth of the Sun celebrations. Then in order to equalize the calendar so that the lunar and solar years agreed they arbitrarily added a day every fourth year.

Although the Peruvians may not have possessed such an advanced knowledge of astronomy as the Mayans, yet they could determine the times of the solstices and also checked their calendar by the moon and the Pleiades. In fact the exact time of the Birth of the Sun ceremony was determined by the position of this constellation.

For their solar observations they used a simple but accurate device known as the *Inti Tihuayana* which may mean "Resting place of the Sun," or "Place where the Sun is fixed." This consisted of a seat or bench for the observer, a stone sun dial and, at a distance and standing clear-cut against the sky at the top of a hill or ridge, eight vertical stone columns or *Pachata-unanchac,* arranged in four groups, two toward the east and two toward the west. By sighting across the gnomon of the sun dial at the stone posts they could determine the exact time of noon, the variations of sunrise and sunset, and could record the variations in the angles of the sun's rays at different periods of the year. In order to obtain an accurate sight the observer used a metal disk or *Tepu* attached to a short handle and perforated by two very fine slits, one vertical, the other horizontal, very similar in effect to the cross hairs in any modern transit or theodolite.

The Nascans of the coastal area near Pisco had an entirely different method of establishing their calendrical dates. It was a most remarkable system, the most gigantic and complicated system ever devised by man. On the level surface of an elevated plain they removed the dark colored stones to leave light colored lines, bands, symbols and figures by means of which they could take observations and check on the sun's position. Many of the lines are miles in length yet as absolutely straight as though laid out with a transit by a modern surveyor. No one has yet determined exactly how the ancient Nascans made use of the enormous layout and it is most interesting to note the general resemblance between it and the strange devices used by the Pacific Islanders in navigation. These to the white man are incomprehensible although perfectly simple to the islanders. No doubt to the Nascans their strange desert astronomical arrangement was just as simple as the navigating devices are to the natives of the Pacific islands.

As I mentioned above, it would seem obvious that the Incan lineal measures must have been derived or evolved from the degrees of a circle, but whether they had actual knowledge of the earth's circumference, or worked the measurements from the orbit of the earth is impossible to say. It would of course be a simple matter for anyone with even a rudimentary knowledge of astronomy and mathematics to realize that the days of the years and the hours of the day constituted circles divided into three hundred and sixty parts or degrees. And if the Incan mathematicians and astronomers ever discovered that the diurnal circle of twelve hours was one thirtieth of a three hundred and sixty degree circle they might have worked out the sixty minute to a degree system and their measurement of a *tupu* of 6250 feet. But to have done so would have required a very advanced knowledge of mathematics which apparently was the case, for their entire political and economic system was based on a mathematical cone or pyramid divided into five vertical, and innumerable horizontal sections. At the very apex was the Inca, a position that never altered, next below were the five wise men or *Amatus*. Below them the ten princes and so on down through priests, governors, mayors, divisions of land, families, individuals, areas of land for each, llamas, etc. With such a theoretical mathematical cone it was a very simple matter to adjust any and every detail of the entire government to maintain a perfect balance, for every detail from births and deaths to the number of officials and llamas, the amount of lands, even to the proportionate number of priests and nobles and the amount of food to be stored for emergencies, could be calculated and determined with mathematical accuracy, yet all arranged and built upon the simple digital five.

RECORDING DEVICES

It was of course essential to keep accurate records of all these various mathematical and astronomical matters, the calendrical data, the surveys, the building, road-making, irrigation and other plans, and the theoretical mathematical cone or pyramid of the social and political organization.

It has been claimed that the Incans had no written or recorded language. Perhaps that is true in a way, but according to the old Spanish accounts the entire history of the people was recorded by pottery vessels in the Temple of the Sun at Cuzco, and the late Dr. Julio Tello, a native Peruvian of pure Indian blood, believed and had quite conclusively proved, that much of the Chimu or Mojica pottery if properly arranged formed a record or story. However, we do know that the Incans kept very accurate and detailed accounts of many events, traditions and other important matters by means of their *quipos*.

Sarmiento de Gamboa, a famous navigator as well as chronicler, who was familiar with the native Peruvian aristocracy following the Spanish Conquest, wrote a History of the Incas (*History of the Incas*, 1572, edited by C. Markham, Hakluyt Society, II. Ser. Vol. XXII, Cambridge, 1907).

In this he states (p. 40):

Before entering upon the history of the Incas, I wish to make known, or more accurately speaking, to answer a difficulty which may occur to those who have not been in these parts. Some may say that this history cannot be accepted as authentic, being taken from the narratives of these barbarians, because, having no letters, they could not preserve such details as they give from so remote antiquity. The answer is that to supply the want of writings they had a curious invention which was very accurate. This was that from one to another, from father to sons, they handed down past events, repeating the story many times, just as lessons are repeated from a professor's chair making the hearers say these historical lessons over and over again until they were fixed in the memory. Thus each one of the descendants continued to communicate the annals in the order described with a view to preserving their deeds and history, their ancient traditions, the number of their tribes, towns, provinces, their days, months and years, their battles, deaths, destructions, fortresses and "Sinchis." Finally, they recorded and still record, the most notable things which consist of their statistics, on certain cords called "*Quipo*," which is the same as to say reasoner or recorder or accountant. On these cords they make certain knots by which, and by different colors, they distinguish and record each thing as by letters. It is a thing to be admired to see what details may be so recorded, for which there are masters like our writing masters. Besides these they had, and still have, special historians in these nations, an hereditary office descending from father to son. The collection of these annals is due to the diligence of Pachacuti Inca Yupanqui, the ninth Inca, who sent a general summons to all the old historians throughout these provinces he had subjugated, and even to many others throughout those kingdoms. He had them in Cuzco, for a long time, examining them concerning their origins, antiquity and the most notable events in their history. These were painted on great boards and were deposited in the Temple of the Sun, in a great hall. There such boards, adorned with gold, were kept as are books in our libraries and learned persons were appointed who were well versed in the art of understanding and declaring their contents. No one was allowed to enter where these boards were kept except the Inca and the historians, without special order of the Inca. . . .

In its simplest form the *quipo* consisted of five strings representing the five fingers of a hand with knots representing the joints. The thinnest cord represented the index finger with the knots having the value of units totaling ten. The next or second finger string knots represented decimals or tens. The third cord represented hundreds and the fourth thousands while the fifth or thumb string indicated fractions. By using more numerous and variously colored strings, knots and groups of knots, as well as inverted knots, innumerable combinations capable of recording any events or other matters could be preserved. Many of the ancient *quipos* have hundreds of strings of many colors often with supplementary pendant strings and with countless single, double, triple and quadruple knots, inverted knots and combinations of knots.*

* It has repeatedly been stated that the Incans had no written language. This, however, is not the case. All of the Spanish priests and chroniclers agree that the Incans did have an ideographic language which was written on cloth, leaves or other material. However, its use was restricted to temporary or inconsequential matters, for the material on which the characters were inscribed was not of an

In addition to the complicated record *quipos* there were the debit and credit strings known as *hankos* and *charas*. The credit accounts were kept on the *hanko* strings and the debit accounts on the *charas*. Quite frequently the *hankos* were made up of strings of pearls, gems, or gold beads representing decimals with a shorter string of nine beads as units. The *charas* or debit strings were usually of seeds or shells strung decimally on a cord with a pendant string carrying nine pearls as units. In effect these account strings were very similar to the abacus. Many of the living Indians can use these *charas* and *hankos* and calculate debits and credits with amazing speed and accuracy. But no one can read or interpret the complicated, involved recording *quipos* with their multitudinous strings and innumerable knots. Prior to the disruption of the Incan Empire there were official *quipo* readers or translators who held a very exalted and respected position. They were usually members of the high priesthood and their intimate knowledge of the deciphering of the *quipos* was kept a secret and handed down from father to son. But the knowledge was gradually lost or forgotten, although as recently as 26 years ago, there was at least one Peruvian Indian who could interpret the ancient *quipos*. I met him a number of times, and painted his portrait. He was an aged man, a fine, intelligent Huanca of noble lineage who frequently was summoned to Lima by the President to determine areas and boundaries of land and controversial matters by his knowledge of the *quipo* records and the ancient Incan measurement systems. His decision was always accepted as being based on the *quipo* records which he read as easily as a person can read a book. From him I obtained the tables of measurements I have given.

In effect the *quipos* are a form of cypher and like a cypher code they doubtless could readily be deciphered once the key is shown. It would seem as though men capable of discovering the keys to secret code messages and deciphering them would find it possible to discover the secret key that would unlock the meanings of the *quipos*. Were it possible to interpret the many *quipos* we undoubtedly would learn much of Incan and pre-Incan history and lore of which we are totally ignorant and which might solve many of the

---

enduring type and for all important and permanent matters the Incans used their pictographic pottery and their *quipos*.

puzzles and mysteries of the ancient Peruvians. Somewhat similar strings are in use by the Guaymi Indians of Panama and although at first they appear very complicated and quite meaningless they are easily read and understood once the key to the system is known. Each color of a string denotes the nature of the message, double knots convey the place or location, single knots give the date or time and pendant strings identify the person to whom the message is sent and the name of the sender.

Perhaps the key to the ancient Incan *quipos* is just as simple.

In addition to their *quipos* the Incans used wooden or pottery trays divided into two sections representing credits and debits with eleven compartments or hollows in each section, each hollow containing ten pebbles or beads.

Each bead in ten of the hollows had a value of ten or a total of one hundred for each depression, while the pebbles in the eleventh compartment represented units with a total value of ten. By this simple method of taking pebbles from compartments on the credit side and depositing them in corresponding compartments on the debit side or *vice versa*, accounts of almost any size could be accurately calculated. These are still in use by the Indians and the rapidity with which they can figure accounts is only equaled by a Chinaman with an abacus.

AGRICULTURE

As agriculturists the Incan people have never been equaled. They were veritable agricultural wizards and had developed agriculture into a fine art. By means of vast irrigation systems, in a land that mainly is arid and dry, they cultivated over eighty per cent of the vegetables and fruits we know today.

From native but undetermined wild plants they had developed and hybridized maize, potatoes, sweet potatoes, peppers, tomatoes, pumpkins, melons, squashes, beans, lima beans, peanuts, cotton, avocados, cherimoyas, a peach-like fruit, the *durazno,* and many other food plants rarely seen in our markets. Maize, potatoes, and peanuts were their principal and most important food crops and ears of maize, shriveled potatoes, and peanuts are found in the most ancient pre-Incan graves. Moreover, even centuries before the arrival of the Spaniards, they possessed every variety of corn and potato we know today and many that we do not have. Popping corn, sweet corn, black corn, and field corn of many varieties were cultivated and in addition they had a dwarf variety with a small ear that withstood frosts and at the other extreme a gigantic variety known as *moti* with kernels an inch in diameter that are parched and eaten like chestnuts. In addition to maize they had another cereal known as *quinoa* which yielded a fine nutritious flour. Besides our many varieties of potatoes they cultivated an insect-resisting, purple-flowered potato with tubers having a purplish skin and another variety with mealy yellow flesh, as well as a small potato that is frost-resistant and must be frozen to render it edible. Numerous varieties of sweet potato were raised and in addition to the ordinary tomatoes they had frostproof varieties, tree tomatoes of half a dozen different kinds, and tomatoes that grow in bunches like currants. They cultivated over a dozen different varieties of sweet peppers or *chire* as well as various forms of the hot pepper or *ajie*. Their varieties of string and shell beans were almost endless as were innumerable kinds of lima beans, and they had produced several distinct varieties of peanuts or *mani*. Pottery replicas of vegetables prove that they raised a number of kinds of squashes and pumpkins and pottery molds of a netted-rind cantaloupe are evidence that they knew and raised these melons. In addition to the cherimoya and *durazno* they cultivated many other fruits and their avocados or *paltas* were as fine and even larger than any we raise today. Cotton of course was a highly important crop and the native Peruvian tree cotton is one of the most highly prized varieties at the present time and when crossed with sea-island cotton yields the finest of all known long staple cottons.

Although the greater portion of their crops were cultivated on the irrigated plains and valleys between the western slopes of the Andes and the ocean, vast quantities of produce were raised on the terraced gardens of the mountains. In many places entire mountain sides are completely covered from base to summit with tier after tier of the ancient stone retaining walls of these gardens now abandoned and forgotten.

For tilling the soil and cultivating their crops, the Incans used bronze hoes, planting sticks, narrow-bladed bronze spades and a true plow. Among all American pre-Columbian races the Peruvians were the only people who knew and used the plow which was almost identical in form with the ancient plows of the Old World. Even today when more modern agricultural implements are available many, indeed most, of the Indians still use the ancient plows of their forefathers.*

When tilling the fields a man and his wife work together, taking turns at pulling and guiding the plow, hoeing and planting and forming an ideal team with the labors equally divided.

Farmers as a rule breed and raise livestock as well as vegetables and the Incan husbandmen were no exception. They had domesticated an unidentified member of the camel family and by selective breeding had developed the llama as a burden bearer and the alpaca for its long, silky, highly prized fleece. Also, from some long-lost wild ancestor they had developed the cavy or Guinea pig whose flesh was and still is highly prized and forms an important part of the Peruvian's diet. And from some fox-like creature they had produced a delightful, attractive breed of dog unlike any other anywhere. Although they did not possess our types of poultry they had domesticated the Muscovy and tree ducks, and the curassow, several species of pigeons, and doves, and a partridge or quail.

Although they had no draught animals for drawing vehicles these were scarcely needed for the Indian cargo carrier or *yanacona* can carry an incredible load upon his back. In Cuzco and other Andean towns it is not unusual to see an Indian porter carrying a piano or several cases of machinery or other goods weighing as much as four hundred pounds with apparent ease, and keeping it up for hour after hour and day after day. In addition to these professional burden bearers there were the llamas. Although a llama cannot or at least will not carry a load of more than one hundred pounds, a drove of a hundred of the creatures will transport nearly five tons over the steepest, most difficult mountain trails, and droves of from two to five hundred llamas, each with its burden of one hundred pounds, are not unusual. Not only will llamas thrive at altitudes where even burros cannot survive, but like their cousins, the camels, they can do without water for long periods and are as

---

* These were of wood with a vertical or slightly inclined blade very much like plows still in use by many of the Mexican farmers. In all probability some of the ancient Peruvian plows had metal blades or at least had the wooden blades edged with bronze, for bronze objects that scarcely could have served other purposes, have been found.

much at home on the burning deserts as among the Andean peaks. Moreover, they require no special feed but will graze contentedly upon barren hillsides apparently devoid of all verdure and will subsist and thrive upon lichens and stunted desert plants. They are one of the most useful of all domestic animals and like the reindeer they provide their owners with transportation, food, wearing apparel, fuel, and leather as well as milk.

ARTS AND INDUSTRIES

No race or people have ever excelled or even equaled the ancient Peruvians in the matter of textiles. They were familiar with and used every type of weaving known to us as well as several that are "lost."

They used cotton and llama, alpaca and vicuña wool, spinning the threads by means of simple spindles consisting of a slender shaft with a broad disk near one end, and weaving their fabrics on the crudest of hand looms. Even at the present time the Indians are most adept and skillful weavers, still adhering to the spindles and looms of their ancestors.

But no textile produced by the present day Indians can approach those of the pre-Incans in color, art, technique and fineness. Many examples have from two hundred and fifty to three hundred threads to the inch, which is finer than the finest cloth produced by our machine looms today.

They were almost if not equally adept at pottery making. No other South American race modeled more beautifully proportioned, artistically decorated, and harmoniously colored pottery than that of the immeasurably ancient Nascans, and no other race ever produced such lifelike animal figures and human portraits as did the Moujiks and the Chimus. But the potters' art deteriorated after the arrival of the Incas and the later Incan ware does not compare either in technique, beauty or quality with that of the pre-Incans, especially the races who inhabited the area near the Pacific coast.

Metallurgy was also very highly developed by the Incans. They mined, smelted and refined copper, tin, lead, silver, and gold and knew the secret of combining copper and tin to form bronzes of varying degrees of hardness. Every known method of producing gold, copper, and silver work was employed by the ancient Peruvians, and they even possessed a secret or "lost" process of plating copper or silver with gold. The objects have all the appearance of having been electro-plated and various theories have been advanced to explain the process used. Some have claimed that it was done with a mercury-gold amalgam, others have suggested some sort of lacquer, while the most reasonable is that it was accomplished by fuming. No one, however, has been able to duplicate the results obtained by the metal workers of the pre-Columbian Peruvians.

Fig. 32. Nasca pottery jars

Another "lost" art is the beautiful lacquer work on wood peculiar to the Andean area. Cups, jars, mugs, dishes of various kinds and *pachas* or ceremonial drinking vessels are found. They are carved from hard wood and are completely covered with beautifully drawn figures of birds, human beings, deities, various creatures, flowers and geometrical designs in contrasting colors on a highly polished jet-black ground. No known solvent will soften or effect the pigments which, after the lapse of countless centuries, are as clear and brilliant as on the day they were made.

The implements and weapons of the Incans were far superior to those of any other American race. Silver, gold and bronze spoons were made with handles ending in a sharp point to be used as a fork. These spoons also did double duty as pins and the Indian women of today still use them for the dual purposes. Small, sharp bronze knives of various shapes and sizes were also used. Their weapons were of a very superior type and were fully equal to those of Europeans before the use of fire arms. They used powerful bows and feathered bronze-headed arrows, bronze-bladed throwing-spears hurled by the *atlatl* or throwing stick. Their long-handled, broad-bladed, single or double headed battle axes were terrible weapons and they had heavy sword-like clubs of exceedingly hard wood as well as heavy hard wood clubs studded with bronze or stone points. They also used stone and bronze maces, either with conical or star-shaped heads, as well as maces with free-swinging heads attached to the hafts by chains or thongs. But their favorite and most deadly weapon was the sling. These were identical in form with the Biblical sling and were made of braided and woven llama wool cords. Some were of immense size and capable of hurling a projectile weighing several pounds for a long distance, but the majority were designed to use stones or copper or lead balls about an inch in diameter.

The slings were not only used in battle but were employed in hunting. There is scarcely an Incan man's grave in Peru that does not contain the sling or slings of the deceased. Neither did the slings pass out of use with the conquest by the Spaniards, but are in universal use today. Every Indian man or boy invariably carries his sling, looped in his belt or draped over the shoulders, and his pouch of selected sling stones. The accuracy with which a Peruvian Indian can hurl a sling stone is absolutely astounding. I repeatedly have seen them knock over a viscacha or a grouse at a distance of fifty yards and using ordinary stones picked up at random. Often, too, the slings are used in herding llamas grazing on almost precipitous hillsides. Hurling stones about the animals' feet the Indians drive the llamas from a distance but never have I known an Indian to make a poor shot and strike a llama.

Undoubtedly the Incan's slings were more accurate weapons than the clumsy arquebuses and ponderous crossbows of the Spaniards, but they lacked the penetration of bullets and crossbow bolts. Against Indian foes they were very deadly but when used against the armor-protected Spaniards they were almost useless.

Although far from a warlike people the Incans were valiant fighters when necessity arose and were absolutely fearless. Moreover, the warriors were always led by the Inca in person. No wonder they would hurl themselves upon a foe in suicidal frenzy when led by the personification of a deity.

Nearly all the American aborigines had their warriors or fighting men who could be called upon when needed but nowhere else in the New World was there a regular, well-drilled, well-officered standing army in addition to thousands of trained reserves who could be summoned as reinforcements if necessity arose. The Inca's army of several thousand soldiers was made up of picked men selected for their strength, their endurance and their skill with weapons. Each regiment or company wore a different uniform and they were officered by princes and nobles who were trained for their military career in the school or college at Cuzco with a three year course. At this Incan West Point they were taught military strategy and warfare, the construction of forts, earthworks, etc., and were intensively trained in the use of weapons, for unlike our "top brass" the officers of the Incan army, regardless of rank or station, were compelled to take an active part in battle and to be the first to fight. Prowess with the various weapons was essential and sham battles and sham duels were important features of the officers' training. Each strove to become more expert than his fellows, prize contests were held and the champions were regarded in much the same way as so many of our people regard the champion prize-fighter or the winners of football or baseball series.

There was also a course for training men for various government positions, such as governors of provinces, royal surveyors, architects, etc., and in addition there was a theological school maintained by the Church where novitiates were instructed in religious matters.

To sum up the outstanding achievements of the Incans were many, yet the greatest, most outstanding achievement of all was that they maintained a commonwealth of happy, contented, industrious, law-abiding people without money, without taxation, without exports or imports, and without politics or graft. No other race on earth has ever achieved so much.

CHAPTER 24

Songs and Proverbs of the Incans

Probably no other aboriginal American people were as poetically inclined or as musical as were those of the Incan Empire. Although the subjects of the Incas were of many tribes and races varying greatly in temperaments and musical or poetical tendencies, the enforced use of the Quechua language resulted in the verses, music and proverbs of one tribe becoming common to all or nearly all, although each community retained its own while adopting those of others. This was largely due to the *checollos* or wandering minstrels who traveled about, teaching the people new verses and songs, carrying the music and poems and proverbs from one place to another, improvising new lyrics to perpetuate any event or to deal with local conditions. To some extent this custom still holds and on one occasion while in a remote Indian village, one of these troubadours composed a song devoted to myself and, presently, all the villagers were singing and dancing the new song in which I formed the central figure. Hence it is not surprising that many Quechua verses deal with individuals or local people, their lives, occupations, arts, thoughts, customs and religions. Despite the fact that the verses and music vary more or less with the locality and tribe where they originated, still certain characteristics are common to all. They are notable for their sentiments, their beauty and expression of thought, their vivid picturization of scenes and of characters and in many cases for their parody and satire. Very often the Quechua verses are symbolic, a song or poem dealing with one subject or occurrence yet actually referring to something quite different. Also, in nearly all cases, even in songs and verses of a gay or satirical type, there is an underlying note of pathos or sadness, a character-

istic of the race that is notable in their language, their lives, and
their appearance, although they are by no means a lugubrious lot
in reality.

It has been stated by some persons that the Incan people had no
songs, no music, no drama of their own but that all of the so-called
Incan verses, songs and music were adapted from Spanish songs
and poetry. Anyone thoroughly familiar with Incan or rather Quechua music will realize how utterly false this is. The Incan music
was in an entirely different scale from that of Europe and was
played on musical instruments wholly unlike those of the Spaniards.
These were the flutes or *quenas* of reed, bone or silver, the trumpets
or *huancaras* of pottery or bronze, Pan-pipes or *antaras,* ocarinas
or *pututus,* rattles of calabashes and the remarkable and unique
double-toned drums or *tinyas.* The lyrics were adapted to the Quechua musical scale and to the instruments, and in order to sing the
songs to the accompaniment of the instruments and in accordance
with the scale, the singer had to possess a voice covering at least
four octaves. Anyone who has heard the amazing voice of Yma
Sumac must realize this, for the voice must range from the lowest
contralto to the highest coloratura. Moreover, the words of a great
many of the most popular of the Quechua songs were in the ancient
Colla language, proving that they were very old.

To have adapted the Spanish scale and the Spanish lyrics to the
Quechua scale and lyrics, and to rearrange the music to suit the
native instruments, would have been a tremendous, almost impossible undertaking even for a highly trained, expert musician. But
to adapt the Quechua songs and music, or rather to embody some
portions of them in Spanish music, was a very simple matter. Yet
in doing this much of the original beauty and expression of the
words and music have been lost. There are a great many so-called
Incan musical compositions based on the Incan music and songs,
among them *Celita Linda, Ollantay, Cuando El Indio Llora,* and
Cachaspare, and it has been stated that a large portion of the best
European music contains certain features adapted from the ancient
Quechua music.

One of the most notable and most famous of the Quechua musical compositions was the operatic drama *Ollantay.* In this ancient
drama hundreds of the Indians take part and if it were carried out
in its entirety a full week would be required for its performance.

Unfortunately many popular songs and verses from the United States and Europe are supplanting the true Incan songs, and guitars, violins, harps, cornets and other similar instruments are taking the places of the instruments of the Indians. At the present rate of progress it will not be long before it will be impossible to find a truly Incan song, verse, musical composition or dance in the whole of Peru.

A few Peruvians interested in the Indians and their lore have recorded some of their songs and poems, some like Señor Juan Durand, have preserved them in the form of stories in prose, others, as I have said, have attempted to adapt them to Spanish or English music, but as far as I am aware no one hitherto has attempted to translate them in such a way as to preserve their original beauty of thought, their simile, their allegory and their rhythm. To accomplish this has been a far more difficult undertaking than might be thought. In meter, construction, rhythm and technique, the Quechua songs are totally unlike ours and while many may rhyme, this, I should say, is the exception rather than the rule. The great majority were intended to be sung or chanted to Incan music and when apart from the musical scores they seem to be as lacking in harmony or rhythm as many of our own lyrics would appear without the music. An example of this is the Sun Chant, "Taita Inti!"

> Taita Inti! Taita Inti!
> K-ontykypa unanchasc-can
> Apu-Inti, uaksha cuyac
> Causechun-llapa-Ima
> Onanchasca-cuyiqui!

which becomes a haunting melody when sung to the Incan scale by such a truly Incan songstress as Yma Sumac, accompanied by Incan instruments.

Another difficulty is that the Quechua language had no words to express wealth or riches for they had nothing of intrinsic value, their nearest equivalent denoting blessings or well being. Also a great many Quechua words have several meanings, thus *willa* may mean blood, beauty, sacred, creator, corpulence, etc. depending upon its relationship to other words. *Mara* may denote a star, time, year, etc. *Kora* meaning verdure, may be used for a wild flower or any certain plant and *chawi* may be used for death, dead, empty, ruins or lacking in density.

Finally the Quechua grammar, the syntax, construction and phraseology, are totally different from our own, and hence it is impossible to make a literal translation and retain the meter, rhythm and meaning of the originals. I have therefore used words which as far as possible convey the same ideas, thoughts and sentiments as the Quechua verses and have rearranged the purely lyrical compositions to form verse.

As I have said, the Incan songs were carried from place to place by the checollos, who were held in a great deal of respect by the people and who were sponsored by the government as a means of entertainment for the public. The position of the chief checollo or Poet Laureate, as we might say, was very important and was eagerly sought, for during his term of office he was a member of the royal household. He was appointed or elected each year at the time of the Birth of the Sun festival and bards from all over the land flocked to Cuzco to compete for the coveted position.

The contest was of intense interest to the people, the most exciting feature of the afternoon for unlike the other awards and prizes given the winners of athletic and other contests and bestowed by the Inca, the decision as to the winner of the checollo contest was left to the public who signified their choice by applause.

The ceremony was very completely described by Cheko, a Christianized Incan prince who at seventy years of age imparted a vast amount of information to the Viceroy Toledo who had become greatly interested in gathering all possible knowledge of Incan history. Having described the religious celebration of the Incan New Year or Birth of the Sun Festival he stated: "Accompanied by his people of the Court and by the public the Inca in his golden litter was borne on the shoulders of the princes to the great *Pampa* not far distant from Cuzco, where were held various contests, games of skill, sham battles, races and dances. These having been accomplished and prizes given by the Inca to those most worthy of reward, the choosing of the checollos took place." Freely translated into English his account is as follows: Accompanied by their musicians, two of the competing minstrels advanced, bowed to the ground before the Inca and stepped back. Then while his musician played an accompaniment on a silver flute or *quena* one of the contestants sang the words of a new *sarawi* or love song he had composed.

As with the last verse his voice died away and the bird-like notes of the *quena* ceased, cheers burst from the audience. The rival candidate would then sing his composition which, perhaps, would be full of satire and quips that would bring bellows of laughter, clapping of hands and shouts of approval from the onlookers. There was no question of which contestant had won the round and the Inca nodded twice. Couple after couple of the competing *Checollos* appeared and sang their songs until the last had been heard and judged and the fifty-two runners-up stood apart. Each of these would receive a silver mounted staff which would be his badge of royal favor. But in the meantime the fifty-two would have to compete until, in the end, one would be elected the official minstrel of the Court and the Poet Laureate of the nation.

This meant a real game, a battle of wits, for victory depended entirely upon the contestants' knowledge of countless proverbs and songs and their skill in using them. As they were permitted to use proverbs or verses of their own, which might be thought up on the spur of the moment, the public looked forward with keen enjoyment to the elimination contest. For this supreme test there were three judges, one selected by the Inca, another by the public and the third representing the competing *checollos*.

Cheers, laughter and shouts of delight greeted the repartee and witticisms of the contesting men.

Finally the first bard quoted an ancient proverb such as: "From one grain of corn come many ears of maize. From one woman may come many sons. From one worthy deed comes great happiness. From one day of laziness may come weeks of want." Instantly the other would reply: "One worm may destroy a tree. One evil deed may destroy a man's life."

The first might come back with, "One yarn does not make a poncho. One event does not make a life."

The other then might suddenly shift the theme by quoting: "The condor in the sky seems no larger than a gnat, but the gnat in one's eye seems larger than a condor."

If his rival hesitated, striving to think of an apt proverb to match this, he would lose and by the rules of the contest the winner would have the right to speak first when the next contestant came up.

But before the winner could be appointed each of the two finals was obliged to pass still another test. One of the duties of the royal bard was to act as the Court Jester and to entertain the Inca and his household by propounding puzzles and conundrums. Also the rules decreed that in order to secure the position he must ask the Inca a riddle that the monarch could not answer. So having won on all other counts one of the two champions touched the ground with his forehead and begged permission to ask the riddle which was:

> He lurks beside the mountain pass
> He hides within the avalanche
> He makes his home amid the snowfields white.
>
> He waits within the jungle deep
> He watches from the precipice
> He seizes whom he will wher-e'er they are.
>
> He hurls down rocks from mountain sides
> He fells the tree that crashes down
> He whispers to the serpent when to strike.
>
> He guides the spotted tiger's spring
> He hides within the rushing stream
> He seizes those who cross and drags them down.
>
> He rides upon the wings of storm
> He hurls the lightning's blinding flame
> He hovers in the air above the home.

For a brief space the Inca hesitated. Then he smiled. "The answer" he said "is Death."

A bit shamefaced and chagrined the *checollo* withdrew and the other stepped forward, requested the Inca's permission to ask his riddle and recited:

> Across the land I wander far and wide, without a home
> I wander over deserts bare and bleak, without a path
> I cross the frozen ice field white with snow, without a rest
> I travel through the mountain passes wild, but cannot stop
> I hurry onward through the long dark night and cannot sleep
> I move through jungles dark and forests deep and there I weep.

The Inca frowned, rested his chin upon his hand and pondered. At last he shook his head. "What *is* the answer?" he asked.

The *checollo,* sure of his triumph bowed. "The answer, my lord, is the wind."

A thunderous applause greeted his words and a courtier stepping forward handed him a hard wood staff bound with gold and with an immense head of massive gold.

Stationed in the palace for his term of a year he would send out the other *checollos* with silver mounted staffs to the various provinces, to go from place to place teaching the people songs and proverbs.

In addition to these official bards there were numbers of independent traveling minstrels who wandered over the land reciting verses, singing songs and teaching proverbs and for their livelihood depending upon the people they visited.

Among the most popular of the songs and poems of the Incans were the *Sarawis* or love songs, for despite their regimentation by the government, the people were very sentimental and love played a very important part in their lives. Typical examples of these Sarawis are the following:

WINI-SONKO
(Hard Heart)

Oh would that I might know your love—
　That you might yield yourself to me
Oh would that you might be my own—
　Would that such happiness might be.

The shadows of the night lie in your eyes
　The blackness of despair is in your hair
The gold of Inca's crown is in your skin
　Your teeth the whiteness of the snowfield hold

Your lips are red as crimson berries ripe
　The singing of the bird is in your voice
Your skin is soft as plumage of the dove

　The rippling of the stream is in your laugh
Your body is as graceful as the deer
　The perfume of the rose is in your breath
Your feet tread earth as lightly as the breeze.

Would that such beauty might be mine—
To love, to fondle, to caress
That I might have you for my own
But underneath your beauty lies—
Heart unresponsive as a stone.

CHUQUI-SANKO
(If You Are A Widow)

O lovely maid
With moonlight in your eyes
If single you should be
Then come and give your love to me.

O lovely maid
With sunshine in your smile
If married you should be
Stop not but go upon your way.

O lovely maid
With music in your voice
If a widow you should be
Fly to my arms for I will marry you.

THE FIRST LOVE

I love you, I want you—my dear little dove
Can't you flutter your wings and come into my arms?
I will build you a nest and guard you from harm,
For I love you, I long for you, dear little dove.

I'm a poor little dove—just learning to fly
Throughout the long night I do nothing but cry
For the lover I want, to reach whom I try
I spread out my wings, I fly there and here
But never can fly to my loved one so near.

You poor little dove—just learning to fly
I love you, I want you so once again try
To fly to your lover who unto you sings
Be brave, little dove and spread out your wings
Just turn in your flight, just turn and fly here.

I'm a poor little dove—just learning to fly
   Throughout the long night I do nothing but cry
   Oh I long for a lover to keep me from fear
   But I'm lost in the forest so dark and so drear
   The river is wide, my wings are not strong
But I'll pray unto Inti and follow your song.

I love you, I have you—my dear little dove
   You have fluttered your wings and come to my arms
   I will build you a nest, and guard you from harm
For I love you, I cherish you, dear little dove.

LONELINESS

   My heart is empty, lonely is my soul—
      Since you, my love, have gone—
   My life is like the desert sere and brown.

   My eyes are blinded, deafened are my ears—
      Now you, dear love, I've lost—
   I wander in the darkness, all alone.

   There is no beauty in the world for me,
      Since you, beloved, have gone—
   My life is always night; there is no sun.

   No longer do the stars shine in the sky,
      Now you, my love, I've lost—
   There is no music in the world; no song.

   Life holds no joys for me; death holds no fear,
      Since you no longer love—
   The days, the nights are endless without you.

   My heart has turned to stone; my soul is dead
      Now I have lost your love—
   There is no pleasure in the world for me.

   Lonely my heart; my soul is filled with pain
      Now that your love is dead—
   It matters not whatever may befall.

My dream is over; sorrow now is mine
  Since you, beloved, I've lost—
Always my thoughts are of you; of your love.

My heart is empty; lonely is my soul
  Now you, my love, have gone—
My life with aching loneliness is filled.

THE PONCHO

Into the warp I weave my inmost thoughts.
  Into the woof I weave my deepest love
With every thread I weave into thy poncho goes a prayer.

The colors tell of all my hopes and fear—
  The blue for constancy and lasting love—
The red for ever ardent love and burning passion's flame.

The green for years of love to come to us—
  The yellow that the sun-god's smile we win
The black for mourning in my heart when thou art far away.

The patterns are the symbols of our lives—
  The flowers for the budding love of youth—
The birds for freedom and for happiness and joyful song.

Condors to show the god of heaven guards—
  The tiger—symbol of the god of earth,
All watching over us and ever guarding us from harm.

Of ears of maize a border I shall weave—
  That always crops in plenty may be ours,
That never may the pangs of hunger dim our lives or love.

So, my beloved one, when upon thy back—
  This poncho that I weave shall find its place
Remember that its folds hold all my love and prayers for thee.

These verses are from the ancient drama of *Kora*. The story is
of a girl, Kora, who became—at her father's wish—a novitiate of the
mamacunas or Virgins of the Sun. An Incan noble demanded, as
payment for services rendered the Inca, the most beautiful of the
Virgins as his wife. Kora was selected and as Mara Willa (Divine
Star), she became his bride. She had a youthful lover—Kespi—who

visited her during her husband's absence and the *Poncho* is the song she sings as she weaves the garment, ostensibly for her husband but in reality for her lover. It was largely from this drama of Kora that the Spanishized musical score of *Yaravi'* was adopted.

Verses and songs of a satirical type or philosophical character are very different from the *Sarawis*. Unlike the Aztecs and many other American races, the Incans had no fear of death. They considered it a mere passing from one phase to another and they believed in eventual resurrection. Many of their songs and verses deal with this theme, among them the following:

WHAT MATTERS DEATH?

The end must come to all in time—
  To Inca and to husbandman the same.
  No man may stay the hand of death,
Yet what is death but life again?

To some death comes with glory in the wars
  Others find death in sickness and in pain.
  Others by accident come to their death—
And some who break the law must die in shame.

The end, no matter how 'tis met—
  To peasant or to Inca comes in time.
  When Inti orders life to cease—
Man bows unto his will sublime.

What matters it how death comes unto us?
  What matters it if ever by our side—
  He stalks with icy hand stretched out to seize?
What matters death or what death may betide.

If death comes to us as we sleep,
  If death comes to us on the battlefield,
  If death is filled with agony—
What matters how it stands revealed?

Earth is no fairer than Hanak-Pachac.
  Life here no better than in Heaven above.
  And if we leave all we hold dear on earth—
Our souls will find in Heaven those we love.

THE WORLD

The worm upon the cotton leaf
  Thinks all the world is green, and made to eat.
The busy ant upon his hill
  Thinks all the world is sand, a place for toil.
The mole who never sees the sun
  Dwells in a world of everlasting night.

The fish knows all the world is sea—
  The desert lizard thinks it all is land.
The frog thinks all the world a pond
  With reedy banks and swampy, quaking bogs.
The cricket thinks the whole world grass—
  He gaily chirps from morn till night, content.

The desert is the marmot's world—
  The squirrel dwells within a world of trees.
The snail crawls o'er his world of stone—
  The scorpion's world lies underneath a log.
The jungle is the Chuncho's world,
  Where tigers roam, where giant serpents lurk.

So, many men think all the world
  Lies in their native village or their hut.
But he who ever wanders far
  And visits other men, and learns their ways,
Will find the world lies far and wide—
  May find, the world of happiness is—love.

AMAUTU [1]

(The Wise Man)

Wise the Amautu above all other men.
He knows the law. He judges those who sin.
Yet can he say when death will come to us?

---

[1] Amautu. A wise man, a member of the Cabinet of four whose decisions could only be revoked or revised by the Apu-Auquis or tribunal of princes.

He gazes at the stars and moon and knows,
When she will hide her face in her travail.[2]
But can he say when rotted rope will part?

Words of great wisdom issue from his lips.
To him the knotted quipos tell their tales.
But can he say when clouds will give us rain?

The secrets of Pachacta-unanchac [3]
Reveal to him the day of Inti's birth.[4]
But can he say if crops will bounteous be?

Wiser is he than Inca or high-priest;
He knows the omens of the earth and air.
But can he tell if man-child will be born?

Wise the Amautu above all other men.
He knows the law. He judges those who sin.
Yet can he say what follows after death?

The Amautus or "Wise-men" corresponded to our judges of the Supreme Court. The Council of Amautus was supreme and passed upon all important matters of law and state and their verdict was superior to the Inca.

In their ability to paint a word picture in verse the Incan people were highly skilled. Such a descriptive song is the "Ancash-Tica" or Blue Flower, Cherisona and others.

ANCASH-TICA

Upon a mountain bleak and bare,
Within a cleft among the stones,
A flower grew.
A flower delicate and rare—
A flower blue.

[2] The Incans believed that when there was an eclipse of the moon she was in the throes of childbirth.

[3] Pachacta-unanchac. An astronomical device of stone columns by means of which the solstices were calculated.

[4] The "Birth of the Sun" or Kapak-rimi, was the Incan New Year and took place on the first of September, the time of the summer solstice in Peru.

Above it gleamed the snowfield white—
Below it yawned a precipice,
But where it stood,
The sunshine fell with grateful warmth
A golden flood.

A condor soaring in the clouds
Gazed down and saw the flower there.
He thought a fleck
Of sky had fallen to the earth,
So blue the speck.

A butterfly on weary wings
Dropped down to find the flower blue.
He could not miss
Her upturned face awaiting him—
Begging his kiss.

A gorgeous humming-bird flashed past,
With jewelled throat and flaming crest.
He saw the blue.
Swiftly he darted to her side—
Her love to woo.

A buzzing bee, all black and gold,
Searching for honey far and wide,
Espied her there.
He blundered down the sweets to rob—
From lips so fair.

A herder, searching for his flock—
His llamas that had strayed away,
Passed by the spot.
He plucked the flower from her stem—
How sad her lot!

A maiden fair with starry eyes
Greeted the herder with a kiss—
Her lover true,
When he returned and gave to her—
The flower blue.

Blue for the symbol of our love—
He said, and gently laid the bloom,
Upon her breast.
Far from its home amid the rock
It came to rest.

CHERISONA
(Song of the Herder)

I play on my quena the tunes of my fathers
Until the birds wonder then silence their song.
I play on my quena from dawn until darkness
The songs of our greatness, the songs of our wrong.

For I am a herder, a care-free young herder
With nothing to do but to watch o'er my flock.
My home is the mountain wherever night finds me
My roof is the sky and my bed is the rock.

The coca and lime in the pouch at my side
My poncho and sandals, my quena and hat
Some parched corn and barley with meat and amani *
Are all that I own, but what matters that?

For I play on my quena the tunes of my fathers
Until the birds wonder then silence their song.
Oh, I play on my quena from dawn until darkness
The songs of our glory, the songs of our wrong.

At the other extreme are the martial or war songs such as this
Warrior's Song.

THE WARRIOR'S SONG

Look well upon the foe, my battle axe, and smile!
For soon his blood shall redden thy bronze blade.
Hold muscles taut and ready, trusty bow!
So when I fit an arrow to thy string—
And strain my arms to bend thy arching back—
The missile may speed true to foeman's heart.

* Amani. Peanuts.

And thee—O gleaming spear—fail not to pierce
　　Through shield, to bury deep thy head in flesh.
And if I call on thee—my trusty sling—
　　See to it that thy singing stone deals death.

Beat loud the war-drums, and unfurl the rainbow flag.
　　Whose bright folds flaunt defiance at the foe
And warn him that the Inca's armies come!
　　Pray unto Kamak for such souls as speed
Shout loud our war-cry and lift high our shields!
　　Of victory sing—O children of the Sun!
For under Inti victory shall come
　　Then hurl ourselves upon the Chimu's hosts!
Strike for the Inca, for our lord the Sun!
　　For gods, for homes, for land, for all we love!

Heed not the blows that rain upon us in return!
　　Heed not the agonies of gaping wounds!
Heed not if death walks grinning by our sides!
　　Death comes to all in time—our glory lies
In dying for our Inca and our gods.
　　Let no man live to say the Children of the Sun—
Born of the mountains and the snow-clad peaks—
　　Showed fear of death in facing Yungas clans
Nor dreaded hordes of howling Chimu men—
　　Spawn of the sea, reeking of fish and dung.

Look well upon our foes, my battle axe, then smile!
　　For soon their blood shall trickle down thy haft,
To run until it reddens all the streams.
　　To bathe the earth, to dye the sea with red!
Speed swift, my arrow, on thy deadly flight!
　　Speed swift and true and strike the foeman down!
And thee—O spear—shine brightly in the light
　　Until thy gleam is dimmed with blood of men
Beat loud the war drums that like thunder roll!
　　Lift high the rainbow banner—let all know—
The armies of the Inca march to war!

Behold! how Inti looks with favor on his sons
　　How shields and weapons gleam beneath his rays!

Behold! the Inca comes! Chants to him praise!
  Clash shields on spear-hafts, till the welcoming din
Startles the condor on the mountain top
  Then grasp our weapons for the moment comes
When battle rages over field and plain,
  Then on! The Inca's pathway lies ahead!
There is no other road, no turning back!
  Our way lies forward—over Chimu dead!

Like all Indians those of Peru were very fond of chants. In fact
a very large proportion of their songs were chanted. Sometimes one
or two individuals would sing or chant a line. Then the next two
or three lines would be chanted by a chorus of fifty or even one
hundred singers. At the time of the *Kapak-Rimi* or Birth of the Sun
festival thousands of voices joined in the "Chant to the Sun."

KAPAK-RIMI
(Chant to the Sun)

Kapak-Inti-illariymun!* Thus we greet thee—
  Lord of day, O glorious Inti—god of all things.
  Unto thee we offer prayers, we sing in praise to thee.
  Unto thee we sacrifice, bow in reverence holy.
We raise our voices loud, we chant thy glory, we beseech
  That blessings may descend upon us with thy rays.
Smile kindly on us, holy Inti. Accept our prayers—
  And unto us, thy faithful children, give thy favor.

Punchao-Pakariycumin, Inti!
  Once more unto this world and unto us thou art reborn,
  Upon this glorious morn of Kapak-Rimi.
  Let all rejoice for now another year of life
Is given unto us by thee, most holy Sun.
  Let all chant loud the praises to our Lord—

* Kapak-Inti-illariymun. A salute to the sun. Freely translated it would be:
Holy Inti thy children salute (hail) thee. Punchao-Pakariycumin-Inti. "Bestow
thy blessings and favors upon us Inti." Pacha-Kamak. Almighty God. Although
classed as sun worshipers, the Incans did not adore the sun but regarded it as
the visual manifestation of a deity who was the son or spirit of the Supreme god,
Kamak.

Who unto us gives life, gives bounteous crops, who blesses us—
  With light, with warmth, with all those things his people need.

Kapak-Inti-illariymun, Inti!
  Great thy glory, O our Lord, son of Pacha Kamak.
  Bless us, thy children, and into thy temple shine,
  And shed thy rays upon the altar, that thy breath
May light the sacred fires that through the long dark night
  Have burned not throughout the land, nor light has shown
In house or palace or in temple while we prayed and waited,
  Not knowing if our blessed Lord would come again.

Punchao-Pakariycumin! Thus we hail thee—
  Once again the sacred fires burn throughout the land.
  Thy children now rejoice, they loudly chant thy praises.
  Great is our rejoicing; up to the heavens rise our chants.
Sound loud the drums! Upon the quenas sound—
  Gay music, sounds of joy that Inti smiles upon us
Let Mamacunas lift their song in voices sweet to Inti,
  For blest are we, the Children of the Sun, blest is our land.

SARA-HUAYNA
(Corn Dance)

Sara-huayna, sara-huayana—
            Chant the song,
Sara-huayna, sara-huayna—
            To the music of the corn.

Kollo-sara, kollo-sara—
            For the chicha, that we drink.
Chocli-sara, chocli-sara—
            For the sancu soft and white.

Choque-sara, choque-sara—
            For the hanca, that we eat.
Sara-huayna, sara-huayna—
            Cherisona dance and sing.

Sara-huayna, sara-huayna—
            Bring the rope.
Sara-huayna, sara-huayna—
            Bind the golden stalks of corn.

Panca-sara, panca-sara—
> Makes the sayri, that we smoke
Kauso-sara, kauso-sara—
> Sound the kepas for the dance.

Sara-huayna, sara-huayna—
> Quenas play
Sara-huayna, sara-huayna—
> Gaily sing like cherriampos.

Kollo-sara, kollo-sara—
> Hanca-cancha, for my food,
Kollo-sara, kollo-sara—
> Drink the aka, step the dance.

Chocli-sara, chocli-sara—
> Men and maids together sing.
Choque-sara, choque-sara—
> Dance and sing the lover's song.

Sara-huayna, sara-huayna—
> Sing the music of the corn.

Sara-huayna: Corn song (Music). Kollo-sara: Black maize. Chicha: A drink made from the black maize. Chocli-sara: White or sweet maize. Sabcu: A cake made of corn. Choque-sara: Yellow corn. Hanca: Parched corn. Cherisona: A song or chant. Panca-sara: Corn husks. Kauso-sara: Golden-flowered corn. Sayri: A corn-husk cigarette. Kepa: A shell trumpet. Hanca-cancha: Popped corn. Cherriampo: Crickets. Aka: A sweetened chicha.

SOME INCAN PROVERBS

The Quechuas were and still are very fond of proverbs. Very frequently they will reply to a question or will make a statement in the form of a proverb. On one occasion when I was trying to induce an Indian to act as a guide he replied: "Does the llama go far when grass is near at hand?" Then as I offered him twice as much as he expected, he grinned and remarked: "The lizard may bask in the sun but he lets no fly pass him by."

During my travels and my ethnological work in Peru I gathered several hundred of the Incan proverbs, yet I expect there are hundreds of others, for the Indians have a remarkable knack at making up some proverb to suit almost any occasion. It may seem strange that so many of these proverbs are quite similar to our own, but in their meaning and application many are common to people in various other parts of the world.

The condor soars above all other creatures, yet he must come to earth to eat.

Sell not thy cloth before thy llamas have been shorn.

Pray unto Inti for favors, but expect not he will replace the arm thou hast lost nor give unto thee a new eye for the one that is blind.

The frog dwells in the pond but he does not drink it up.

Wait not until hunger gnaws at thy belly before parching thy corn.

Once the arrow leaves the bow thou cannot alter its course. Once thy son leaves thy house thou cannot guide his footsteps.

Complain not of thy lot in life. If all were Incas there would be none to rule.

To win a woman's love give her each day a gift. To hold her love give her each day two gifts.

Many men are like the owl and win a name for wisdom by looking wise and saying little.

The wise man listens to all others. The fool expects all others to listen to him.

The ways of the dove are not those of the eagle. The ways of a woman are not those of man.

Does the tiger wait for the deer to walk into his jaws? Expect not to have crops without labor.

Trust not too greatly thy woman's words. The Maiko sings sweetest as he steals thy fruits.

In crossing the desert look not backward at thy footprints in the sand, but gaze forward to the mountains ahead.

If there were no thorns there would be no flowers. If there were no bees there would be no honey. If there were no sorrows there would be no joy.

Even the Inca cannot plow the ocean's waves nor tie knots in the wind.

CHAPTER 25

Who Were the Pre-Incans?

The origin of the ancient Peruvians has always been a most intriguing mystery. They seem to have had no beginning, no evolutionary development, no intermediate steps from barbarism to high cultures and from cultures to an advanced civilization. As far as any known evidences to the contrary are concerned they seem to have sprung spontaneously, fully developed, from the deserts and the Andes. In the Andean region where the ancient civilization reached its peak, no traces of a primitive or archaic culture have ever been found; the most ancient remains showing a cultural development equal to if not ever superior to the latest pre-Columbian remains.

Innumerable theories, suppositions and fanciful ideas have been offered in explanation of this mystery, but even the most plausible of these have never been substantiated by facts. As we know that a civilization cannot be developed all at once it is obvious that the Peruvian civilizations must have been introduced from some other area, and the only localities where a similar civilization existed thousands of years ago, were the Near East, India and some other portions of Asia. But any suggestion that there had been contacts between America and Asia in prehistoric times was derided, scoffed at, and utterly discredited by practically all leading archaeologists and anthropologists. In fact to propound any such theory was regarded as archaeological heresy. No, according to those who should have known, *all* the ancient American cultures were purely one hundred per cent American Indian.

But their previously mentioned opinions, like times, change and within recent years, a number of our achaeologists have had the good sense and the temerity to declare that in their opinions there were numerous contacts between the civilized Asiatics and the Americans by way of both the Atlantic and the Pacific.

One of the strongest arguments against this theory was the archaeologists' claim that no pre-Columbian American race knew the wheel. But about a year ago, when this allegation had been challenged by Mrs. Verrill, who called attention to evidence to the contrary, an article appeared in *Natural History,* the official organ of the American Museum of Natural History, in which it was admitted that the ancient Americans *did* know and use the wheel, that wheeled toys of pre-Columbian origin had been found, but that no "practical use" was made of the wheel by these early Americans.

For the past seventeen years Mrs. Verrill has devoted her time to intensive researches and studies of the ancient Sumerian civilizations of Asia, even learning to decipher inscriptions in Archaic Sumerian Linear Script.

Her findings, including detailed genealogies of the ancient Sumerian god-kings, quotations from ancient inscriptions and a wealth of other material all apparently linking the Sumerian and Peruvian civilizations, were embodied in a two hundred and fifty page volume and copies were sent to various archaeologists. She confidently expected that her work would be discredited, derided and cast aside. But to her intense satisfaction and astonishment several leading archaeologists and scientists accepted her findings. One copy of the volume was presented to Dr. Ernest A. Hooton who placed the work in the Peabody Museum reference library and another, sent to the Department of Archaeology of the American Museum of Natural History for their consideration, was placed in the reference library of their department.

The results of Mrs. Verrill's work in conjunction with the author's wide first-hand knowledge of the ancient civilizations of Peru, would seem to prove conclusively that the pre-Incan civilization was brought to Peru ready made and fully developed by Sumerian (Phoenician) explorers and colonists 2000 to 2500 B.C. In the following pages I present the evidence we have accumulated and the established recognized facts all tending to substantiate the ancient Sumerian origin of the pre-Incan races in South America.

One of the oft-repeated objections to the claim that voyagers of

2000 or more B.C. reached America was the belief and statement
that these ancient Sumerians did not possess vessels capable of crossing the Atlantic.

As a matter of fact the Sumerians of 2000 or more B.C. possessed
excellent ocean-going ships well rigged, with large sails and with
three decks. Some had two or more sails controlled by sheets and
braces and a short bowsprit and were steered by a rudder. Carvings
and sculptures of these vessels show them in great detail, while the
inscribed records on their tablets speak of boats nearly one hundred
feet in length. Many of these vessels were of large size. In the Third
Dynasty of Egypt, about 2400 B.C., King Snefru sent a fleet of
forty ships to a Syrian port to secure cedar lumber, and the length
of one of these was not less than one hundred and seventy feet
(Baikie, Sea-Kings of Crete, 1920.P.146). It is also recorded that
King Gudea of Lagash, about 2370 B.C. imported timbers of cedar
and other woods seventy-five to ninety feet in length, and that from
Mount Barshib he brought great blocks of stone. Also that his ships
brought stone from lands distant "a year's journey."

It is a well known fact that these ancient voyagers circumnavigated Africa about 600 B.C. and had maintained constant trade
with India by ship centuries earlier, and that regular voyages were
made to England to procure tin, perhaps as early as 2600 B.C. Compared to such voyages, that across the Atlantic from Gibraltar to
South America would have been little more than a pleasure jaunt.
Barely one thousand miles of ocean separates Africa from the coast
of Brazil, it is perhaps the calmest section of the whole Atlantic
Ocean and the trade winds as well as the ocean currents would have
made it easy sailing both westward and eastward. Moreover, all
the ships were provided with numbers of rowers as auxiliary power.*

It also has been claimed that these early voyagers would never
have dared to sail into unknown seas for fear of falling over the
edge of the earth, that they did not know the earth is a sphere and

* Within the past few years several small sailing boats, from 25 to 40 ft. in
length, poorly rigged and in bad repair, have crossed the Atlantic from Scan-
dinavia to Florida, bringing crowds of refugees in safety.

Numerous small boats from 18 to 25 ft. in length, often with a single man,
have made the Atlantic crossing both eastward and westward between America
and Europe. Others equally small have circumnavigated the globe. Within the
past month (Dec.-Jan. 1953) a man made the crossing from Europe to Florida
in a 16 ft. rubber life raft.

had no knowledge of navigation out of sight of land. These arguments are without foundation.

In the first place the Sumerians were not only aware that the earth is round but actually had pottery spheres representing the earth and marked with the equator, the tropics and the parallels of latitude. One such sphere was found at a depth of twenty-six feet beneath the surface at the third and burnt city of Ilios and hence dates from about the time of Sargon of Agade and his son, King Menes. (Schlieman's "Ilios")

Undoubtedly they relied largely upon the pole star as a guide in navigating and checked on their direction by the stars, but among the countless records of their voyages there are references to an "established course," the "full course" and some sort of contrivance to aid in navigation. (No. 10477, Sheet 28, British Museum papyrus.)

This sheet says: "His cordage has been completed and the instrument wherewith he maketh his way he grasps firmly. I have protected the implements of the gods and I have delivered the boat Kha." The implement referred to may have been similar to the strange grid-like affairs of sticks used by the natives of the Pacific islands for navigating their canoes over vast distances. But even had they been wholly lacking in nautical instruments they easily could have sailed to South America, guiding their course by the sun and the pole star.

That they did make this voyage not once but many times is pretty conclusively proved by the ancient inscribed tablets and by certain papyrus sheets in the British Museum. In one of these (No. 10477, Sheets 21-22) it says: "Tell me thy name saith the wood whereat I would anchor—." "—the prince of the red beings. I am brought along like him who hath suffered shipwreck."

Ancient inscriptions found in the Near East record voyages to the "Land beyond the Western Sea" and to the "Land of the Sunset." One of these states that in the eleventh year of his reign, Sargon of Agade returned from a three years' voyage after subduing the "Western Lands" and having established a "Holding" and erecting statues there. The "Omens" inscription of Babylonian records states, that when on his voyage to the "West Lands beyond the Western Sea," Sargon set up statues. In many inscriptions relating to Sargon his name symbol is a crab, the Gan symbol of Archaic

Sumerian Linear Script, and it is very significant that some of the monolithic statues at Tiahuanaco have belts bearing crab-like crustaceans.

Sargon was succeeded by his eldest son, Menes, who, according to the inscription on his cenotaph at Abydos, "made the complete course to the end of the Sunset Land, going in ships. He completed the inspection of the Western Lands. He builded a holding at Urani Land, at the Lake of the Peak. Fate pierced him by an insect. He was buried in the Land of the Sunset." The name of the place where the deadly insect bit or stung King Menes is given as "Ia-aru" and in the Colla and Aimara dialects "Uru" is the name of a poisonous insect, especially the Black Widow Spider.

Naram-Sin was a son of Menes and on an Egyptian face paint palette there is an inscription which calls him the "King of the Western Sunset Lands and of Tianu and Ammaru' Land." The similarity between these names and Tiahuanaco and Aimara is very striking.

Naram-Sin was succeeded by his son, Shar Gani, who was "Under King Commander and Companion" to his father as well as to his grandfather, King Menes, a position that may be compared to that of rear admiral, viceroy or governor. One of his signatures was *Gin-ti*, the "Ti" being the "stone symbol."

If these ancient Sumerian explorers actually visited Peru and erected statues and buildings why, it may be asked, did they not leave records or inscriptions in Peru? As a matter of fact they did. At Sachuayacu, about one hundred and fifty miles north of Cuzco, in a field near Urubamba, a stone tablet bearing these twenty-two incised characters was discovered.

Another, almost identical, tablet was found in Bolivia. The characters are readily identified as the Gangetic (India) form of Archaic Sumerian Linear Script of the type in use at the time of Menes. They are quite easily deciphered and read as follows:

"Lower Sunset Land (at the) Divine temple of the Sun God of fire enthroned. Under Commander of Deep Waters, Under Commander (to) Gin-ti, God of fire of the Land Below, Gan (and) second shagman (or) Under Companion (to the) God of Fire, Men, of the Indus Valley Colony of India, Under Companion from the Rising Sun of the Eastern Waters."

According to the historical records on incised tablets and stelae, Gin-ti or Shar-Gani was ruling as Vice-Admiral or Under Companion to Menes who was known also as "Men," God of Fire, and was the ruler of the Indus Valley Colony in India. Hence the inscriptions on the stone tablets found in Peru and Bolivia agree perfectly with recorded Sumerian history.

In the innumerable inscriptions dealing with Sumerian history frequent references are made to the "Land of Manu" sometimes associated with a "cloud lake," and usually designated as being in the "Mountains of the Sunset," a semi-fabulous or traditionary land which, apparently the Sumerian explorers were seeking on their voyages to the "Sunset Land."

Lake Titicaca is the only lake that fits the description and the most ancient remains of pre-Incan civilization are those on the Island of the Sun at Tiahuanaco.

In all the ages-old traditions of the Peruvian races, it is related that white men came from the "Sunrise across the water" (the Lake) and erected temples and statues on the Island of the Sun and on the mainland near the lake. Also that a second lot of white men arrived and called themselves the "Stone People" and that the leader of these stone people (The symbol of King Menes) was accompanied by his Governor, his servants and many men, women and children. According to these same traditions the first of these white strangers transformed men to stone to serve as statues, and as proxies, to guard his newly acquired land after he left. As the natives regarded these strange white men as deities it seemed perfectly reasonable that they should be able to do this.

When telling of these "Lands Beyond the Western Sea," one First Dynasty Egyptian inscription refers to them as "Urani" or "Urani Land." In the Colla (Aimara) dialect Indians as an entity are often called Urani which means literally "People of Ur."

In the famous so-called Egyptian "Book of the Dead" much of which is preserved in the British Museum, there are constant references to the "Land of Amentet" and to "Amenti" which was the land or abiding place of souls, and where King Menes was buried.

In Peru there are several places called Amencay or Abencay. One of these is near Cocacabana, another is about 40 miles southwest of Cuzco and a third is close to Lima. In all instances the Indians believe these areas are the "abode of spirits" of long-dead Incans and their rulers and at stated intervals they hold ceremonial dances and other festivities in honor of the dead, to show their reverence and to please the spirits. At Abencay, on the outskirts of Lima, the annual ceremony has become a veritable carnival and fiesta for the white inhabitants as well as the Indians, even the President of Peru taking part. Thousands of people crowd the pampa, races and sports of all kinds are staged, and at a little chapel solemn ceremonies are held and prayers offered.

Although throughout most of the year the area is sere barren desert surrounded on three sides by arid barren mountains, each year, at the time of the celebration, the plain becomes covered with golden yellow flowers which spring, almost magically, from the sand. The Indians believe that these are the visual manifestations of their dead ancestors. Whether or not this and the other Amencays or Abencays are hallowed ground because rulers of the Incans were interred there, is impossible to discern, but the striking similarity of the Sumerian "Amenti" and the Peruvian *Amencay* or *Abencay* and the fact that both names are applied to "abodes of souls" cannot be lightly cast aside or regarded merely as a coincidence.

It is true that coincidences occur far more frequently in real life than is permissible in fiction, but it is beyond all reason and logic to believe that hundreds of coincidences in scores of matters relating to the Sumerians and the ancient Peruvians should occur consistently and regularly.

CHAPTER 26

The Identity of the Bearded God

Among the remains of all the Ancient American civilizations there are figures in sculptured stone, pottery or in frescoes representing bearded men. At the Temple of the Jaguars at Chichen Itzá there are innumerable bas-reliefs, both on the exterior and interior, of men with beards. As the temple was dedicated to Kukulcan, the Plumed Serpent god, who was always depicted as bearded, it has been suggested that the figures represent priests of Kukulcan, especially as the beards on some are obviously false. It must not be forgotten however, that the Incans and some of the Mexican Indians had heavy beards and that the Spaniards found excellent barber shops in Mexico.

But among the Mayas, the Aztecs and the Incans there was an identical legend or tradition of bearded men from the "sunrise" having reached South and Central America ages before the coming of the Spaniards.

All of these traditions of the "Bearded Ones" agreed that they were white men. Both the Aztecan Quetzalcoatl and the Mayan Kukulcan were traditionally white, while in Peru, Wira Kocha, the greatest of deities in human form, was also reputed to have been a bearded white man.

Among the innumerable specimens of pottery obtained from the graves and tombs of the ancient Moujiks of Chan Chan and vicinity there are vast numbers of so-called "portrait" jars. These obviously are of a ceremonial or record type and are beautifully made and modeled to represent actual men, the features being reproduced with the utmost care and fidelity. They are so accurately modeled, so complete in detail—even showing the warts, moles, scars and other blemishes of the originals, that it is evident they were modeled from life to serve as portraits. Among these a few represent a bearded man, a figure so entirely different from all the others, so obviously not an Indian but a white man, and so strikingly life-like that it is impossible to believe they were products of the potter's imagination.

The figure is seated, with hands resting upon the knees, or in some cases clasped against the stomach. The nose is large, high-bridged and aquiline, the eyes full and the expression serene and usually benign. A luxuriant moustache and full beard cover the cheeks and upper lip, and in every case the head is covered with a close-fitting cap with two upstanding "ears." The full, heavy-lidded eyes, the strongly aquiline nose and other facial characteristics are unmistakably Aryan or Hittite and indicate a personage of great mentality.

Across the shoulders there is always a cape-like garment decorated with spots like those of the jaguar. Statues and bas-reliefs of a deity or god-king found in Egypt show him with a full beard, an eared cap made from the skin of a lion's head and with features almost identical with those of the Peruvian figures, which unquestionably were portraits of Wira Kocha, the supreme deity of the pre-Incans. Wira Kocha was also known as the Tiger or Jaguar god whose spots appear on the effigy jars.

Moreover, many vessels, carvings and decorations show the "Tiger God" with huge canine teeth, as well as beard and moustache, and with the head of a jaguar above the forehead and with the jaguar's or "lions'" ears to the headdress. In countless representations of the Tiger god on pottery, carvings, decorations and woven in textiles, the deity is invariably represented with beard and moustache and with the cap with the feline's ears. Moreover, a few of these have the mark T, the symbol of the Stone People of King Menes. Hence the only conclusion we can reach and which explains these figures of a bearded tiger god and his apparel, is that Wira Kocha and Sargon of Agade or his son, King Menes, were one and the same.

There is also additional corroborative evidence of Sumerians having visited Peru. Carvings and sculptures, as well as designs on pottery, show a man standing between two felines. These are found both in the Old World and in Peru and form one of the most convincing evidences of the Sumerian origin of the ancient Peruvian Civilizations for they apparently represent the Sumerian "Keeper of the Cats," or "Double Lion god," known as Ishi, Tashia, Tas, Tascia, Indar, Indara, Indra, etc., probably symbolical of dominion over both the "eastern" and the "western" lands. Among the Peruvians the deity was known as "Mishi." Some of the Old World "Keepers of the Cats" are bearded but as far as I am aware no bearded specimens have been found in pre-Incan territory, therefore it is doubtful that the figure represents Wira Kocha.

Among the various names by which Sargon of Agade was known were Pra-Vira, Su-Vira, Kunti-Jit and Sharrukin which might easily be altered to become Wira-Kosha, Cuntur (Condor god) and Saycunin, names that may have applied to various attributes of but one Peruvian deity. Among the ancient Peruvians a secondary deity believed to be the son of Wira Kocha was known as Urcon. Menes' grandson, Shar-Gani, was also known as Urukn-gina and Uru-kn, and Ur-kon may be interpreted as King of Ur.

Urkon was also known as Kuntur-Tiksi or the Condor god and King Menes also bore the title of "Kutir" and members of his royal family wore a diadem bearing the figure of a vulture, or similar bird of prey. It is also noteworthy that the Sumerians' ancestors worshiped the Sun-god under the name of Indi, Indar, Indra (the latter is pronounced Engur or Engah) while the Hittite "Bull of the Sun" was called Inti, and that the Peruvians called their Sun-god Inti and occasionally Inga and their Incas (also pronounced very much like Engah) were traditionally Sons of the Sun.

I have in previous chapters referred to the repeated mention of the "Land of Manu" in several ancient Sumerian inscriptions and there is a locality known as Manu at the headwaters of the Madre de Dios River about one hundred and twenty miles east of Cuzco. If the Sumerian explorers actually reached Peru and Lake Titicaca it is highly probable that they ascended the Amazon and thence followed up the Madre de Dios River to its headwaters where a tributary named Manu passes through the area designated as Manu and a small town of the same name is located at the junction of these two rivers. But we have no means of knowing if in those far distant days the rivers were as they are today. In fact it is not impossible or even improbable that a large portion of what is now the Matto Grosso was inundated and that the Madre de Dios, at one time known as "The River of the Serpent," and other rivers were broad, deep estuaries.

The careful and intensive studies of the late Dr. Julio Tello of Lima, Peru, has in his monumental work, *Wira Kocha*, established the fact that Manko-Kapak the first Inca was a member of the Panaka family or clan and came from Zapala, a district about fifty miles east of Cuzco and about midway between Cuzco and Manu. Koshalla was the name of a royal sun-worshiping clan or tribe related to the "Panchala" or Aryan Phoenicians, at one time under the rule of East Indian kings.

According to legend, when Manko-Kapak first appeared on the scene he declared himself to be "Tihuantasuyo Kapa" or King of the "Four Corners of the Earth." One of the titles of Narām-sin was "Lord of the Four Regions of the Earth."

In view of all the above material it would seem a pretty firmly established fact that King Sargon of Agade reached Peru and Bolivia about 2500 B.C. and set up monuments and built temples on the Island of the Sun, and that he and Wira Kocha, the bearded god, are the same; that Sargon's son, Menes, established a colony near the shores of Lake Titicaca, that he was killed by the bite of a poisonous insect and was buried in Bolivia or Peru, probably the former, that he was deified by the Peruvians as a Father-god presiding over the land of the dead, or "souls' abode," and that his son Narām-sin, and grandson Shar-Gani contributed to the cultural development and enlightenment by introducing arts, religion, and other features into the pre-Incan civilization.

In addition to the evidence of the ancient Sumerian records, the ancient Peruvian traditions, the identical or very similar names of the deities of both races and the portrait jars representing Wira Kocha, there are a great many other evidences of the Sumerian origin of the ancient Peruvian civilization.

Perhaps, most important of all are the engineering feats and the stonework of the two peoples. The remarkable Cyclopean walls already described in Chapter 22, built of enormous stones of many angles and fitted together with mathematical precision, are found in Peru, Boghaz Koi in Asia Minor, and at Mycenae, Greece. Moreover, in all these widely separated localities the surfaces of the walls slope inward toward the tops and both the Asian and Peruvian polygonal type walls have small nipple-like projections on their outer surfaces. Peruvian door lintels made of a single huge slab are the same as in the famous twin lion gateway at Mycenae. Also, just as in Peru, the massive multiple-angled stones gave way to simpler masonry of rectangular type walls surmounted by tiers of smaller, more roughly cut, rectangular stone.

No one comparing photographs of the two can believe that they were merely a coincidence, that two races, separated by thousands upon thousands of miles of ocean, could have chanced upon the unique type of masonry, so identical in every respect that the structures in Peru and those in Asia Minor might well have been planned and erected by the same artizans.

Equally convincing is the type of architecture at Tiahuanaco where massive slabs of stone were locked together with metal keys of staples. Nowhere else in America is there any similar method of building and in only one other spot in the world is it known to have been duplicated in early times. In the ruined palace walls of Ashur-nasir-apal's residence at Calah or Nimrud in Assyria are enormous stone slabs with niches for metal staples cut in the same manner as those found at Tiahuanaco, Bolivia. Can anyone believe that this method of construction was invented independently in South America and in Mesopotamia? The fact that King Menes and his immediate family called themselves the "Stone People" and that the ancient Peruvian traditions tell of the arrival of the "Stone People" at Lake Titicaca, taken in connection with the unique and identical architecture of the pre-Incans and the Sumerian races, would seem to prove that these types of stone work were introduced to Peru by the Sumerians.

There are many other cultural features of the Sumerians and the Peruvians that are just as striking and which cannot logically be explained by any other hypothesis. No other race in America used the plow and the wide-bladed, short-handled hoe exactly like the ancient Sumerian implements. No other American race used the long-handled, broad-bladed battle axe; or maces with star-shaped heads and maces with free heads attached to the haft by thongs or chains, all of which were closely similar to those used by the Sumerian people. In no other portion of the Western Hemisphere did the Indians use the Biblical type of sling. In addition the Incans used a peculiar form of wooden shield exactly like the shields shown on bas-reliefs of the ancient Sinjarli warriors of Asia Minor, a territory once under control of the Sumerians. Neither did any other pre-Columbian American race possess balance scales, steelyards and standards of linear measurements, and nowhere in America except in Peru did the people use shears, precisely like those of the Old World, for shearing the wool of llamas and alpacas. Even the tight-fitting woolen caps with extended crown and ear-tabs worn by the Incan men, and still universally worn by their descendants of today, are duplicates of the "Phrygian caps" worn by Phoenician sailors in southwestern Asia from time immemorial.

It has been claimed that the ancient Peruvians had no recorded calendar, but in the Museum of the American Indian, Heye Foundation, in New York City, there is a gold calendrical sun-disk found in Peru, and a similar calendrical disk of gold was found near Cuenca, Ecuador (once Incan territory) in 1859. The Peruvian disk is five and one quarter inches in diameter and divided into eight sections. The center bears a conventionalized jaguar's or puma's face and in the spaces about the margin are human heads and various symbols. The disk reveals a number of features which indicate it is of Sumerian origin, such as "cup marks" in accord with those of the Sumerians and which had various meanings depending upon the arrangement and number of the marks. On the tiara of the symbolized face are two groups of four each of these cup marks, which, if interpreted correctly, would read: "Tas, the Field of Tas" (Heaven or the sky), *Tas* being another name for *Tasia* or *Mishi*, the "Keeper of the Cats" already described. The outer portion of the circumference of the plaque is divided into twenty equal sections bearing representations of the "seven pillars of the setting sun" and other typically Sumerian symbols. Double spirals, one on either side of the central face, indicate the day sun and night sun, the whorls or coils running in opposite directions, while the conventionalized plume in the center of the forehead was the family symbol of the house of Sargon of Agade. All of this checks perfectly with the known Sumerian calendrical and zodiacal symbolisms. Finally, we know from Sumerian inscriptions that the name Prithu-Rukhma, an early Sumerian-Phoenician prince, meant "Keeper of the Golden Disk," a sacred, precious object supposed to have been of calendrical character (Fig. 33).

As an acceptable rule, striking similarities in the religion of different tribes or people indicate a relationship or an influence and in the religions of the Sumerians and the Ancient Peruvians there were not only similarities but exact duplications. Both the Sumerians and the Incans held the Birth of the Sun ceremony and both celebrated the event, that marked the beginning of a new year, in September. Records do not give detailed descriptions of the Sume-

Fig. 33. Gold calendrical sun disk, Cuenca, Ecuador.
Now in Museum of American Indian, New York City

rian ceremonies but inscribed ancient Babylonian tablets state that as the sun appeared above the horizon the king drank from a ceremonial vessel. This ceremony was also held in early Egypt and their sacred drinking vessel was called a "pacha" exactly the same name that was applied to the Peruvian drinking vessel of the Incas. In both cases the pacha was of phallic significance. The Egyptian form was, according to tradition, created by Isis as a symbolism pertaining to Osiris, or deified King Menes. Also, as in the Incan ceremony, the sacred fires were re-kindled by means of a "burning glass" which was probably a concave mirror like that of the Incas.

One description taken from the cuneiform (Assyrian and Baby-lonian Literature) is as follows: "The king then rises, takes the sacred glass and holds it in the sun before the mass of waiting fuel on the altar piled. The centering rays the fuel quickly gild with a round spot of fire, and quickly spring above the altar curling while they cling."

Although it is probable that the "sacred glass" was a mirror, yet it is not impossible that it may have been a lens, for a true lens made from quartz was discovered by Dr. Layard at Nimrud, near Nineveh in Assyria (Museum of Antiquity by L. Yaggy and T. L. Haines, A.N., Page 346).

In 1853 Sir David Brewster, F.R.S., exhibited this lens at a meet-ing of the British Association for the Advancement of Science. Sir David, who had devoted a lifetime to optics, declared it to be an exceptionally finely and accurately ground lens. It is now in the British Museum.

Both the Sumerians' and the Incans' year was of three hundred and sixty days divided into twelve months or *Quillas* as they were called in Peru, each consisting of thirty days. As the *Quillas* were computed from the moon's rotation or were lunar months, and the lunar rotation is completed in three hundred and sixty-four days, eight hours and forty-eight minutes of our time, the *Quillas* lacked approximately five days of the solar year. In order to bring their solar year to coincide with the lunar year, the five days were un-named and were devoted to festivities attending the rebirth of the sun. Thus the old year ended on the night preceding the sun's rebirth and the new year began when the ceremonies ended five days later. Then, to make their lunar year exactly coincide with the solar year, an extra day was added every fourth year.

In taking their astronomical observations the Sumerians used a device almost exactly like the *Inti Tihuayna* of the Peruvians and a number of these have been discovered in widely separated areas.

Following the religious ceremonies attending the Birth of the Sun the holidays were given up to merry making, contests and games and the same procedure was followed by the Sumerians.

Whether or not a court minstrel or poet laureate was selected by the Sumerians at this time we do not know, but we do know from various inscriptions that there was a court bard just as at the court of the Inca and that he was a very important personage.

Both the Sumerians and the Incans held the rainbow as a sacred emblem and both the Sumerian kings and the reigning Incas wore the rainbow emblem above their foreheads. Both, also wore the artificial bangs or fringes known as a *borla*, among the Incans as a pad to ease the pressure from the weight of their crowns, and both

Fig. 34. Rainbow symbols

wore an upright plume of white feathers surmounted by scarlet feathers.

Many animals and inanimate objects were revered or held sacred by the Incans and the Sumerians. In Peru the most sacred creature was the big Andean goose and among the Sumerians and Egyptians the goose was also considered sacred.

There were many striking similarities between the Incas' and the Sumerian kings' forms of government. Inscribed records on a black diorite obelisk now in the Louvre in Paris gives full detail of the free institutions, the divisions of lands and the liberal government by the king of that era. Other records tell of the wise system of Sargon, which was followed when a race or territory was conquered and was very similar to the system employed by the Incas. The Sumerian king did not possess absolute power but was subject to an assembly or *Pankus* composed of warriors and nobles who had the power to ratify or to reject the rulings and edicts of the king, just as the five *Amautus* and the Tribunal of Princes could ratify or annul any decree of the Inca. Also, as in the case of the Inca, the Sumerian king was compelled to lead his troops in warfare and to expose himself to the same dangers as any common soldier.

In the Incan empire it was obligatory for the Inca to be the first to break ground and turn the earth with a golden spade whenever a new temple or public building was to be erected, and exactly the same custom prevailed among the Sumerians and several other civilized races of the Old World. Also, as in the Incan Empire, the monarch was obliged to listen personally to complaints of his subjects.

Even if the socialistic and governmental systems of the Incans and the Sumerians were not identical in every detail, we must remember that fully two thousand years had elapsed between the time of King Menes and the beginning of the Incan regime in Peru, and that during that period great changes would have been made and that the rulers, profiting by the experiences of their forebears and their own, would undoubtedly have devised a governmental system best adapted to the people, the conditions and the environment. Far more revolutionary alterations have been made in European governments, and in our own, for that matter, within the space of a century than existed between the ancient Sumerian and the Incan forms of government.

All descriptions of the Incans, and innumerable carvings, paint-ings and designs on pottery, prove that the Inca rode in a litter or sedan chair borne on the shoulders of nobles who considered this service a great honor, and this method of transporting royalty was a very ancient Old World custom.

Many of the burial customs of the two races were very similar and both the Sumerians and the Incans of certain cults placed a metal disk in the roof of the mouth of the corpse and placed arti-ficial tears of various materials on the face-covering or mummy mask.

Ceremonial and folk dances are very important clues to the re-lationship of races, for details of costume and other matters persist unchanged through hundreds of years. In the highlands of Peru and Bolivia the men who take part in one dance wear strange cape-like affairs of jaguar skin attached to two sticks resting upon their shoulders and in some of the ancient Sumerian religious dances or rituals the same type of capes made of leopard skin were worn. Several Pacific Island tribes also wear ceremonial capes of animal skin formed like those worn in Peru and Bolivia.

Although early Sumerian textiles are very rare and the few that have been found are fragmentary, those from Susa or Shushan are practically identical with those of the pre-Incans in the type of weaving and the technique.

As mentioned in a preceding chapter, the ancient Peruvians had an advanced knowledge of medicine and surgery. Many of the medicines that they employed are among our most valued and efficacious drugs and remedies. Such for example as quinine, co-caine, sarsaparilla, aloes, rhubarb, iodine, borax, etc. They were also very capable and expert surgeons and dentists. They successfully trepanned skulls, amputated limbs, performed abdominal opera-tions, practised plastic surgery, filled, extracted and crowned teeth, and designed efficient artificial limbs and hands. No other Amer-ican race ever equaled them in these matters and it would seem as if they must have acquired their medical and surgical knowledge from some outside source. According to their records the Sumerians also were famed for their medical and surgical knowledge and skill and King Menes wrote the first of all books on human anat-omy, medicine and surgery. He dealt in great detail on anatomy, the symptoms of many ailments and their remedies, and it is said that he even instituted and taught a special priesthood concerning these matters, probably the earliest of all medical schools, in order that they might benefit his subjects. Some of his medicines were efficacious and are still in use while others of course were nostrums. After his death and deification he often was referred to as the "god of Healing." He died in "Urani land at the lake of the peak at the end of sunset land" and on a wooden cenotaph from Egypt it is recorded that he met his death in this far distant land through the bite of an insect called the *laur-au*. In the Aimara dialect of Bolivia any poisonous insect is known as a *pu-uru* although the name is more especially applied to the Black Widow spider.

It would not seem possible or within the realms of chance that all of these many resemblances between the Sumerians and ancient Peruvians could be merely coincidence. And there are many times more. In the following pages I have listed forty-two important matters that were identical or very nearly so, in both these ancient civilizations.

1. Bearded figures representing a deity wearing a headdress made of the skin of a feline's head with upstanding ears.
2. Lion and jaguar gods with humanized faces.
3. A human figure standing between two felines occasionally accompanied by similar symbolic emblems.
4. Figures of a vulture or condor-god with a head mask resembling the likeness of a bird of prey.
5. Walls of the Cyclopean type composed of enormous, many-angled stones fitted together without cement or mortar. Peculiar to Peru, Asia Minor, and Greece.
6. Secondary walls, often on the above, made of plain rectangular blocks laid in regular tiers.
7. Blind niches or recesses in the walls.
8. Structures built of huge stone slabs locked together by means of metal keys or staples hammered into recesses cut in the stone. So far as known found only in Bolivia and Assyria.
9. Wide-bladed, long-handled battle axes. Not used by any other American race.
10. Maces with star-shaped or many-pointed heads. Not used by any other American race.

11. Maces with free-swinging heads attached to the haft by chains or thongs. Not used by any other American race.
12. Slings of the Biblical type not in use by any other American race.
13. Wooden shields of a peculiar type carried by warriors of Peru and Asia Minor.
14. Short-handled, heavy-bladed hoes.
15. Plows of identical form not employed by any other American race.
16. Shears with blades actuated by a spring used in shearing llamas and alpacas. Not used elsewhere in America.
17. Balance scales, steelyards and standards of linear measurement.
18. Caps of the "Phrygian" type with long crown and ear tabs.
19. A calendrical system precisely the same.
20. Similar devices for astronomical observations.
21. The "Birth of the Sun" ceremony and celebration of the New Year.
22. Method of rekindling the sacred fires by concentrating the sun's rays.
23. Sacred vessels used in ceremonial libations and drinking, known as *pachas*.
24. Holidays at the time of the Birth of the Sun.
25. Court bards or minstrels.
26. Adoration of the rainbow and the use of the rainbow symbol by the Sumerians of royal blood and the reigning Incas.
27. The *borla* or royal fringe worn on the forehead of both the Sumerian and Incan monarchs.
28. Plumes or white and red feathers on the front of the crown of Sumerian and Peruvian rulers.
29. The goose considered a sacred creature by both Sumerians and Incans.
30. Similarities of governments of Sumeria and ancient Peru.
31. Free schools or colleges where military officers, astronomers, civil engineers, etc. were trained. Established and maintained by the Incan and Sumerian governments.
32. Regular standing armies fully equipped and in uniform and a reserve force of trained soldiers maintained by Sumerians and Incans.
33. Both the Inca and the Sumerian king were obliged to lead the army in battle and to take equal risks with the soldiers.
34. Neither the ruling Inca nor Sumerian king were absolute mon-

archs. Both were subject to a tribunal or assembly of nobles who could ratify or reject any edict of the monarch.

35. Many burial customs of the Sumerians and ancient Peruvians were the same, such as the use of masks or false faces, placing a metal disk or plate in the roof of the mouth of a corpse, placing artificial tears on the mask.
36. The use of a jaguar's skin made into a peculiar cape-like affair worn by the Incans in certain dances and precisely the same sort of garment worn by natives of certain South Pacific islands once under Sumerian rule.
37. The same types of weaving and techniques found in textiles of the Sumerians and the pre-Incans.
38. Great knowledge of medicine and surgery common to both the Incans and the Sumerians.
39. Over one hundred identical or very nearly identical words with the same meanings in both the Sumerian and Peruvian languages.
40. Names of gods and lesser deities the same or very similar in both languages.
41. Sacred objects and matters pertaining to religion the same or very nearly the same in both the Sumerian and Peruvian languages.
42. Sumerian inscriptions and records agreeing perfectly with the traditions of the Peruvians and Bolivians.

Among the more noteworthy examples of duplicate or very similar words, names, etc., that have the same meanings in the Sumerian and Peruvian languages are the following:

SUMERIAN	PERUVIAN
VIRU—KASHA: King Sargon of Agade	WIRA KOCHA: The Bearded god
SHAKUNI: Another name for Sargon	SAYCUNIN: The Bearded god
URUKN: Menes' grandson, Shar-Gani	URKON: "Son" of Wira Kocha
ENKI or EA: God of Waters	ENKI: pre-Incan deity
INDAR (pronounced Engur): The Sun god	INGA or INTI: The Sun god
MISHI: The dual Cat or lion god	ISHI: "Keeper of the Cats"
KON: God-King father of Sargon (also Shar-Gani)	KON-WIRA: Jaguar god

SUMERIAN	PERUVIAN
Kutir: King Menes as the Vulture god	Kuntur-Tici: The Condor god
Tonen: King Menes after deification	Tonapa: A secondary deity
I-ri-ja: A Cultural god	Iraya: A lesser deity
Go-a: Mother goddess	Goya or Ccoya: Mother goddess
mica-iah: Like unto Jehovah	micay: Divine, Godlike
Panasa or Pank-alla: A royal family	Panaka: The Inca family name
mettiyo: A noble	metiyok: A noble
kuter: Incanting priest	Kutur-tiksi: A lesser deity
Amatya: Council of wise men	Amautu: Councillors, Wise men
miok: Sacred New Fire	mosok: The New Fire
imenti: Sacred or occult	imentin: Sacred or occult
choucha: A stone tower	chulpa: A stone tower
yasi-kaya: Shrine or temple	kalasaya: A temple
ilu: A talisman. God's proxy	illi: A charm or talisman
apacha: Hill with reservoir	apakana: Hill with reservoir
e-absu: Baptismal font	apasu: Baptismal font
pacha: Sacred drinking vessel	pacha: Sacred drinking vessel
ya: A priest	ya-ya: Priest
amenti: Royal cemetery	amencay: A burial place of nobles
Nuna: The sacred goose	Nun-una: Sacred Andean goose
pankus: Council or assembly	pankus: Tribunal or council
kosher: Pure or holy	kocha: Pure or holy
inini: Creed or belief	inny: Creed or belief
tyana: Throne or seat	tyana: Throne or seat

Miscellaneous Words

SUMERIAN	PERUVIAN
aba: Negative word	iba: Negative word
alla: Capable or able	alli: Capable or able
amara: A race	aimara: A tribe or race
atium: Great or mighty	atun: Mighty or great
apu: Head of a family	apu: Head of a family

SUMERIAN	PERUVIAN
AK: Affix meaning many	AK: Affix meaning many
AKIS: Eye	AKIS: Eye
ATUN: Mighty or great	ATUN: Mighty or great
CALI: A house	CALI: A house
CUSH: Happiness or joy	CUSHI: Happiness or joy
CATA: The end or a remnant	KATA: Remnant or end
CA: You or thou	CCAU: You or thou
CA-AI: This or that	CHAI: This or that
HALA: The plow	HACLA: The plow
HAM: We or us	HAM: We or us
IAUR-AU: Place of the stinging or biting insect	URU: Poisonous insect
ISHME: Safe or secure	ISHMI: Safety
ISTER: A star	ISHTAR: Star
IMA: Something	IMI: Something
IMENTI: Mysterious	IMENTIN: Mysterious
KAYA: A corpse	KAYA: A corpse
KALA: The moon	QUILLA: The moon
KENYA: A ditch	KENKA: A ditch
KIPI: Monkey	CHEPI: Monkey
KASIKIKI: Chief, Governor	CAZIQUE: Chief
MITTANI: Shore, coast	MITANA: Shore
MA: The world	MAI: The world
MAK: River	MAK: River
KHUNAS: More than one	KUNA: More than one
MUKTA: Pearl	MUYU: Pearl
NUNA: Water	UNA: Water
PAITA: Father	TAITA: Father
PUNCU: A kind of door	PUNKA: A door
SAHKI: Friend	SAHAKA: Friend
SIVAS: Ring or circle	SIVI: Ring or circle
TINYA: Drum	TINYA: Drum
TAG: The earth	TEKSI-MUYU: The earth (Muyu means round, a pearl, etc.)
TIANU: Lion or tiger	TI-TI: Jaguar or puma
URANI: Below, Beneath	URANI: People below. People of Ur Indians as an entity
URMANA: To fell or to destroy	URMANI: To destroy. To go down

SUMERIAN	PERUVIAN
URACUY: Setting sun	INTI-URUCY: Setting sun
UMMA: The head	UMA: The head
UTU: Home	UTU: Home
VINCA: A farm	FINCA: A farm
AIJA: Ruined-place name	AIJA: Destroyed. A place name
CADZU: Place name	CUZCO: Place name
CHANAAN: Place name	CHAN-CHAN: Place name
ILLI-MANI: "Shining jewel"	ILLI-MANI: Mountain in Bolivia
KANAH: A place name	CANA: A place name
PURU: Pharaoh	PERU: Place name
PURU-NUNU: Euphrates River	PURUS: A river in Peru
RECAH: Place name	RECUEY: Place name
RIMAC: Place name	RIMAC: Place name

Bibliography

Album Historico Civilizacion Nazca-Peru, Edad de Bronce. Lima, 1921.

Antiguedades Mexicanas. La Junta Colombina de Mexico. Mexico, 1892.

Baessler, Arthur, *Ancient Peruvian Art.* Leipzig, 1902-03.

Bancroft, Hubert H., *Conquest of Mexico.* New York, 1883.

Bandelier, Adolph F., *Report of an Archaeological Tour in Mexico.* Boston, Cupples, Upham and Co., 1884.

Baranda, J., *Recordaciones Historicas.* Mexico, 1907.

Bardin, J. C., *Yucatán Develops a Truly American Art.* Bull. Pan American Union. Washington, D. C., July 1926.

Bennett, Wendell C., *Handbook of South American Indians.* Vol. 5, *Comparative Ethnology of South American Indians, Bulletin L43,* Bureau of American Ethnology, Smithsonian Institution, Washington, D. C., 1949.

Benzoni, H., *Novae Novi Orbis Historae, id est, Rerum ab Hispanis in India Occidentali.* Geneva, 1600.

Beyer, Hermann, *Apuntes Sobre el Jeroglifico Maya-ek "Negro."* Anales del Museo Nacional de Arqueologia. Mexico, 1925.

—, *Apuntes Sobre el Jeroglifico Maya Muluc. Memoria Revista de la Sociedad Cientifica Antonio Alzate.* Mexico, 1926.

—, *Las Dos Estelas Mayas de Chila Chis. El Mexico Antiguo.* Mexico, 1926.

—, *Las Inscripciones del Lintel 30 de Yaxchilan.* Mexico, 1927.

—, *La Cifra Diez en el Simbolismo Maya. Revista Mexicana de Eustudios Historicos.* Mexico, 1927.

BIBLIOGRAPHY 317

Beyer, Hermann, *Dos Fechas del Palacio de Palenque.* Mexico, 1927.
—, *La Cifra Tres en el Simbolismo Maya.* Mexican Folkways. Mexico, 1927.
Bingham, Hiram, "Type of Machu-Picchu Pottery." *American Anthropologist,* N.S. Vol. 17. April-June, 1915.
—, *Machu-Picchu, a Citadel of the Incas.* New Haven, Yale University Press, 1930.
Blom, Frans, "Notes from the Maya Area." *American Anthropologist,* 1924. *Conquest of Mexico.* Boston, 1936.
—, *Archaeological and Ethnographic Expedition to Middle America.* Tulane University, New Orleans, 1925.
Bordone, Ben, *Isolario Nel Qual si Ragiona di Tutte le Isole del Mundocopia Delle Lettere del Prefetto Della Indra Alla ces. Maesta rescritte* (the first account of Pizarro's arrival in Peru.) Venice, 1537.
Brinton, Daniel G., ed., *The Maya Chronicles.* Philadelphia, 1882.
Budge, E. A. W., *The Book of the Dead,* Vols. I, II, III. London, 1901.
Cartas de Indias. Publicadas por primera vez el ministerio de fomento. Madrid, 1887.
Caso, Alfonso, *Las ruinas de Tizatlan.* Mexico, 1927.
—, *El Teocalli de la guerra sagrada.* Mexico, 1927.
Catherwood, Frederick, *Views of Ancient Monuments in Central America, Chiapas and Yucatán.* London, 1844.
Cervantes De Salazar, Francisco, *Cronica de Nueva Espana escrita por Cronista de la Ciudad de Mexico, etc.* Madrid, 1914.
Chico, Domingo, *Accounts of the Incans' customs, ceremonies, beliefs, etc., as related to the Viceroy Toledo.* Archives, Madrid.
Cieca, De Leon, Pedro, *Parte primera de la cronica del Peru.* Seville, 1553.
Cieca, F. Lopez De Gomara, *Historia de Peru y conquista de Yucatán.* Venice, 1560-1599.
Codex Magliabecchiano XIII (facsimile). Rome, 1904.
Codex Nuttall (facsimile). Cambridge, Mass., 1902.
Codex Osuna (facsimile). Madrid, 1878.
Codex Peresianus (facsimile). Paris, 1888.
Codice Kingsborough (facsimile). Madrid, 1912.
Codice Mendoza (facsimile). Mexico, 1925.

Coleccion de documentos ineditos relat. al descubrimiento, conquista y colonizacion de las posesiones Espana en America, sac del Archivo de Indias. Madrid, 1864.

Cortes, Hernando, Historia de Nueva Espana. Mexico, 1770.

—, Letters of Cortes. London, 1908.

De Landa, Friar Diego, Yucatán before and after the Conquest. Translated by W. Gates, Baltimore, 1937.

Delafield, John, An Inquiry Into the Origin of the Antiquities of America. New York, 1839.

De Leon, Cieza, Letters and documents describing Chan Chan, Cajamarca, etc., and the capture and execution of Atahualpa. Archives Real de España.

Diaz del Castello, B., Historia verdadera de la conquista de Nueva España. Madrid, 1632.

Diego, Lopez De Cogolludo, Historia de Yucatán. Merida, 1867.

Durand, Juan E., Leyendas Incaicas. Antofagasta, Chile, 1923.

Ekholm, George F., "Is American Indian Culture Asiatic?" Natural History Magazine. October, 1950.

Ekholm, George F., and Heine-Geldern. Significant Parallels in the Symbolic Arts of Southern Asia and Middle America. Proceedings of the 29th International Congress of Americanists, Vol. I. University of Chicago Press, 1951.

Fancourt, Charles St. John, The History of Yucatán From Its Discovery to the Close of the Seventeenth Century. London, 1854.

Farabee, Wm. Curtis, Ancient American Gold. Museum Journal, University of Pennsylvania, September, 1920.

Fernandez De Navarrete, Coleccion de los viages y descubrimientes que hicieron por mar los Españoles. Madrid, 1829.

Fernandez, Miguel A., El Templo de los Tigres, Chichen Itza. Ethnos. Mexico, 1925.

Feyjoo De Sosa, Don Miguel, Corrigedor y Tesorero General del Tribunal y Comision Real. Verdad Historia de Trujillo. Lima, 1632.

Field, Henry, The early history of man with special reference to the Cap-Blanc Skeleton. Field Museum of Natural History. Chicago, 1927.

Foster, John W., Prehistoric Races of the United States of America. Chicago, S. C. Griggs and Co., 1874.

Frejes, Fr. Francisco, Historia breve de la conquista de los estados independentes del imperio Mexicano. Guadelajara, 1878.

Gamio, Manuel, *Las excavaciones del Pedregal de San Angel y cultura arcaica del Valle de Mexico.* Lancaster, Pa., 1920.

—, *La poblacion del valle de Teotihuacan—su evolucion etnica y social.* Mexico, 1922.

Gann, Thomas. *In an Unknown Land.* New York, C. Scribner's Sons, 1924.

—, *Mystery Cities. Exploration and adventures in Lubaantum.* New York, 1925.

—, *Maya Jades.* Twenty-first International Congress of Americanists. Gottenborg, 1925.

—, *A New Maya Stela With Initial Series Data.* Man. London, 1926.

—, "Slowly the Past Emerges." *Scientific American.* New York, 1928.

—, and J. Eric Thompson, *The History of the Maya From the Earliest Times to the Present Day.* New York, C. Scribner's Sons, 1931.

Garcia, Gr., *Origen de los Indios del Nuevo Mundo.* Madrid, 1729.

Garcilasso De La Vega, *Historia des Yncas, rois du Perou.* Amsterdam, 1737.

Gayton, Anna H., and Kroeber, A. L., *The Uhle Pottery Collections from Nazca.* Berkeley, University of California Press, 1927.

Gomez, Robelo Ricardo, *El significado esoterico de algunas simboles Nahua.* Mexico, 1925.

Gordon, G. B., *Examples of Maya Pottery in the Museum of the University of Pennsylvania,* etc. Philadelphia, 1925.

Gordon, Thomas F., *The History of Ancient Mexico.* Philadelphia, 1832.

Guia para visitar le ciudad arqueologica de Teotihuacan. Mexico, 1927.

Guzman, D. J., *Interpretation de la escritura hieratica de Centro America. Estudio sobre el sistema grafico de la lengua Maya.* Boleten de la Academia Salvadorena. San Salvador, 1925.

Hartman, Carl V., *Archaeological Researches in Costa Rica.* Stockholm, 1901.

Helps, Arthur, *The Spanish Conquest in America.* London, 1855.

Herrera, Moises, *Las representaciones zoomorfas en el arte antiguo Mexicano.* Mexico, 1925.

—, *Esculturas zoomorfas y fitomorfas de Tlotihuacan.* Mexico, 1919.

Hewett, Edgar L., *Ancient Life in Mexico and Central America.* New York, Tudor Publishing Co., 1943.

Historia de las Indias. Madrid, 1875-1876.

Historia de los Yncas. Sarmiento de Gamboa. 1574. Edited by Sir Clements Markham. Hakluyt Soc. Ser. II. Vol. XXII, Cambridge, 1907.

History of Art In Phoenicia and Cyprus. Vols. I, II. London, Perrot and Chipiez, 1885.

Hrdlicka, Ales, *Anthropological Work in Peru in 1913.* Smithsonian Misc. Collections. Washington, D. C., 1914.

Idiomas y Dialectos Indigenas Del Continente Hispano Sud-Americano Con La Nomina De Las Tribus Indianas De Cada Territorio. Carlos Prince. Lima, 1905.

Joyce, Thomas A., *An Example of Cast Gold Work From Palenque.* Proceedings of the Twenty-first International Congress of Americanists. The Hague, 1924-25.

—, "The Paccha of Ancient Peru." *Journal Royal Anthr. Inst.* London, 1922.

—, *The Hieroglyphic Stairway at Naranjo, Guatemala. Ibid.,* 1925.

—, *South American Archaeology.* New York, 1912.

—, "Report on the Investigation at Lubaantum." *British Museum Quarterly.* London, 1927.

Joyce, Thomas A., *Mexican Archaeology.* London, 1914.

—, *Maya and Mexican Art.* London, 1927.

Karsten, Rafael. *The Civilization of the South American Indians with Special Reference to Magic and Religion.* New York, 1926.

King, Leonard W., *A History of Sumer and Akkad.* New York, F. A. Stokes, 1910.

Kingsborough, Lord. *Antiquities of Mexico.* London, 1830.

Kroeber, Alfred L., *Archaeological Explorations in Peru.* Part 1. "Ancient Pottery from Trujillo." Field Mus. Nat. History, Chicago, 1926.

—, *The Uhle Pottery Collections From Chancay.* University of Cal. Publ. in American Arch. and Eth. Berkeley, 1926.

Larde, Jorge, *Arqueologia Cuzcatleca.* Contrib. al III Congreso Cientifico Panamericana. San Salvador, 1924.

Ledon, Luis Castillo, *La fundacion de la Ciudad de Mexico; 1325-1925.* Mexico, 1925.

Long, Richard C. E., *Some Maya time Periods.* Proceeds. Twenty-first Int. Congress of Americanists. Gottenberg, 1925.

Long, Richard C. E., *A Link Between the Earlier and Later Maya Chronologies*. Man., London, 1924.

Lothrop, Samuel K. *Tulum, an Archaeological Study of the East Coast of Yucatán*. Carnegie Institution, Washington, D. C., 1924.

—, *The Museum's Central American Expedition*. Indian Notes, Museum of the American Indian, Heye Foundation, New York, January, 1925.

—, *Pottery of Costa Rica and Nicaragua*. Contr. Museum of The American Indian, Heye Foundation, New York, 1926.

—, *Stone Sculptures From Finca Arevalo, Guatemala*. Indian Notes, July, 1926.

Luna, Carlos, *Apuntes sobre arqueologia nacional*. Sociedad de Geografia y Historia de Guatemala. 1925.

Madrid Royal Archives. 1530-1750. *Letters, Reports*, etc., *from Ponce de Leon and others*.

Markham, Sir Clements, *Incas of Peru*. London, 1910.

Martinez, Fray Alonzo, *Los Habitos Incaicos y Los Tesoros Fundado en El Cuzco*. Madrid, 1535.

Mason, J. Alden, *Native American Jades*. Museum Journal, Philadelphia, March, 1927.

—, *Mirrors of Ancient America*. Ibid. June, 1927.

Matthewson, Capt. Archibald, *Account of a Voyage to the Spice Islands Of the South Sea*. London, 1750. (Captain Matthewson never reached the Spice Islands. Shipwrecked on the coast of Peru, he lived there several years and devoted much of his time to digging for treasure at Pachacamak, Chan Chan and elsewhere.)

Maudslay, Alfred P., *The True History of the Conquest of New Spain*. Hakluyt Society. London, 1908.

—, *Collection of Maya Sculptures from Central America*. British Museum Publication 1923.

McBride, George McCutchen, *The Agrarian Indian Communities of Highland Bolivia*. Am. Geo. Soc., Research Series, No. 5. Oxford University Press, New York, 1921.

Mead, Charles William, *Old Civilizations of Inca Land*. American Museum of Natural History, New York, 1924.

—, *Peruvian Art As Shown on Textiles and Pottery*. Am. Museum Nat. Hist. New York, 1925.

Means, Philip Ainsworth, *Ancient Civilizations of the Andes*. C. Scribner's Sons, 1931.

Means, Philip Ainsworth, *Peruvian Textiles*. New York, 1930.

Meba, Ramon, *Arqueologia; Monolitos*. Mexico, 1924.

Mendijabal, Miguel O. de., *El Lienzo de Jucatacats. Se verdadera significacion*. Museo Nacional, Mexico. D. F., 1926.

Mesopotamian Archaeology. P. S. P. Handcock. New York, G. P. Putnam's Sons, 1912.

Mexico. Museo Nacional de Arqueologia, *Historia y Etnografia. Album de colecciones arqueologicas anegladas* por Franz Boas. Mexico, 1921.

—, *Opiniones y juicios critices sobre la obra La poblacion de valle de Teotihuacan, etc.*, Tacubaya, 1924.

—, *Informe general de los trabajos, realijados de septiembre de 1925, a augusto de 1926*. Mexico, 1926.

Moreda, Jose De, *Relacion historica y cronologica de las Companias Coloniales para Indias occidentales*. Cartagena, Colombia, 1764.

Morley, Sylvanus G., *The Earliest Mayan Dates*. Proceedings of Twenty-first International Congress of Americanists, Gottenberg, 1924.

—, *New Light on the Discovery of Yucatan and the Foundation of the New Maya Empire*. Am. Journal of Archaeology. Concord, N. H., 1927.

—, *The Ancient Maya*. Stanford, Cal., Stanford University Press, 1946.

—, *An Introduction to the Study of the Maya Hieroglyphs*. Bureau of Am. Ethnology, Smithsonian Institution, Washington, D. C., 1915.

Nognera, Eduardo, *Los altares du sacrifico de Tizatlan*. Tlazcala, Mexico, 1927.

Novella, Gustavo, *Clasificacion del estilo Maya entre los demas estilos de arquitectura que se conocen. Anales de la Sociedad de Geografia y Historia de Guatemala*. Guatemala, June, 1925.

Nuttall, Zelia, *The Aztecs and Their Predecessors in the Valley of Mexico*. Philadelphia, 1926.

Ordonez De Zevallos, P., *Historia y viage del Mundo—A America*. Madrid, 1691.

Oviedo y Valdes, Gonzalo Fernandez De, *La Historia general de los Indias*. Seville, 1535.

Pachacamac. Max Uhle. Dept. of Archaeology, University of Pennsylvania, 1903.

Pacheco Cruz, Santiago, *La tumba tesoro. Leyenda Yucateca escrita en el ingenio Dziuche por el Señor J. Baltagar Perez. Vertida a la lengua Maya.* Merida, 1913.

Palacios, Enrique Juan, *Interpretaciones de la piedra del calendario.* Mexico, 1924.

Paleveceno, Enrico y Imbelloni, J., *Dos notas preliminares sobre la lengua Quechua.* Buenos Aires, 1926.

Pan American Union, *Summary of Archaeological Work in the Americas in 1926.* Washington, 1927.

Pedrahita, Fern L., *Historia general de la conquista del Nuevo Reyno de Granada.* Hamburg, 1688.

Peñafiel, Antonio, *Teotihuacan. Estudio historico y arqueologico.* Mexico, 1900.

Peralta, M. M. De, *Costa Rica, Nicaragua y Panama en el siglo XVI.* Madrid, 1883.

Pizarro, Hernando, *Account of Pachacamak and the treasures obtained there.* Royal Archives, Madrid.

Popul Vuh. Goetz, Morley, Recinos. University of Oklahoma Press, 1950.

Posnansky, Arthur. *Tiahuanacu.* New York, J. J. Augustin, 1946.

Pottery of Costa Rica and Nicaragua. Contributions from the Museum of the American Indian, Heye Foundation. Vol. III.

Prescott, William H., *History of The Conquest of Peru.* New York, E. P. Dutton and Co., 1924.

—, *The Conquest of Mexico,* Philadelphia, J. B. Lippincott Co., 1899.

Pre-Spanish Art of Mexico. Instituto Nacional de Antropologia e Historia. Mexico, D. F. 1946.

Proceedings of the Twenty-third International Congress of Americanists, 1930.

Raegan, A. B., *Indian Pictures in Ashley and Dry Fork Valleys in Northeastern Utah.* Art and Archaeology, Vol. 34, No. 4, 1933.

—, *The Petroglyphs of Ashley and Dry Fork Valleys In Northeastern Utah.* Transactions of the Kansas Academy of Sciences, Vol. 34, 1931.

Reygadas Vertiz, Jose, *Ruins de Zayi.* Anales del Museo Nacional de Arqueologia. Mexico, April-June, 1925.

Ricketson, Oliver G., *Burials in Maya Area.* Am. Anthropologist. July, 1925.

Rivet, Paul, *Les Australiens en Amerique.* Paris, 1925.

Rocha, Diego A., *Carta al Excmo. Señor Don Baltasar de la Cueva.* Lima, 1675.

Safford, William E., *An Aztec Narcotic.* Washington, D. C., 1915.

—, *The Isolation of Ancient Americas Established by the Cultivated Plants and the Languages of its Aborigines.* Rio de Janeiro, 1924.

—, *Foods Discovered With America.* Garrison, N. Y., 1925.

Sahagun, Fray Bern. De O. S. F., *Historia general de las cosas de Nueva Espana.* Mexico, 1829. Pub. for the Mexican Govt. by Francisco del Paso y Troncoso.

Salazar y Olarte, J. de, *Historia de la Conquista de Mexico.* Cordoba, 1743.

Saville, Marshall H., *The Manabi Culture.* Contrib. Museum of the American Indian, Heye Foundation, New York.

—, *Turquoise Mosaic Art In Ancient Mexico.* Contrib. Museum of the American Indian, Heye Foundation, New York, 1922.

—, *Mayan Sculpture from Guatemala.* Indian Notes, Museum of the American Indian, Heye Foundation, New York, 1924.

—, *The Wood-Carvers' Art in Ancient Mexico.* Contrib. Museum of American Indian, Heye Foundation, New York, 1925.

Schliemann, Henry, *Ilios,* New York, 1880.

Schuller, Rudolph, *The Native Country of the Maya K-ici Indians.* Am. Anthropologist, April-June, 1927.

Simoens Da Silva, Antonio Carlos, *Los des Incas dans la prehistorie du Brazil.* Rio de Janiero, 1926.

—, *O Continente Americano propulsor de paz.* Rio de Janeiro, 1926.

Solis y Rivadeneira, Antonio de, *Istoria della conquista del Messico.* Venice, 1733.

Solis Alcala, Emelio y Solis Mendiburu, Ermilio. *Los ahau-katunes del manuscripto de Mani.* Merida, Yucatán, 1925.

Sotomayor, Damaso, *La conquista de Mexico, efectuado por Hernan Cortes segun el codice jeroglifico Troano-Americano.* Edicion especial, Mexico, 1897.

—, *El siglo jeroglifico Azteca en sus 52 calendrios.* Mexico, 1897.

Spence, Lewis. *The Myths of Mexico & Peru.* London, 1920.

—, *Mythologies of Ancient Mexico & Peru.* London, 1907.

—, *The Civilization of Ancient Mexico.* Cambridge University Press, 1912.

Spinden, Herbert J., *The Reduction of Maya Dates.* Paper, Peabody Museum of American Arch. and Eth., Cambridge, 1924.

Spiro Mound Collection in the Museum; E. K. Burnett, and *Historical Sketch of the Spiro Mound* by F. E. Clements. Museum of the American Indian, Heye Foundation, New York, 1945.

Squier, Ephraim G., *Nicaragua, Its People, Scenery, Monuments, etc.* New York, Harper & Bros., 1860.

Stahl, Ferdinand A., *In the Land of the Incas.* Mountain View, Cal., Pacific Press Publishing Assoc., 1920.

Stephens, John L., *Incidents of Travel In Central America, Chiapas and Yucatán.* Vols. I, II. New York, Harper Brothers, 1841.

Steward, Julian, *Petroglyphs of the United States.* Annual Report of the Smithsonian Institution, Washington, D. C., 1936.

Strube, Leon, *Arte rupestre en Sud America—los petroglifos de la Provincia de Coquimbo,* Chile. 1926.

Stuebel, Alfonse and Max Uhle, *Die Ruinenstaette von Tiahuanaco.* Breslau, 1892.

Susto, Juan Antonio, *Panama en el Archivo General de Indias.* Panama, 1927.

Teeple, John E., *Maya Inscriptions.* American Anthropologist. January-March, 1925.

—, *Maya Inscriptions; the Venus Calendar, etc. Ibid.* April-June, 1926.

Tello, Julio, *Wira Kocha. Jaguar-God.* (*El Div Tigre*) Lima, 1931.

Thomas, Cyrus, *A Study of the Manuscript Troano.* Washington, 1882.

Thompson, Eric, *The Meaning of the Mayan Months. Man.* London, 1925.

—, *A Correlation of the Mayan and European Calendars.* Field Museum of Natural History, Chicago, 1927.

—, *The Civilization of the Mayas. Ibid.* Chicago, 1927.

Toledo, Don Francisco, Viceroy of Peru, *Letter dated 9th October, 1572, telling of the discovery of the gold sun-disk hidden in the Willea Pampa.* Spanish Archives in Madrid.

Toro, Alfonso, *Compendio de historia de Mexico, Historia antigua desde los tiempo mas remotos hasta antes de la llegada de los Espanoles.* Mexico, 1926.

Townsend, Martin Ingham. *Prehistoric Structures of Yucatán.* Troy, N. Y., T. J. Hurley, 1900.

Tozzer, Alfred M., *Time and American Archaeology.* Natural History. May-June, 1927.

Tozzer, Alfred M., *Chronological Aspects of American Archaeology*. Proceeds. of the Mass. Historical Society. Boston, April, 1926.

Triana, Miguel, *Petrogifos de la mesa central de Colombia*. Bogotá, 1924.

Tribes, and Temples. A record of the expedition to middle America conducted by the Tulane University of Louisiana in 1925. New Orleans, 1926.

Uhle, Max, *Los elementos constitutivos de las civilizationes Andinas*. Quito, 1926.

—, *Zur chronologie der alten culturen von Ica;* Journal de la Société des Americanistes de Paris, 1913.

Ulloa, Antonio de, and Jorge Juan, *Relacion historica del viaje a la America Meridional*. Madrid, 1748.

Valera, Fray Blas, *Relaciones de los Freyes y Los* (locano defaced) *de los Yncas Juira Gocha y el Ynca Rocca* (locano defaced), Madrid, Royal Archives of the Indies.

Van Den Bergh, Henry, *The Incas and Their Industries*. London, G. Routledge and Sons, 1921.

Vocabulario Castellano-Zapoteco. Mexico, 1893.

Vocabulario Castellano-Quechua-Pano con Sus Respectivas Grammaticas. Fr. Manuel Navarro, Lima, 1903.

Vocabulario Poliglota Incaico, Compuesto por algunos Religiosos Franciscanos Missioneros de los Caligios de Propaganda. Fide del Peru, Lima, 1905.

Waddell, Lt. Col. L. A., *Makers of Civilization in Race and History*. London, 1929.

Waterman, Thomas T., *The Architecture of the American Indian*. Am. Anth., April-June, 1927.

Weigall, Arthur, *Glory of the Pharaohs*. New York, G. P. Putnam's Sons, 1923.

Willard, Theodore A., *The City of the Sacred Well*. New York, The Century Co., 1926.

Wilson, Robert W., *Astronomical Notes on the Maya Codices*. Papers of the Peabody Museum of Arch. and Eth., Cambridge, 1924.

Wisler, Clark, *The Relation of Nature to Man in Aboriginal Am.* New York, 1926.

Whymper, Edward, *Travels Amongst the Great Andes of the Equator*. New York, C. Scribner's Sons, 1892.

Index